COLLEGE DRINKING

COLLEGE DRINKING

Reframing a Social Problem/
Changing the Culture

BY *George W. Dowdall*

REVISED EDITION

Sty/us

STERLING, VIRGINIA

Published by Stylus Publishing, LLC
22883 Quicksilver Drive
Sterling, Virginia 20166-2102

Library of Congress Cataloging-in-Publication Data

Dowdall, George W.
  College drinking : reframing a social problem/changing the culture /
by George W. Dowdall.
     p.   cm.
  "Revised edition"—Pref.
  Includes bibliographical references and index.
  ISBN 978-1-57922-813-2 (pbk. : alk. paper) — ISBN 978-1-57922-814-9 (library networkable e-edition) — ISBN 978-1-57922-815-6 (consumer e-edition)   1. College students—Alcohol use—United States.   2. Young adults—Alcohol use—United States. 3. Alcoholism—United States—Prevention.   I. Title.
  HV5135.D69   2013
  362.292088'3781980973—dc22

                                                                                  2012031227

13-digit ISBN: 978 1 57922 813 2 (paper)
13-digit ISBN: 978 1 57922 814 9 (library networkable e-edition)
13-digit ISBN: 978 1 57922 815 6 (consumer e-edition)

Printed in the United States of America

All first editions printed on acid free paper
that meets the American National Standards Institute
Z39–48 Standard.

Bulk Purchases

Quantity discounts are available
for use in workshops and for staff
development.
Call 1-800-232-0223

First Paperback Edition, 2013

10 9 8 7 6 5 4 3 2 1

To Jean
CA
J

Contents

Figures and Tables

FIGURES

TABLES

Preface to the First Edition

College drinking has been recognized as one of the most important problems facing today's college student. Even though excessive drinking has increased only modestly over the past few decades, concern about its health, behavioral, and safety consequences has risen exponentially. As the concern grew, so did the controversy about how to study college drinking and how to respond to it.

This book examines college drinking as a social problem within higher education. It is based on a large body of research and on interviews with many figures leading the way in addressing the problem. It assesses the evidence about how many students drink or drink excessively and what kinds of behavioral and health problems they have as a consequence. College drinking reflects an individual student's choice, but it also reflects a social context. This book answers the crucial questions of why students drink and what mixture of personal and environmental factors shape college drinking. The complex links to campus crime and sexual assault are discussed fully. Key practical questions about effective prevention programs and countermeasures are answered in detail. Students and parents can take action to lower the risk of binge drinking by consulting appendix D, which presents information about college policy, drinking levels, and alcohol violations at nearly 400 leading institutions, and appendix A, which explains how to gather information about the full range of American colleges and universities. Anyone concerned with higher education today—students, parents, and college personnel—will find a full discussion of the scope of the problem and what can be done about it.

THIS BOOK'S PERSPECTIVE

This book differs from other treatments of college drinking by probing behind the facade of consensus surrounding the issue that obscures the real conflicts among those who study or treat this problem. This book contrasts the image of a single national higher education problem with the reality that drinking varies enormously across colleges. It compares how higher education—the national social institution, its national leadership and organizations, and individual colleges—has responded and what options individual students and parents have for coping with the problem.

As I walked into an alcohol research agency to conduct one of the interviews on which this book is based, an experienced observer of the college drinking problem exclaimed to his colleagues, "Here comes the man from Switzerland!" I was mystified, until he went on to explain that I was the one person in the college-drinking field "who could talk to both sides." Although I cannot claim to be fully neutral, I do claim to have tried hard to understand the competing approaches and to treat each side fairly.

College drinking is experienced as "friendly fun," chosen freely by individual college kids.[1] But I think we should look "upstream" at broader cultural, organizational, and social forces that shape this behavior.[2] Much of the rich literature about college drinking looks at downstream behavior at individual colleges, well after students have begun drinking and after they've chosen a particular college. College drinking is part of a pervasive and deep-rooted college culture, one that shapes individual student behavior as well as the responses of higher education to this behavior. But like all real cultures, this one is filled with contradictions and serves different interests in different ways. Students and their parents place it at the top of a list of problems colleges face; presidents, administrators, and faculty treat this problem differently.

My argument rests on a body of evidence cited in the references, but it was shaped as much, if not more so, by a series of learning experiences over my career; both evidence and experience are discussed in greater detail in appendix B. So this book is not only "data driven" but also shaped by my own academic and personal history. I have been a regular faculty member at Indiana University, Buffalo State College, and Saint Joseph's University (a major research university, a comprehensive public college, and a selective private liberal arts university, three important segments of the vast collection of institutions making up American higher education). I have held visiting appointments at the University of California–Los Angeles, the University of Pennsylvania, the Brown University School of Medicine, and the Harvard School of Public Health, giving me a glimpse into other parts of the higher education world.

Over the past 15 years, I have worked with many people who have shaped the field of research about college drinking, including arguably the most important researchers in the field of college alcohol studies and the leader of the most significant organization in higher education dealing with college drinking. I have contributed my research to a federal agency task force that redefined college drinking. I served in the office of U.S. Senator Joseph R. Biden, Jr., when his office prepared a report on college drinking.[3] Recently, I had the opportunity to interview dozens of leaders in the field and to visit many campuses across the country. I believe that I have been in a unique position to understand how the field developed, why it became so divided, and where it is headed now.

PLAN OF THE BOOK

Chapter 1, "College Drinking as a Social Problem," examines how this issue has evolved over the past few decades. College drinking has increased only modestly over that time, yet it now has become recognized as the major public health problem facing students. In a rapidly changing institution such as higher education, the rise of a social problem reflects changing drinking behavior only in part.

Why do students drink? Chapter 2, "Reframing College Drinking," answers that question by reviewing what has been discovered about the roots of college drinking. Conflicting ways to name the problem have been offered—should it be called binge drinking, high-risk drinking, or dangerous drinking?—and efforts to respond to it have had a real impact on higher education. Data indicate how widespread college drinking is and how it has changed over time. College students drink differently than their noncollege-going peers. Why do students who have been educated about the risks of drinking often end up drinking excessively?

Is college drinking simply a harmless rite of passage, as traditional college and popular culture often depict it? Chapter 3, "The Impact of College Drinking," examines the health consequences—1,700 deaths each year, according to the most recent reliable estimate. The consequences for the individual drinker are not the only ones, and many nondrinking college students and nonstudents are also affected. The impact over the long term is more complex but reaches a far larger population. A whole range of family, personal, and college factors have been found to raise the risk of drinking and excessive drinking. A deeply entrenched culture shapes student alcohol consumption, and public policy plays a complex role as well.

Chapter 4, "The 'Dark Figure' of Alcohol-Related Campus Crime: The Gap Between Reported Incidents and Victimization," looks at one of the most troubling consequences of college drinking. Alcohol plays an important but complex role in campus crime. Many of the college crime incidents reported to the police are alcohol related, and many if not most of the serious crimes on college campuses involve alcohol. Students who abuse alcohol are more likely to be victims of crime than nonusers or nonbingeing users. Is alcohol the engine that drives most campus crime, or is it merely one of a number of factors, and perhaps a minor one at that, that play limited roles? Should preventing alcohol abuse be seen as a way of preventing campus crime?

Chapter 5, "Work Hard, Play Hard: College Drinking, Social Life, and Sex," looks at the ties among these central parts of the college experience. In an era in which "hooking up" has become a dominant theme in social life, alcohol use has taken on a new meaning for students, including drunken sex and intoxicated rape. This chapter takes a close look at the notorious alleged rape case at Duke University to assess what lessons can be learned from it.

The role of public policy is examined in Chapter 6, "Public Alcohol Policy and College Drinking." National and state policy shapes overall alcohol consumption, and that in turn shapes college drinking. Public policy informs decisions about alcohol, and so this chapter examines the most important developments. State alcohol policies prove to be important in setting the rate of college drinking.

Chapter 7, "The College Response: Reframing Prevention," discusses the response of higher education to this problem. For decades, colleges and higher education have been trying to moderate college drinking. Some programs have been demonstrated not to work at all, even though they were used widely. Others show more promise but also cost much more. Many students with alcohol use disorders fail to get adequate attention, signs that a treatment gap exists in higher education.

In Chapter 8, "What More Can Colleges Do?" we discuss what colleges can do to deal with the social problem of college drinking, now successfully reframed as higher education's most serious public health problem. How has higher education responded? How can presidents lead change in the future? Should the minimum drinking age be changed?

Chapter 9, "How to Cope with College Drinking: What Students and Parents Can Do," takes up several practical questions about contemporary college life. Since college binge-drinking rates vary from almost nothing to more than 70 percent, choosing a college would seem to be a crucial decision, but it is one that requires much more information than colleges readily provide. For students who had problems with alcohol in high school or earlier, or who have been trying to stay sober as part of a 12-step program, college choice is perhaps even more critical. How can you use college guides, as well as federal data about alcohol violations and campus crime, to help choose a college?

Data and resources presented in appendices to the book can help as well. Several appendices take up issues of how to cope with or how to understand college drinking as a social problem:

- Appendix A, "Sources for Further Information," includes a whole range of resources available on the Internet that can help in understanding college drinking or in helping students and others cope with it.
- Appendix B, "Methods and Data," provides sources of evidence about college drinking.
- Appendix C, "Timeline of Important Events Shaping College Drinking," highlights major dates in the history of alcohol and the culture of college drinking.
- Appendix D, "Alcohol and Crime Data for Selected Colleges and Universities," presents extensive data about drinking, crime, and alcohol violations at nearly 400 major colleges.

Finally, I sometimes present in the text the voices of key people, usually quoting them by name with their permission. In appendix D, institutional names listed in publicly available data are used. But elsewhere in the text, I omit the names of people or institutions when confidentiality seemed more appropriate, and so some individuals, such as the rape victim discussed in Chapter 5, are not identified.

NOTES

1. The phrase "friendly fun" is used by Moffatt (1989) to capture the essence of the student culture he studied at Rutgers University a generation ago.

2. McKinlay, in Conrad (2004). The upstream-downstream metaphor helps frame much of this book's argument, and I want to acknowledge my debt to both of these sociologists of health.

3. Biden (2002).

Preface to the Revised Edition

Publication of this Stylus book, a revised paperback edition of *College Drinking* (originally published in 2009 by Praeger Publishers), provides me with a welcome opportunity to take note of some recent developments in college drinking as a social problem. In the few years since the first edition came out in hardback, several notable changes have taken place in college drinking, higher education, and American drug and alcohol use. This revised edition includes this new preface, an afterword titled "Afterword: 2013—Changing the Culture of College Drinking," and a new version of appendix D, which includes current data on alcohol and crime.

The afterword emphasizes the student culture of college drinking, drawing on several important studies published since the first edition. It also summarizes research that allows us to update data in the book, although the majority of new data points are not much, if at all, different from the previous trends. We end up concluding that little has changed in either the facts of college drinking or the ways in which they have been constructed into a social problem. Arguably the major reason why college drinking hasn't changed is the organizational culture of the contemporary American university. Although universities have redefined college drinking as a social problem, the problem is largely tolerated; that is, it has not become the target of transformation. Few leaders have been willing to take on that culture; the afterword discusses how one courageous university president was able to change the culture on his campus in the face of considerable opposition.

I am grateful to a number of people and institutions that helped with this revised edition. Without Susan Slesinger's editorial guidance, *College Drinking* in both its hardback and revised editions would never have been published. I also want to thank Stylus Publishing's John von Knorring for the opportunity to work with his very innovative company. Alexandra Hartnett was a superb production editor.

John Sloan and Bonnie Fisher asked me to revise a chapter for the third edition of their excellent book *Campus Crime*, and that experience helped me sharpen the argument in the 2013 afterword. Claire Renzetti and Jeff Edelson asked me to write about college drinking for their *Routledge Handbook of Gender and Crime Studies*, which also helped me to frame an argument for the afterword, and I thank them as well.

I am also in debt to the staff and board of directors of the Clery Center for Security on Campus, Inc., and especially to its founder, Connie Clery, and her wonderful family, and to Alison Kiss, its dynamic new executive director. The afterword builds on some of the arguments advanced during an October 2011 conference that the Clery Center organized along with Lehigh University; video and text of that conference are available on the Clery Center's website (www.securityoncampus.org).

My interest in how the 50 states could play more of a role in moderating college drinking increased when I participated in the work of the Pennsylvania Advisory Council on Drug and Alcohol Abuse. My thanks go to my colleagues on the council and to the staff of the Pennsylvania Bureau of Drug and Alcohol Abuse. I also presented a paper to the European Sociological Association 2011 meeting in Geneva; the paper gave me the opportunity to study youth drinking across the 50 states and 35 European countries.

I also owe my thanks to Vice President Joseph R. Biden, Jr., for the honor of serving as a fellow in his Senate office in 2000. He has continued to address college safety and security issues, and his leadership on the role of Title IX in dealing with sexual violence is reflected in my comments in the afterword.

I once again want to express my gratitude for the many comments about college drinking that my students, especially those at Saint Joseph's University, have shared with me. Working with them has made me a "realistic optimist" about college drinking. I am optimistic because most college students manage to navigate their way through the sometimes rough seas of undergraduate life. Another cause for optimism is the rich body of practice and scholarship that has addressed this issue. But I am a realist, and it is clear that there has been little progress in the actual amount of binge drinking among college students, at least on the national level. University and college presidents, faculty, staff, and students will all have to address this issue more effectively in the future.

George W. Dowdall

Acknowledgments

This book was written the old-fashioned way, a lone scholar at his laptop surfing the Internet (to bend a phrase from Paul Starr). Much of my research was done online, though it also depends on extensive interviews with college administrators, researchers, and activists (please see appendix B for details). Although I am its sole author, I have learned so much from so many people that I must acknowledge their contributions, even while I free them from any responsibility for the results. I want to thank, in particular, all those persons I interviewed for the book. I also want to thank the key staff members at the National Institute on Alcohol Abuse and Alcoholism and the Higher Education Center for Alcohol and Other Drug Abuse and Violence Prevention.

My more formal learning about college alcohol resulted in publications or presentations, which I coauthored with the following people, and I owe each of them greatly: Melissa Abraham, Bryn Austin, I. Baik, Catherine Bath, Kathleen Bogle, Sonia Castillo, Robert Chapman, Mary Crawford, Andrea Davenport, William DeJong, Charles Deutsch, Karen M. Emmons, J. Gledhill-Hoyt, S. J. Grossman, Mary Koss, Joseph LaBrie, SJ, Hang Lee, Barbara Moeykens, Meichun Mohler-Kuo, Eric Rimm, Henry Wechsler, and S. I. Zanakos. I owe a great deal to Henry Wechsler for introducing me to the field of college drinking. Barbara Ryan, Tom Colthurst, Bob Saltz, and Andrea Mitchell were my key informants about its history. William DeJong has always supported my work in this field. Robert Chapman has been a fine guide to practitioner concerns.

The idea for this book first emerged while I served as the American Sociological Association's congressional fellow in the office of Senator Joseph R. Biden, Jr. My thanks to him and members of his superb staff at the time, especially Allan Glass, Alan Hoffman, Marcia Lee Taylor, and Jane Woodfin. Senator Biden's report on college drinking is the basis for several of this book's chapters.

For their continued support of my academic work, I owe special thanks to Concha Alborg, Raquel Bergen, Robert Chapman, Dan Curran, William De-Jong, Jean Dowdall, Bonnie Fisher, Janet Golden, Michael S. Goldstein, Kim Logio, Randall Miller, Lois Monteiro, Claire Renzetti, Eric Schneider, Elissa Weitzman, and Marsha Zibalese-Crawford. My colleagues in the Sociology Department at Saint Joseph's University continue to be uniformly the best I've ever had. I thank Saint Joseph's University (and especially its Board of Faculty Research and Development chaired by Roger K. Murray) for providing a sabbatical and summer support during which most of this book was written, and for a series of leaves of absence that allowed me to work at the Harvard School of Public Health. Jenna White transcribed most of the interviews for this book and helped in countless other ways. Mary Martinson filled an endless set of interlibrary loan requests, and her colleagues at the Saint Joseph's University Library answered other questions. Denise Shaw and Christina Hobson responded to many other requests. Enrico Capitan and Anne Szewczk provided invaluable computer support, including replacing a laptop that I managed to run over. Several colleagues deserve thanks for educating me about college alcohol: Joan Bradley, Nancy Komada, Linda Lelii, and Ellen Trappey.

My thanks to Praeger/Greenwood for publishing the book, and especially to editors Susan Slesinger (for early encouragement and feedback) and Elizabeth Potenza (for accepting the proposal and shaping the final manuscript). Randy Baldini and Maureen O'Driscoll did a superb job in final editing.

I also want to thank the thousands of college and graduate students that I have had the pleasure of teaching and talking with at seven different institutions: Indiana, University of California–Los Angeles, Buffalo State, Saint Joseph's, Penn, Brown, and Harvard. I hope this book honors them by taking them as seriously as it has been a pleasure to work with them. Corinne Lemon and Annie Savage were inspirations.

I owe special gratitude to parents of students who died while in college or graduate school and who went on to try to prevent future tragedies: Catherine Bath, Connie and Howard Clery, Jeffrey Levy, and Bryce Templeton. The great contributions that Security on Campus, Inc. (S.O.C.) and Mothers Against Drunk Driving (MADD) have made to addressing college safety issues are wonderful memorials to their children. It was an honor to serve as an officer of Philadelphia MADD and continues to be a pleasure to serve on the board of S.O.C.

Almost all of this book was written during the past two years, but several chapters contain brief portions of material originally published elsewhere and used here with permission:

- Dowdall, G. W. (2006). "How Public Alcohol Policy Shapes Prevention." In Chapman, R. J. (ed.), *When They Drink: Practitioner Views and Lessons Learned on Preventing High-Risk Collegiate Drinking*. Glassboro, NJ: Rowan University.
- Dowdall, G. W. (2007). "The Role of Alcohol Abuse in College Student Victimization." Portions reprinted from Fisher, B. S., and Sloan, J. J., III (eds.), *Campus Crime: Legal, Social, and Policy Perspectives* (2nd ed.). Springfield, IL: Charles C Thomas, Publisher, Ltd.
- Dowdall, G. W. (2009). "Alcohol Consumption by College Students." Portions reprinted with permission from Seigel, M. (ed.), *Race to Injustice: Lessons Learned from the Duke Lacrosse Rape Case*. Durham, NC: Carolina Academic Press.
- Kuo, M., Dowdall, G. W., Koss, M. P., and Wechsler H. (2004). "Correlates of Rape while Intoxicated in a National Sample of College Women." Portions reprinted with permission from *Journal of Studies on Alcohol, 65*, 37–45.
- *National Lampoon's Animal House* (1978). Universal Pictures/Photofest.

CHAPTER 1

College Drinking as a Social Problem

Most college students don't drink heavily. But many do, and they create problems for themselves, their fellow students, and their colleges and universities, and these institutions should play a role in addressing the problem.

Those assumptions have been the starting points over the past decades to frame a social problem about college drinking and then take action about it. This book explains how the problem came into being and what options exist for dealing with the problem of college drinking.

That college students drink, and often drink excessively, is hardly news. But during the past several decades, college drinking went from being higher education's dirty little secret to being an openly acknowledged social problem. A series of activists, researchers, university and government officials, and others successfully argued that college drinking was tied to the most dangerous and harmful aspects of college life. Excessive drinking, they argued, contributed to the saddest and most troublesome parts of college life, including violence, sexual assault and date rape, and even death. Thus, college drinking was reframed as a pressing social problem for higher education.

Go to any campus now and you probably will hear many stories about alcohol. As the journalist Barrett Seaman reports in his bestselling *Binge: What Your College Student Won't Tell You: Campus Life in Age of Disconnection and Excess:*

> In the course of two decades, Americans have gone from being generally blasé about underage drinking to being obsessed with it. Amid all the challenges that higher education faced at the turn of the twenty-first century—from

controlling costs, making diversity work, and modernizing the curriculum to revitalizing teaching and rebalancing the role of athletics—it was the drinking issue that dominated the conversation around the tables of academia.[1]

The headlines tell another part of the story:

- At Georgetown, drunk students pour out of a sports bar well after midnight. A fight in a parking lot leaves one student dying of head injuries. The police call the incident a homicide.

- At MIT, the top technological university, a brilliant freshman engineering student dies after a long night of heavy drinking.

- At Rider University, a freshman pledge dies at a fraternity house; his blood alcohol level reached 0.426. A prosecutor initially brings criminal charges against two college administrators, but later drops them. His parents sue the fraternity and the college.

- At Duke, a sensational scandal about a rogue district attorney prosecuting lacrosse team members for a rape that never happened reveals a widespread pattern of excessive drinking.

But we have to go beyond anecdotes to get a more comprehensive picture of the problem. What is new or different about this book? While college drinking is as old as colleges, the way colleges look at the problem has changed considerably in the past few decades, and college drinking is framed quite differently than it once was. Several decades ago, it was primarily viewed as a personal aberration (Joe drinks too much, Joe is an alcoholic or soon will be). Now it is more likely to be seen as a problem for higher education as a social institution (binge drinking is the number one public health problem for college students) or for a specific college (State U. is ranked the number one party school by the *Princeton Review*). Where once Joe's drinking was the central focus, now it has become a social problem for colleges across the country. This book explains how that social problem came into being, what it is like today, and how it may change in the future.

This book explains how high-risk drinking is defined, and assesses the evidence about how many students are binge drinkers and what kinds of behavioral and health problems they have as a consequence. The book answers the crucial questions of why students drink, and what personal and environmental factors produce binge drinking. Key practical questions about effective prevention programs and countermeasures are discussed in detail. Students and parents can take action to lower the risk of binge drinking by following the book's recommendations and by consulting its appendices, which explain how to use data about alcohol violations and crime presented for 400 leading institutions and available online for several thousand colleges. Administrators, trustees, and faculty will find a full discussion of the scope of the problem and what can be done about it. The book is written for a broad audience, with endnotes, appendices, and a bibliography available for those who want to examine the published research on which it is based.

College drinking has been studied empirically since the 1920s, including the groundbreaking work of Straus and Bacon in their 1953 book *Drinking in College*.[2] Well over a thousand studies have been completed, with particular frequency in the period since Henry Wechsler first published the Harvard School of Public Health College Alcohol Study (CAS) findings (in papers that I coauthored) in the mid-1990s.

What makes this book different from these other treatments of the problem? First, I examine how the understanding of the issue has changed over time, using a "social constructionist" framework to illuminate how higher education, the alcohol industry, and professional and scientific figures have shaped the way the problem is framed and addressed. I evaluate the evidence about how much change has taken place in college drinking, and how some have tried to define the problem. Second, I focus on how the organizational and institutional context of higher education (during an era of increasingly conservative politics) shifts responsibility onto the individual student, making what might have been defined as a public issue into a personal trouble.[3] Finally, I assess why, while the scientific evidence points toward the need for broad comprehensive and long-term programs to reshape the environment of college drinking, prevention programs tend to adapt short-term and individually focused efforts.

Issues come to be defined a social problem when they draw attention from the mass media, such as newspaper headlines. But the headlines tell only a part of the story because they miss some of the worst about college drinking. Some college deaths associated with drinking do not make the headlines, sometimes because the colleges want to spare the family further embarrassment or dodge the bullet of bad press. For example, Jeremy, a sophomore at a small suburban college, comes home to his off-campus apartment after celebrating his 20th birthday with a friend. Friends find his body later in the morning, and his death is attributed to drugs and alcohol. Other than a brief story in the college newspaper, area newspapers do not cover the death when it occurs. This may be the typical form of college alcohol-related death, and so the extent of this most serious part of the college binge drinking problem remains at present a "dirty little secret."

Much of the cost of college drinking is paid in problems that are far more common than death. One such consequence is violence against women.

Among college women, violence includes physical abuse, dating violence, rape, and sexual intercourse without consent. But the media rarely report on these incidents. Binge drinking is associated with a higher risk of having ideas about suicide. Students who binge have lower grades. And alcohol abuse in college casts a long shadow. There are long-term consequences too: people who abused alcohol in college have a significantly higher risk of alcohol-related problems in middle age. But few of these problems make headlines and nor do the substantial and (some would argue) growing costs of dealing with these issues, which often are hidden inside the growing tuition and other fees that have made college less affordable. These are among the most serious and widespread consequences of drinking.

To be fair, the headlines also miss some of the good news: most college students *do not* binge drink, and the percentage of those abstaining from alcohol has actually *increased* since the late 1990s. Moreover, many colleges are working hard to address the problem of alcohol abuse. Many resources are available for students, parents, and colleges, and more on the way (I've listed some of the most helpful resources in appendix A). Finally, many students who abuse alcohol simply do not have long-term or serious problems with alcohol and look back on their college binges as just a part of growing up. But always keep this in mind: more than 1,700 students die each year because of drinking.

This book goes beyond anecdotes to ask and answer the following questions:

- What is college drinking? How has it changed over time?
- How widespread is it?
- What consequences does college drinking have for the individual drinker and for those nonbingeing students in the immediate environment?
- What can be done to address excessive or binge drinking?
- What is the link between drinking and sexual activity, including sexual assault?
- What policy changes might be considered?
- How can parents and students choose safer colleges?

This book discusses an issue most people experience in personal terms by looking at some of the broader factors that shape such personal experience. Where disagreements exist, this book tries to present both sides fairly, so that the reader has the opportunity to reach his or her own conclusion. This book also addresses questions of public policy, in contrast to most previous discussions of the topic that tended to dwell only on the individual student and not the entire social environment.

I examine college drinking from several angles as a *cultural* issue. A groundbreaking report from the lead federal agency in investigating alcohol issues, the National Institute on Alcohol Abuse and Alcoholism (NIAAA) in 2002 concluded that college drinking was an entrenched subculture in American higher education, with the report's title (*A Call to Action: Changing the Culture of College Drinking*) underscoring the necessity of a cultural explanation for individual student behavior. In this book, I expand that argument to say that cultures operate more broadly at both the institutional level (all of higher education) and organizational (this specific college or that particular professional group) level. Culture powerfully shapes the way those seeking to study or to change college drinking operate.[4]

THE IMAGE OF COLLEGE DRINKING

The image is iconic: A young John Belushi wearing a sweatshirt that simply says, "College," holding a bottle of Jack Daniels he has just drained. The still photograph from the film *Animal House* (1978) is a fair introduction to our topic: how did college drinking become labeled as a public problem? How did conduct once considered private become a public issue, discussed in college admissions books, advice to the college student, newspaper editorials, scientific journals, congressional legislation, and government action?

The Belushi image also poses some of the book's central concerns (see figure 1-1). Most of us experience college at a single institution, where we are students, administrators, staff, faculty, alumni, or parents. But defining college drinking as a public problem means a concern with more than 4,000 different organizations enrolling 17 million students, linked together as much by shared culture and identity as by any formal ties. College drinking is part of a huge, complex, and rapidly changing social institution, American higher education. This book looks at how this public problem affects both individual organizations as well as an entire social institution.

Finally, the Belushi image (and *Animal House* as a whole) point to much of college drinking as some kind of game. After the film's release, drinking games became popular across the country, and more recently "pre-gaming" or drinking a lot quickly before going out for the night came into play. Talking about college drinking as a game is not meant to indicate that it cannot

College Drinking

Figure 1-1.

John Belushi appeared in *Animal House* (1978); the film's success helped reframe college drinking as a social problem. Universal Pictures/Photofest.

have serious outcomes, like the estimated 1,700 alcohol-related deaths discussed in Chapter 3. But the game metaphor helps us see it as a more or less permanent subcultural feature of undergraduate life, with taken-for-granted rules for its participants. Those of us who do not play the game may find the rules hard to comprehend, like those uninterested in basketball trying to figure out 35-second shot clocks or charging fouls. Aside from not understanding the rules, outsiders simply do not get the reason for spending so much time on the game: why would anyone waste so much time playing rugby, living in a fraternity house, or spending most nights in bars? Clinicians who need to deal with the individual damage done by the games, researchers who study the overall health and social costs, and university and government officials who try to ameliorate the problem also may see the negative side of the game. Whether it dresses up the behavior with the label of a culture—the culture of college drinking—is a matter for further discussion.

My approach to the problem is straightforward. For the past 15 years, I have been a participant in the field. I was a researcher with the Harvard School of Public Health College Alcohol Survey, and coauthored several of the most widely cited papers written about this issue. I was also the senior author of a paper about how to study college drinking, commissioned as part of the NIAAA's Task Force, and I had the opportunity to witness the Task Force deliberations. I have read widely in the popular, professional, and college press about how college drinking is perceived and reported. I attended national meetings of college drinking experts; college presidents, trustees, and other leaders; and public health organizations. I conducted oral history interviews with 50 national experts on the problem, including those who have shaped the main positions on the issue. (Appendix B explains more formally the methods used to do the research for this book.) Finally, I have been a college teacher and researcher for four decades at seven different colleges and universities (Indiana, Buffalo State, University of California–Los Angeles, Saint Joseph's, the University of Pennsylvania, Brown, and Harvard), so college students are (happily) much more than an abstract demographic category to me.

FROM ALMA MATER TO ENABLER

What this book adds to the discussion of college drinking is a focus on the role colleges and college-going have to play. There has been some important work on the impact college has, that is, the question of "college effects." Scholars have created a framework for understanding these issues and then done a great deal of empirical work about what kinds of effects college has.[5] College students drink a bit more than people of the same age who don't attend college, but the fact is that the difference turns out to be smaller than widely believed. However, many believe that rates of drinking and binge drinking are much higher among college students than their non-college-educated peers. This may reflect the unique environment of the contemporary American campus, the different characteristics of those who go to college and those who don't, or some combination of how colleges both "collect" and "create" problem drinking.

An additional important question is, what is the difference between going to college and going to *this college*? Is the issue more about moving to a specific place, occupying a special status, or simply coming of college age?

Whatever the reason, prevention and intervention programs directed at college students are different than those directed at their noncollege peers.

The way we use language captures some of the complexity. Americans talk about an individual "going to college" as well as attending a specific institution. We sometimes label the problem "drinking on college campuses" but sometimes call it "college student drinking." We occasionally limit our discussion to students under the legal drinking age of 21 or those who are of "traditional college age," 18 to 24 years old or so. Sometimes we look only at those students who attend four-year colleges, or go to college on a full-time basis. And finally we focus our attention not merely on those who drink, but also on those who "binge" or drink excessively or dangerously.

How do professional administrators, researchers, preventionists, and treatment specialists construct college drinking as a problem, and what kinds of solutions do they propose? Much of the discourse about the issue, which usually assumes there is just a single way of correctly viewing it, implicitly advocates a position in a field filled with competing arguments. Many in the college drinking field put forward positions that don't admit disagreement. It is assumed that college drinking, however defined, is somehow wrong or unhealthy, and that any right-thinking person would assume so had she or he the facts. In that sense, many in the field assume that the objective dangers associated with heavy drinking are so severe as to remove the necessity of arguing about what the best course of action should be. Instead, I assume that the college drinking issue is *fraught*, by which I mean that there is a great deal of disagreement about its meaning and implications.

Why should there be so many questions about what appears to be the simple problem of college kids drinking too much? First, when it comes to human conduct, there are no simple problems. All the more so with alcohol, which is at once a substance with powerful pharmacological effects, a commercial product pushed by an immense and complex industry, and an idea embedded in an enduring societal as well as college culture. Second, college drinking occurs within an institution, higher education, that has been undergoing major transformations in the past decades, changes perhaps as dramatic as any in American life. Putting college drinking on higher education's agenda during such a turbulent period has been a major challenge for those who want to attack the problem. Finally, the cast of characters who claim expertise or professional responsibility over college drinking has also changed considerably over the past few decades.

This book adds to the large literature on college drinking in several ways. First, I develop a model of how society influences college drinking, looking at both individual behavior and higher education's response to this behavior.

I borrow from the work of sociologists of health who have argued for a rethinking of the society-health relationship. My framework is based in neoinstitutional thinking as applied to higher education, particularly about why organizations like universities tend to adopt similar features and culture. Second, I try to write from a position that acknowledges the unique character of alcohol as a substance and a commodity, *but no ordinary commodity*, in fact one that is regulated in virtually all societies because of its unique impact on human conduct.[6] Third, I pay particular attention to how higher education has responded to college drinking. Much of what has been written about college drinking ignores the history of this practice. We have a series of snapshots, but need to put them together into a film that captures movement over time.

The classic 1953 study, *Drinking in College*, questioned whether there was anything special about college life and alcohol. In fact, its authors struggled with what to name their book. Should it be titled "College Drinking" or "Drinking in College?" The former implies that there was something unique about college drinking, while the latter (the one they chose) indicated that it is a custom shaped by a larger society. In the intervening half century, the amount of college drinking may have shifted a bit upward. But college drinking came to be defined as a problem by universities, higher education, and the alcohol prevention and treatment fields. This book will explain how the problem of "college drinking" came to be defined as a serious one for higher education, and what kinds of solutions came to be popular within the institutions.

BRIGHT COLLEGE DAYS, DARK COLLEGE NIGHTS

Walk across a college campus in the late morning, and you will see little evidence of college drinking as a social problem for higher education. Sure, a few of the students may seem a bit bleary eyed over morning coffee, and some have skipped class because of last night's drinking. In the waiting room of a student affairs judicial officer, a sophomore waits for her hearing about her second alcohol infraction. Two buildings away, a freshman is in the middle of a "motivational interviewing" session with a psychologist, exploring why his straight-A high school grade average has become a bunch of Cs and two Fs. In a dorm, a maintenance worker repairs a door whose lower panel was kicked in last week, and a cleaner mops up some vomit in a communal bathroom. Professors lead the hundreds of classes that meet on campus, only a few of which touch on alcohol as a subject in any way, while a roomful of students sit listening to the lecture, many who were drinking the night before. The president's senior officers hold their weekly cabinet meeting, and far down the agenda is an item about hiring more security staff to deal with a string of fights, some alcohol fueled, after the last home basketball game.

Take the same walk in the early hours of Saturday morning, and a very different picture appears. Although most students are either sober or have had just a drink or two, some students walk visibly drunk toward their dorms, while others party off campus in the student apartments where many of the upperclassmen live. In residential fraternities, heavy drinking began well before sunset the day before. Most students drink moderately or not at all this particular day, but a substantial minority binge drink, a term that during the 1990s came to represent the heavy episodic drinking that defines much of college drinking today. This type of drinking raises risks of a lot of negative outcomes, but for most on any one occasion, the outcomes are often just a hangover or getting sick. For a very few, a trip to the emergency room or being watched over by a roommate might end the night.

What makes the headlines are some—but a surprisingly small fraction—of the estimated 1,700 American college students who die as the result of their or others' drinking. These alcohol-related deaths, along with stories about students killed in their dorms or women raped near campuses, have played a role in the shifting discourse about the American college.

Day and night are different worlds in higher education, perhaps as different as at any time in its long history, and this book describes both worlds and then examines the connections between them.[7] Student conduct at night is often well beyond the scrutiny, let alone guidance, of college authorities, whose planning, assessment, evaluation, and intervention mostly proceeds during daylight hours.

COLLEGE DRINKING AS A SOCIAL PROBLEM

A rich tradition in American sociology has examined why some problems become major issues while others don't. Sociologists initially began with what might be called an "objectivist" perspective. An objectivist approach assumes that the objective facts of harm to society or its institutions explain how social problems arise. In this approach, the facts (of objective harm to society) speak for themselves. As the sociologist Wendy Griswold (2004: 107) argues,

> Some things are clearly wrong and need fixing. Any society produces conditions that are pathological, dysfunctional, cruel, shameful, maybe even evil. Political or moral leadership entails getting people to recognize and

acknowledge the problem and then to set about fixing it. This view of social problems sees them as objective: The situation in question is real, it can be identified, it can be objectively measured, and just about everyone will agree that the situation is indeed "a problem" once they know about it.... Although this objective view of social problems is attractively straightforward, its assumptions are vulnerable.[8]

By contrast, constructionists see a more conflicted and complex route. They assume that facts rarely speak for themselves, that someone has to discover facts or at least assemble forceful evidence of their existence, and then "claims-makers" have to argue for their importance. Griswold notes:

The essence of the constructionist approach is that potential social problems ... are not just objective facts, but instead are producers of meanings. It is only when a solution has meaning for a specific group of people, and that meaning is a negative one, that it can get defined as a social problem.

Some problems wax and wane in importance (such as poverty), not because the objective facts change, but because individuals speak up to define them as problems. Some problems are the products of the work of energized individuals, sometimes called "moral entrepreneurs"; they campaign effectively for framing some set of "facts" as a problem. For example, a single energetic leader, Harry Anslinger, almost singlehandedly created the nation's policy banning marijuana. The contemporary War on Drugs was a more complex creation, but presidential leadership (and in Nancy Reagan's case, leadership by a presidential spouse) was critical.[9]

College drinking was targeted as a problem by a series of claims-makers, beginning with researchers and writers in the 1950s through 1970s; as a by-product of attention to drunk driving and underage drinking, it attracted the attention of alcohol preventionists and education reformers in the 1980s; it expanded with the Harvard School of Public Health College Alcohol Study and the founding of the Higher Education Center for the Prevention of Alcohol and Other Drugs in the 1990s and the growth of the "social norms" approach in the same decade; and it received national attention with the publication of the NIAAA report in 2002. Far from some plan unfolding over the time, the actual development of the college drinking problem was as much a product of competition between approaches that focused on different aspects of the problem. Also important was the changing character of higher education during this period, and even the collective character of its students and staff. This chapter will explain how these factors all came together to produce "college drinking" as a social problem, not just an aggregation of college drinkers but a cultural object in its own right.

What would it take to redefine college drinking as a social problem for higher education? First, college drinking would have to be objectively common enough so that many examples could come to mind in discussing it. Data will show that as early as the 1950s, that common usage was present. But widespread drinking is a necessary but not sufficient condition for the creation of a social problem. Cases of individual drinking would have to be aggregated into a large number; and the case is especially convincing if that large number is found to be increasing dramatically. The drinking would have to cause damage well beyond the individual, perhaps to many in the immediate vicinity of the drinker and maybe well beyond the college campus where it occurs. The damage would have to be serious, involving many deaths of young people. Arguments would have to be crafted that linked something about the college experience to the rise in problematic drinking. Experts who claim specialized understanding or competence in caring for individuals would arise, and their understanding would change how the problem is perceived. The mass media and the media specializing in higher education would have to cover stories about college drinking, portraying it as an urgent and serious problem. Finally, it might help if the more dramatic increases in the problematic behavior affected important subgroups, such as women at a time when they became a majority of college-goers, or students at the most prestigious and competitive institutions.

THE RISE AND FALL OF SOCIAL PROBLEMS ON THE PUBLIC AGENDA

College drinking has risen as a social problem. I borrow from the work of two sociologists, Stephen Hilgartner and Charles Bosk, to create a model of why social problems rise and fall.[10] The model tries to explain how the limited attention society can give to social issues inevitably creates competition among them. Issues rise and fall on the public agenda. Issues that deal with higher education and college students are just one of an almost innumerable set of possible social problems that might attract public attention and discourse.

When Americans are polled about social problems, a handful of issues are at the top of the list. One axis along which issues vary concerns domestic versus international problems. Since the terrorist attacks of September 11, national security and terrorism has risen to the top, competing for attention with problems such as health care, unemployment, and the economy. Over the past few decades, one substance abuse issue, illegal drugs, has sometimes joined that list, though it rarely is identified as a major problem by a large proportion of Americans. Alcohol was once such an issue, culminating in the passage of the 18th Amendment and the onset of Prohibition. Just a decade later with the 21st Amendment, Prohibition ended and control over the problem fell to the individual states. Not until the founding of the NIAAA in 1970 did this issue return to the national agenda, where interest in it continues to fluctuate with a general rise in concern.

College drinking exists as part of several broad discourses about alcohol. Since Prohibition, Americans have viewed alcohol as a legal substance for those above a certain age. Deviant behavior involving alcohol either comes from its abuse (like drinking before driving) or from compulsive or long-term overindulgence (termed alcoholism or alcohol abuse).

Americans long ago became enmeshed in driving cars as part of daily life. As the amount of driving increased, harms associated with alcohol abuse also increased. Young drivers are a particularly critical category, for as relatively inexperienced drivers, they are likely to get into more crashes than their elders. But add to their behavior a tendency to drink in heavy episodes and relative harm increases. In the 1980s, Mothers Against Drunk Driving (MADD) was formed and led a successful crusade against both drunk driving and underage drinking, resulting in changes of the minimum drinking age.[11]

Federal agencies claim jurisdiction over some of these problems. College drinking is part of higher education, so the U.S. Department of Education is a major player. But it is also an issue of the abuse of alcohol, and so NIAAA (research about alcoholism) and the Substance Abuse and Mental Health Services Administration (SAMHSA, specializing in treatment of alcohol problems) are involved. Alcohol abuse is a major cause of death, so the Centers for Disease Control and Prevention is active as well.

Two political scientists, Frank Baumgartner and Bryan Jones, argue that institutions are central to policy:

> Institutional structures in American politics are not easy to change, but when they do change, these changes often lead to dramatic and long-lasting changes in policy outcomes.... The result is that the American political system lurches from one point of apparent equilibrium to another, as policymakers establish new institutions to support the policies they favor or alter existing ones to give themselves greater advantage.[12]

Much of the story of college drinking represents the lengthening shadow of federal policymaking about alcohol and drugs, student conduct, drunk driving, and college governance. Some of the work of constructing a social problem concerns reframing the image of the problem. According to Baumgartner and Jones,

> Policy images play a critical role in the expansion of issues to the previously apathetic.... Policy images are always a mixture of empirical information and emotive appeals. These appeals can be subtle or strong, but they are invariably present. Hence every policy image has two components: an empirical and an evaluative. We refer to the evaluative component of its policy image as its *tone*.[13]

Much of the conflict over college drinking is about its tone: *Animal House* (1978) is the perfect portrayal of college drinking as harmless fun, whereas government reports paint a far darker picture with empirical data about its impact on health and well-being.

Drug or alcohol issues can be seen both as an individual and as a social problem. Baumgartner and Jones suggest that illicit drug use is easier to frame as a problem of government because it is defined as criminal and its use is linked to other crimes:

> In the case of alcohol, there has not always been such a social link. In the 1970s and 1980s the issue seems to have emerged with some significant socializing arguments, however. The most powerful is drunk driving.... Congressional attention to alcohol never receded after 1970 to the levels where have been before the passage of this act and the creation of the NIAAA. In other words, alcohol abuse, like drug abuse before it, was institutionalized on the formal agenda of the federal government. The nationalization of the two problems occurred in the same period of time.... Unlike popular or media attention, no one has ever accused a federal agency of being fickle; they do not "fade away."[14]

College drinking as an issue builds on how society reacts to alcohol use and abuse. College drinking can be defined as a problem in a very narrow way, as the excessive consumption of alcohol by students; narrowly defined, discussion of the impact of drinking might focus on its pharmacological effects on individual students. But it can also be looked at in a broad way, as part of a broader environment or culture, emphasizing how it is correlated with other student issues. It might be expanded, seen as part of a declining sense of morality, or a transformation of students into consumers. Some might also claim that it is at the root of student issues.

HOW HIGHER EDUCATION IS CHANGING

The institution of higher education has changed greatly, reshaping the college experience.[15] Table 1-1 presents some important contrasts between 1966 and 2006, a 40-year period of impressive transformation in higher education. The number of students almost tripled, and the number of colleges and universities almost doubled. Women became the new majority on

Table 1-1.

Changes in American Higher Education, 1966–2006

	1966	2006
Demography of Higher Education		
Number of colleges and universities	2,329	4,216
Total college enrollment	6,390,000	17,648,000
Percent college students female	40%	58%
Percent college freshmen white	91%	74%
Average SAT Scores of College-Bound Seniors		
Males: verbal/critical reading	540	505
Males: mathematics	535	536
Females: verbal/critical reading	545	502
Females: mathematics	495	502
Percent 25 Years and Over Who Completed College		
Total	9.8	27.6
Males	12.5	28.9
Females	7.4	26.5
Whites	10.4	28
Blacks	3.8	17.6
Degrees Conferred Annually		
Doctoral	20,617	50,500
Master's	157,726	603,000
Bachelor's	558,534	1,488,000
Professional	31,695	87,400
Total	768,572	2,228,900
Bachelor's as percent of all degrees	73	67
Finances (in billions of dollars)		
Annual expenditures by colleges	$12.50	$315.40
Federal budget for higher education	$0.71	$39.80
State appropriations for operating expenses	$3.50	$66.60
R&D at colleges and universities	$1.70	$42.90
Research funds from federal government	$1.20	$27.40
Research funds from industry	$0.04	$2.10
Gifts to colleges and universities	$1.48	$25.60
Average Tuition and Fees		
At private four-year institutions	$1,456	$22,218
At public four-year institutions	$360	$5,836
At public community colleges	$121	$2,272

Source: Chronicle of Higher Education, (2006b).
Note: R&D = research and development.

campus, and minorities advanced from less than a tenth to more than a quarter of students. The center of gravity shifted, with the percent of all degrees given at the baccalaureate level falling from 73 percent to 67 percent. Funding for research expanded greatly. Sports continued to professionalize, as indicated by one telling number not found in the table: net income from the National Collegiate Athletic Association (NCAA) men's basketball tournament was estimated at $180,000 in 1966 and at $470 million 40 years later.

During this period, hundreds of colleges renamed themselves universities, signaling an organizational change away from an almost-exclusive preoccupation with undergraduates well under way earlier in the twentieth century. In all, the changes Straus noted in the 1950s and 1960s continued into the new millennium, joined by a rise in age at marriage and a decline in student activism.

One could hypothesize that factors associated with college drinking were changing in a direction associated by and large with higher rates of college drinking and binge drinking. Although some things are changing in a way that might predict less drinking, more things seem to be moving in the direction that might raise drinking levels. What in fact has been the trend in college drinking?

COLLEGE DRINKING AS A RISING SOCIAL PROBLEM

How has the status of college drinking as a social problem changed? To assess this question, figure 1-2 presents data on trends from 1966 to 2007 in national and college media reports on "college drinking." Each series suggests the rise or fall in attention to "college drinking" by the general public, higher education professionals, and college students.[16] One series is drawn from counts of stories that mentioned the terms "college drinking" in the *New York Times*, arguably the most important newspaper covering domestic news. A second series presents the same trend in the *Chronicle of Higher Education*, a weekly newspaper that covers the institution of higher education, regularly read by professional administrators and faculty leaders. The *Chronicle* is the source of "inside baseball" coverage of the industry of higher education. Data are reported from 1989, the first year the *Chronicle*'s full text is available in an online searchable index. A final series represents the trend in the student newspaper the *Harvard Crimson*. (Harvard is in no way a representative college, but it is a strong choice on grounds of being the leading campus in the country; it is also an easy choice for this purpose because its student newspaper is searchable back to its first publication in 1873.)

The *Harvard Crimson* published so many stories on college drinking that its trend line is expressed "per 10" (in other words, the frequency is divided

Figure 1-2.
News Stories About College Drinking, 1966–2007

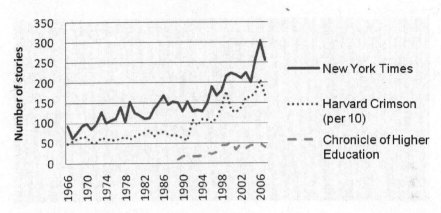

Source: Author; see text.

by 10) so that the magnitude of any one year's number of stories is actually 10 times what appears in the figure. College drinking is much bigger news to students than it is to the general public who read the *New York Times*. But note that the trend lines for the *Times* and the *Crimson* follow similar paths, with a big jump in stories in the early and mid-1990s, and another rise in the early 2000s. By contrast, the *Chronicle*'s coverage rises more slowly: college drinking is hardly big news to higher educational professionals. (The small number of stories in the *Chronicle* relative to the two other newspapers also reflects the fact that it is a weekly, and the others are dailies.)

Newspaper coverage of this issue clearly has increased dramatically in the recent past. This increase supports strongly the social constructionist view of college drinking as a social problem. The greatly increased attention to the issue is not explained by the modest change in behavior, as data reviewed in the next chapter will show. But the issue of college drinking hasn't moved up the higher education agenda commensurate to its standing among students and the general public.

CONCLUSION

A social constructionist view of college drinking stresses how claims-makers successfully raise an issue. But this does not imply that the issue is merely or even mostly a social construction. Before leaving this topic, let me explain my own position. I believe that many of the claims of the objectivist position on college drinking are well founded. I believe that, as I once wrote in a major public health journal, "binge drinking is arguably the No. 1 public health hazard and the primary source of preventable morbidity and mortality ... for college students in America."[17] College drinking is no mere construction of moral entrepreneurs who are the contemporary incarnations of the "drys" who fought for an earlier form of Prohibition. They are no mere "neoprohibitionists" but, I believe, are reacting to a real problem. This puts me squarely in the ranks of those who claim college drinking brings real problems to students, universities, and their communities. I disagree with those who minimize the problem. But the insights of the constructivist position impress me as well, and I agree with those who argue that we need to better understand why so few college students, even those who binge, appear to view their own behavior as problematic or in need of change.

The problem has become a major one within higher education. The newspaper story data partly confirm Seaman's observation that began this chapter: college students are obsessed with college drinking as an issue, and since the 1990s, general newspaper readers are seeing much more about it. But it appears that higher education leaders may not be keeping up with the curve. The next chapter presents a portrait of this rising social problem.

NOTES

1. Seaman (2005: 24).
2. Straus & Bacon (1953).
3. Mills (1959).
4. My thanks to Patrick Carr and Maria Kefalas for stimulating conversations about culture, context, and college drinking.
5. Pascarella & Terenzini (2005); Astin (1993).
6. Babor (2003).
7. Melbin (1978).
8. Griswold (2004: 107).
9. Massing (1998).
10. Hilgartner & Bosk (1988).
11. Reinarman (1988).
12. Baumgartner & Jones (1993: 12).
13. Baumgartner & Jones (1993: 25).
14. Baumgartner & Jones (1993: 164).
15. For a timeline of significant events in higher education since 1966, see http://chronicle.com/weekly/v53/i14/14a00801.htm, accessed December 26, 2007.
16. The phrase "college drinking" was entered into the search box of each archive for the period from the beginning to the end of each calendar year.
17. Wechsler, Dowdall, Davenport, & Castillo (1995: 921).

CHAPTER 2

Reframing College Drinking

That college students drink alcohol is hardly news. But framing college drinking as a social problem for higher education is quite different than simply noting that students drink, sometimes excessively. Defining drinking as a social problem requires moving beyond anecdotes to research. The sheer scale of American higher education requires surveying the almost 15 million undergraduates who study at more than 4,000 institutions spread out across the 50 states.[1] Researchers have been conducting surveys since the 1930s about student alcohol consumption, including a pioneering national study (*Drinking in College*, published in 1953), and systematic reviews of the literature in 1977 and 1986.[2]

But it was not until the 1990s that the movement to reframe college drinking as a social problem drew fully on that research. The new frame claimed college drinking was widespread, linked to the college experience, and might be increasing; this chapter examines how to define binge or heavy episodic drinking, examining how widespread it is and whether it has changed over time, and discussing the difference between college and noncollege drinking. Reframing the issue also involved arguing that far from being a harmless rite of passage, college drinking caused substantial harm to both the drinker and those in the immediate environment, all to be discussed later.

Collegiate illicit drug use had soared in the 1960s and 1970s, but declined in prevalence by the 1980s. Symbolically, the 1978 film *Animal House* might mark a turning point, as alcohol appeared once again at the top of substances used by students. Data reporting the perception that one's friends use marijuana would fall from a high of about 35 percent at the beginning of the 1980s to 10 percent by the end of the decade; the perception of cocaine use fell from 8 percent or so to almost nothing, while alcohol remained at a steady 25 percent or so.[3]

The most significant research on college drinking in the mid-twentieth century tended to downplay differences between college drinking and drinking by youth not in college. Robert Straus and Selden Bacon concluded from their large survey of American undergraduates that "79% of the men who drink and 65% of the women reported that their drinking started before entering college.... It is obvious that the 'when' of early drinking for many students antedates their entering college."[4] What shaped college drinking was the family: "In considering drinking in college, it is important to realize the extent to which early drinking is a form of behavior associated with the family, and the relatively minor role the college plays as a place of first drinking."[5]

The narrative about college drinking would shift greatly. In an influential 1991 white paper summarizing what was then known about college drinking, Lewis Eigen made a strong case for an environmental approach to the issue. "In a rough sense, the college campus may well be a type of environmental hazard. Surely not like a toxic waste dump, but with certain similar properties—namely, that if one spends considerable time there, there is an increased probability of certain negative health consequences."[6]

Eigen explicitly rejected the position that campus alcohol consumption simply reflected the surrounding society's behavior, arguing that colleges had substantially higher rates of drinking: 74.5 percent of students, but only 71 percent of nonstudents of similar age, drank alcohol each month.[7] (He did not explain why a 3.5 percent difference would be taken so seriously.) College students spent more money on drinking than on textbooks.

> The typical college is potentially hazardous to the health of its students. Drinking is the principle hazard. The college campus has cultural traditions and patterns which interact with students who are particularly vulnerable at this point in their lives. The combination is always potentially dangerous, and often deadly ... college communities can take [steps] to diminish the risk and ameliorate the problem, but these steps will mean profound changes in campus tradition, norms, rules, and culture. These changes need to be made. As Robin Wilson, president of California State University at Chico, put it so well, "If this culture of alcohol abuse is not confronted, then what? If not now, when? If not by us, by whom?"[8]

DEFINING BINGE OR HEAVY EPISODIC DRINKING

Reframing college drinking as a social problem involved "discovering" college drinking and making claims about its danger to a large public.

Using the term "binge drinking" facilitated this change—but it also generated controversy within the field of college-drinking prevention that continues to this day. Binge drinking is a particular form of heavy episodic alcohol use. It is generally understood by most people to mean too much alcohol in too little time, often resulting in inebriation. More precise definitions are used by researchers. Beginning with its initial publication in the *Journal of the American Medical Association* (JAMA) in 1994, the Harvard School of Public Health College Alcohol Study defined binge drinking as five drinks or more in a row for men and four drinks or more in a row for women. This definition equalizes the sex differences evident in the risk of alcohol-related problems.[9] It is sometimes referred to as the "5/4" definition.[10] The term "binge drinking" rapidly became popular with the mass media and with much of the field of college-drinking prevention. It also matched definitions used by scientists in other alcohol research and by policy experts in stating national health goals.[11]

Some have taken issue with this definition. One objection is that the definition is too broad and inclusive, in effect making some of those who engage in moderate drinking appear immoderate. But scientists from the National Institute on Alcohol Abuse and Alcoholism (NIAAA) define moderate drinking as only one or two drinks at a sitting, making this "5/4" definition well above moderate levels.[12] Another objection is the use of the phrase "in a row," rather than a more precise statement of the time over which alcohol is consumed. Still others claim that the weight or body mass of an individual has to be factored into the definition; for example, a 300-pound male drinking five drinks over a three-hour period might hardly feel the effects of alcohol, let alone get drunk. But critics tend not to provide detailed alternative specifications for these measures that could be used to survey national samples. Some critics claim that measured blood alcohol concentrations of students returning to their dorms at night seem lower than might be expected from survey results, although other research indicates that drug and alcohol self-reports are reliable and valid.[13] Variations on the "five-drink" or "5/4" definitions of binge drinking are the most commonly used in research studies.

Different views about use of the term "binge" and about the 5/4 measurement shaped different views about policy and prevention. The debate continued into the 1990s. A document on the major Web site serving the field put out four major arguments against using the term:

First, many so-called "binge" drinkers do not reach blood alcohol concentrations (BACs) high enough to cause impairment, due to their weight and the long period of time over which they drink . . .

Second, when considering alcohol-related consequences, there are absolutely no scientific grounds for stating that 5/4-plus drinks is a meaningful cut-off point in defining problem drinking....

Third, research is also beginning to demonstrate that the 5/4 measure is too insensitive to detect real changes in alcohol consumption and its consequences due to new programs and policies.... In many cases, therefore, progress is going undetected when gauged against the 5/4-plus measure.

Another consideration is that using the 5/4-plus "binge" definition creates the errant belief that nearly half of college students use alcohol in a reckless and dangerous way. This puts pressure on campus and community officials to crack down, but at the price of alienating many students and faculty, who will then ignore prevention messages. Focusing instead on consequences helps communicate the idea that there is a majority community, including students, that wants policy change and stricter enforcement to deal with the irresponsible minority of students who drink most of the alcohol and cause most of the problems. This alternative approach invites wide community participation and builds a strong case for changing the legal, economic, and social factors that drive high-risk alcohol consumption.[14]

Figures in the alcohol prevention field also took sides. Drew Hunter, the director of the Bacchus/Gamma Peer Education Network, urged that the term "binge drinking" be dropped.[15] Robert Chapman, a leading figure in the Network, wrote eloquently against the term:

When the media tell us that binge drinking is rampant on our campuses, it does not take much to "hear" that "all" college students are "drunken fools." You know this is not so. I know this is not so. The Harvard research team knows this is not so. But the media nonetheless convey this message, either by design or neglect.[16]

An important research outlet, the *Journal of Studies on Alcohol* (since renamed *Journal of Studies on Alcohol and Drugs*), issued a policy on the term:

In order to avoid the confusion that can potentially arise when different clinical phenomena are being described by the same name, the *Journal* has now adopted a policy that requires the term "binge" to be used in a specific way in accepted manuscripts. According to the policy, the term "binge" should only be used to describe an extended period of time (usually two or more days) during which a person repeatedly administers alcohol or another substance to the point of intoxication, and gives up his/her usual activities and obligations in order to use the substance. It is the combination of prolonged use and the giving up of usual activities that forms the core of the definition of a "binge."

If authors are using the word "binge" to mean something other than the extended period of intoxication with concomitant neglect of activities/obligations as described above, we ask that they change their terminology. Alternative terms for the word "binge" include "heavy drinking"/"heavy use" or "heavy episodic drinking"/"heavy episodic use."[17]

From that point on, the alternative terminologies were used in this one journal, even as other research journals (such as JAMA) and the popular press came to settle on "binge drinking." Enough controversy continued in the field to motivate the NIAAA to finally resolve the issue by convening a panel of experts and leading the Institute to recommend the following:

> A "binge" is a pattern of drinking alcohol that brings blood alcohol concentration (BAC) to 0.08 gram percent or above. For the typical adult, this pattern corresponds to consuming 5 or more drinks (male), or 4 or more drinks (female), in about 2 hours. Binge drinking is clearly dangerous for the drinker and for society.

- In the above definition, a "drink" refers to half an ounce of alcohol (e.g., one 12-oz. beer, one 5-oz. glass of wine, or one 1.5-oz. shot of distilled spirits).
- Binge drinking is distinct from "risky" drinking (reaching a peak BAC between 0.05 gram percent and 0.08 gram percent) and a "bender" (2 or more days of sustained heavy drinking).
- For some individuals (e.g., older people or people taking other drugs or certain medications), the number of drinks needed to reach a binge-level BAC is lower than for the "typical adult."
- People with risk factors for the development of alcoholism have increased risk with any level of alcohol consumption, even that below a "risky" level.
- For pregnant women, any drinking presents risk to the fetus.
- Drinking by persons under the age of 21 is illegal.[18]

In other words, the 1993 Harvard College Alcohol Study "5/4" definition was amended by replacing the indeterminate phrase "in a row" with a period of two hours, which for many people will result in a blood alcohol concentration high enough to constitute driving under the influence. But even with the NIAAA's standing in the field, its definition of binge drinking hardly put the issue to rest.

All the debate about "binge drinking" notwithstanding, the "5/4" definition (or sometimes the older "5/5" definition) remained in use as the usual survey measure of heavy episodic drinking, even though many preferred a different label. Some clinicians still found the term inadequate.[19] The NIAAA issued an update of its Task Force report in late 2007, and repeated its definition of "binge drinking." The mass media continued to use the definition.[20]

Why such controversy over two words? Some of it is explained by the difference between clinical and epidemiological perspectives. Epidemiologists seek words and concepts that have straightforward operational definitions, and that appeal to their primary audiences of mass media, government officials, funders, and administrators. By contrast, clinicians face the daunting task of trying to "treat" students who usually see little or no problem in their own behavior and seek "treatment" only because someone makes them do so. Clinicians avoid words that sharply distinguish (and possibly stigmatize) their clients.

HOW WIDESPREAD IS COLLEGE DRINKING?

With almost 15 million college students, establishing how widespread college drinking is requires large national samples.[21] The largest efforts have produced remarkably similar findings, even though their methodologies differ. In this chapter, the extent of drinking among American college students is assessed, with particular attention toward the amount of binge or heavy episodic drinking. Over the past two decades or so, several national studies of college drinking have been published, such as the four large national surveys produced by the Harvard School of Public Health College Alcohol Study, directed by Henry Wechsler.[22] The College Alcohol Study results have been consistent with other large-scale efforts, but the study uses scientific sampling techniques to produce a representative large national sample of colleges and students, and so we will begin with its findings.[23] For its original survey in 1993, the College Alcohol Study chose 195 four-year colleges and universities using probability proportionate to size sampling (140 colleges were able to participate in the study). Because each participating institution was promised confidentiality, it is not possible to describe the sample's institutions in detail, except to say that the sample is representative of four-year full-time higher education. Each college provided the researchers with a random sample of full-time students, with roughly 60 percent completing a detailed 20-page questionnaire about their alcohol and drug use as well as behaviors and values. The College Alcohol Study conducted surveys of large samples (of roughly 15,000 to 17,000 students) in 1993, 1995, 1997, and 2001.

Using the 5/4 definition of binge drinking, the Harvard study reported that two in five college students were current binge drinkers, with one in five meeting the definition of "frequent binge drinkers" by having three or more episodes of binge drinking in the two weeks before completing the survey.[24]

The percentage of students who were frequent binge drinkers and the percentage who abstained from alcohol completely slightly increased over time, but otherwise little change was seen in the period from 1993 to 2001.

Among the most important contributions of the Harvard College Alcohol Study was to generate insight into the wide variation in drinking rates among the colleges in the study. The College Alcohol Study is unique in its use of a large scientific sample of colleges as well as students within them; this means the study data can shed light on what makes colleges distinct from one another, not just what makes individual students different.[25] The data allow us to take an important step from framing college drinking as an individual issue, to framing it as an institutional issue that occurs in a particular environment.

Drinking rates vary extensively at the colleges in the study. While 1 percent of the students were binge drinkers at the lowest-rate school in each survey, 70 percent were binge drinkers at the highest in 1993 (75 percent in 1997).[26] When the colleges in the 1993 survey were stratified according to bingeing rate, it was noted that several characteristics affected the rate of binge drinking, including location, region, proportion of residential students, and racial composition. For example, women who attend women's colleges have lower rates of binge drinking than women who attend co-ed colleges.[27] Other factors, such as size of enrollment or whether the college was public or private, were not related to the bingeing rate. Individual binge drinking is less likely if no alcohol outlets are located within one mile of campus or if the institution prohibits alcohol use for all persons (even those over 21) on campus.

Figure 2-1 presents the percent of binge drinking on the 140 college campuses in the original study; a similar pattern has marked each of the four surveys conducted since 1993. At one college, almost no students binge, while more than 70 percent do so at the top campus in binge drinking. About a third of the schools had more than 50 percent of their students defined as binge drinkers, and these schools were designated "high-binge" institutions. Figure 2-1 highlights the important point that no single pattern of binge drinking describes college students in general, with each campus having a unique configuration.

The variation in rates of college drinking across American colleges is striking. Just as there is no typical American college student, so too there is no typical American college. This heterogeneity has important implications with regard to prevention, intervention, and treatment of college drinking.

Almost all college students drink occasionally, and most do not binge drink, but roughly two out of every five full-time college students at

Figure 2-1.

Distribution of Colleges by Percentage of Binge Drinking, 1993

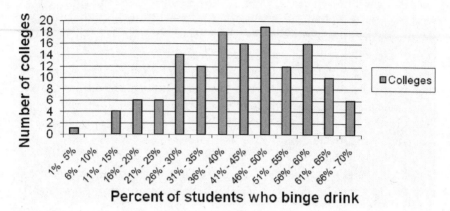

Source: Author; adapted from Wechsler, Davenport, Dowdall, Moeykens, & Castillo (1994).

four-year colleges are binge drinkers. Table 2-1 presents data from the four College Alcohol Study surveys on college drinking, showing that little change has occurred over the years from 1993 to 2001. Roughly one in five college students still meets the definition of "frequent binge drinker" by bingeing at least three times in the two-week period.

Table 2-2 presents important facts about the character of college drinking today. Almost a third of all college students were drunk three or more times in the past month. Almost half of all students drink to get drunk, that is, they report that drinking to get drunk is an important reason for drinking. The data still show significant differences between men and women, but it is clear that women's drinking styles often resemble those of men. Many of the undergraduates at U.S. colleges are under the minimum drinking age, guaranteeing that many episodes of drinking by college students violate various state laws.[28]

The data from the 1993 Harvard survey were published in 1994 in the JAMA. What was unique about the JAMA paper's contribution to reframing college drinking? First, it was the first research to confront the enormous diversity of American higher education. By creating a sample of 140 colleges and universities, the study was representative of four-year colleges and universities in the United States (although it unfortunately had no data on two-year institutions). Previous research had either used data from a single campus or from convenience and not scientific samples. Second, Wechsler

Table 2-1.
Reported Drinking Behaviors Among College Students, 1993–2001
(percent)

Drinking behavior	1993 (N=15,282)	1997 (N=14,428)	1999 (N=13,954)	2001 (N=10,904)
Abstainer	16.4%	19.6%	19.8%	19.3%
Male	15.7	18.9	20.5	20.1
Female	17.0	20.3	19.2	18.7
Drank in past year	83.6	80.3	79.8	80.7
Male	84.2	81.0	79.0	79.9
Female	82.9	79.7	80.5	81.3
Nonbinge drinking	39.7	37.2	35.7	36.3
Male	35.1	32.6	29.4	31.3
Female	44.0	41.4	41.4	40.4
Binge drinking	43.9	43.2	44.5	44.4
Male	49.2	48.5	50.2	48.6
Female	39.0	38.4	39.4	40.9
Occasional binge drinking	24.3	22.2	21.9	21.6
Male	26.8	25.3	24.9	23.4
Female	21.9	19.4	19.2	20.0
Frequent binge drinking	19.7	21.0	22.6	22.8
Male	22.4	23.2	25.3	25.2
Female	17.1	18.9	20.3	20.9

Source: http://www.albany.edu/sourcebook/pdf/t377.pdf, accessed January 21, 2008.

and his coauthors defined problematic college drinking in a different way, using the concept of binge drinking. Third, the paper's publication in one of the foremost international medical journals raised the profile of college drinking as a social problem. Two other supporting papers appeared almost simultaneously in the foremost public health journal (the *American Journal of Public Health*), again raising both the stature of the problem and its framing as a public health issue. Finally, unlike virtually all previous research in this field, the funding organization, the Robert Wood Johnson Foundation, paid for an extensive public relations campaign following publication of the research. The problem of college drinking was discussed on the front pages of the nation's newspapers and in its major television news programs.

Table 2-2.
Drinking Behaviors Among College Students Who Drank Alcohol,
1993–2001 (percent)

Drinking behavior	1993	1997	1999	2001
Drank on 10 or more occasions in the past 30 days				
Total	18.1	21.1	23.1	22.6
Male	23.9	27.2	30.1	29.2
Female	12.3	15.1	16.4	16.8
Was drunk three or more times in the past 30 days				
Total	23.4	29	30.2	29.4
Male	28	33.6	35.8	34.9
Female	18.9	24.4	25	24.6
Drinks to get drunk				
Total	39.9	53.5	47.7	48.2
Male	44.4	59.1	53.8	55.2
Female	35.6	48.4	42.4	42.4

Source: http://www.albany.edu/sourcebook/pdf/t379.pdf, accessed January 21, 2008.

LONG-TERM TRENDS IN COLLEGE DRINKING

Most college students drink occasionally, but it is excessive student drinking that forms the core of this social problem. Researchers attempting to measure excessive drinking usually have employed survey research across large populations, asking whether the respondent has consumed a certain number of drinks in an episode. Unfortunately (and perhaps inevitably), the researchers have differed in the exact details of their questions, making a direct comparison across the years virtually impossible. But we can piece together evidence to yield a fairly robust estimate of trends in college drinking over more than a half-century.

Robert Saltz reviewed the growing body of research on college drinking for the period from 1972 to 1985, finding 12 studies that reported trends in college drinking for time periods of 1 to 11 years.

The reports do not offer support for a single conclusion about drinking trends. Of the nine studies which reported longitudinal data on the prevalence of college student drinking, four found an increase in drinking between the first and last administration.... There were no studies which found decrease. In addition, the three of the remaining five studies reported an increase in either quantity or frequency.[29]

Patrick O'Malley and Lloyd Johnston presented an analysis of college-drinking trends over the half-century since Straus and Bacon published their groundbreaking 1953 study *Drinking in College*. They conclude that a slight increase may have taken place in the monthly prevalence of drinking:

> How much change has occurred since 1950? Straus and Bacon's (1953) study does not allow comparison of heavy-drinking rates, but we can compare monthly prevalence (i.e., the percentage who drank at all in the prior 30 days). According to Blane and Hewitt's (1977) recalculation of Straus and Bacon's data, 65% of college students in 1949–51 drank once a month or more. The monthly prevalences in the early 1990s is very close, perhaps slightly higher than that figure, depending on the source and how one defines the comparable population. The [Monitoring the Future data] estimates that, in 1995, 68% of full-time students (1–4 years past high school) in 4-year colleges in 1995 drank in the past month. For 1995, the NCHRBS estimated 68% of all students and 73% of 4-year college students (full-time and part-time) drank in the past month. The CAS [College Alcohol Study] estimated that 70% of college students did so. Thus there seems fair agreement that the prevalence of past 30-day drinking is slightly higher than it was in midcentury.[30]

Scott Walters and John Baer argue that excessive college drinking hasn't changed much. "Comparing Straus and Bacon's measures of *heavy* drinking to today's (unfortunately the measures are somewhat different) suggests a modest 50-year increase in rates for men and a more substantial increase for women.... Over the past 20 years, though, patterns appear to be more stable."[31] Cook comments that "[t]he adoption of an official ban on underage drinking on campus has not been inspired by an objective increase in the prevalence of drinking or abuse."[32]

Data from the four large Harvard School of Public Health College Alcohol Studies show little change from 1993 to 2001. The most important changes were slight increases in the number of abstainers and also binge drinkers, leading the researchers to discuss a growing trend toward "polarization" among college students.[33]

When the two most reliable series about heavy episodic or binge drinking are put together, a picture emerges of little change over most of the past three decades. Figure 2-2 presents the slightly downward trend in the Monitoring the Future (MTF) data about college student one to three years from leaving high school. Based on a much larger sample than the MTF, the Harvard College Alcohol Study data for binge drinking appear as four points, showing almost no change over the period from 1993 to 2001.

Figure 2-2.
Trends in College Drinking

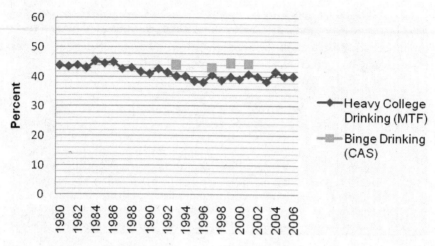

Sources: Johnston, O'Malley, Bachman, & Schulenberg (2007); Wechsler, Lee, Kuo, Seibring, Nelson, & Lee (2002).

Little has changed in the first decade of the twenty-first century. Examination of the data in the 14 American College Health Assessments conducted each fall and spring semester from spring 2000 to fall 2006 show almost no change in the question of whether the student has had "five or more alcohol drinks at a sitting during the past two weeks." In the last semester surveyed, 68 percent of females and 53 percent of males say they never drank at this level; 21 percent and 24 percent, respectively, report one to two times; and 11 percent and 23 percent, respectively, say three or more times. Another series of questions were asked of drinkers only about the number of drinks and the hours over which they were consumed during the last time the students partied or socialized. These data show a slight downward trend, so that in the fall of 2006 females consumed 4.5 drinks over 3.4 hours, for a rate of 1.3 drinks per hour, while males consumed 7.2 drinks over 4.0 hours, a rate of 1.8 drinks per hour. The downward trend for men was sharper than for women: men drank 9.0 drinks over 5.0 hours in the fall of 2000, the highest amount in the 14 surveys.[34]

In the past two decades, colleges have begun to address the problem of college drinking. Interventions designed to moderate problematic behavior were fielded at hundreds of institutions, led by a national center funded by the U.S. Department of Education. A considerable amount of social science research was done. Congressional resolutions were passed and hearings were held. Significant attention from the mass media was directed at the issue. Nonetheless, available evidence suggests little change in rates of problematic drinking across the country, although the situation at individual campuses may vary considerably. Whatever changes did occur took place as far back as the 1960s or 1970s, with less change since then. In the past few decades, almost no change is noted.

COLLEGE VERSUS NONCOLLEGE DRINKING

College students abuse alcohol at higher rates than their noncollege-going peers, though the reason for this difference is not entirely clear.[35] Some of the gap between college and noncollege alcohol use patterns probably reflects the demographic differences between these two populations—with college-goers being more likely to abuse alcohol. Some of the answer reflects the particular environment in which many students live, with large numbers of underage people in proximity to alcohol users of legal age and to bars and other alcohol outlets that vigorously promote heavy alcohol consumption.[36] Differences in rates of binge drinking among colleges may reflect the large variation in these environmental factors. Much of the current thinking about preventing binge drinking begins with the assumption that changing the broad social environment is necessary to lower binge drinking rates.

Bacon and Straus concluded in 1953 that there was nothing particularly unique about college drinking, and that it in fact mirrored what was going on in the broader society. Using MTF data on a sample of college students and persons not in college one to three years after high school, O'Malley and Johnston compared trends over the period from 1980 to 1999 (see figure 2-3).[37]

Two measures were virtually identical between college and noncollege-going users: any use of alcohol in a year (12-month prevalence) and daily alcohol use. Two other measures—any use in the past month (30-day prevalence) and heavy alcohol use—showed a small but consistent difference, with "slightly higher prevalence rates" among college students than their age-mates who didn't attend college. But it is noteworthy that the curves are pretty close together in any one year and that the overall trends follow similar trajectories over the years.

Cook's reanalysis of another data set on young people strengthens the case that the college versus noncollege drinking difference may be less than assumed:

[C]ontrary to the conventional wisdom, attending college does not appear to be a cause of increased drinking, at least on average. An analysis of data from the National Longitudinal Survey of Youth . . . for the year 2000 demonstrates

Figure 2-3.
Trends in Annual, 30-Day, Heavy, and Daily Alcohol Use Among College Students and Noncollege-Goers, 1980–1999

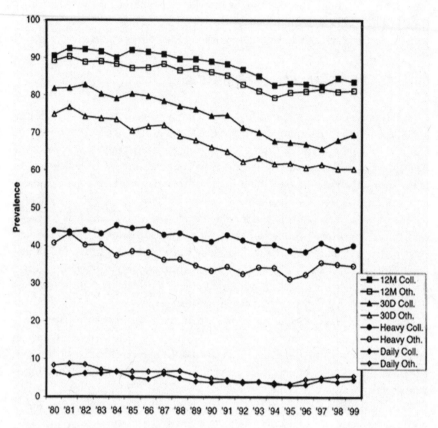

Source: O'Malley & Johnston (2002). *Note:* 12M = annual; 30D = 30 days; Coll. = college students; Oth. = noncollege-goers.

that while college students as a group drink somewhat more than their out-of-school age peers, that difference disappears when account is taken of personal characteristics (including aptitude and family background) and living arrangements. Youths who live in an apartment or house with other youths are more likely to drink (and drink more) than those living at home or in supervised group quarters (such as a dormitory)—regardless of whether they are in college or not.[38]

An important piece of evidence about the college-noncollege divide was provided by an analysis of data from a large national survey, the National Household Survey on Drug Abuse. Joseph Gfroerer, Janet Greenblatt, and

Table 2-3.

Prevalence of Heavy Episodic Drinking Among College and Noncollege-Going Past-Year Drinkers, Ages 18–29 (percent)

Drinking	College	Noncollege Going
Any heavy episodic drinking	56.1	53.1
Heavy drinking >1/month	31.1	27.6
Heavy drinking >1/week	16.7	14.1

Source: Dawson, Grant, Stinson, & Chou (2004: figure 1).

Douglas Wright compared the entire college-age civilian population (17–22 years old) on substance use, examining the impact of living arrangements and student status. [39]

> College students not living with parents had the highest rates of current use and heavy use of alcohol. High school dropouts had the lowest rate of current use, while college students living with their parents had the lowest rate of heavy use. Logistic regression models confirmed that college students not living with parents were more likely to drink heavily than those living with parents ... college students were more likely than high school graduates to have used alcohol in the past month. In contrast with findings among older populations, educational status was not found to be a significant predictor of heavy alcohol use in the college-age population.

Deborah Dawson, Bridget Grant, Frederick Stinson, and Patricia Chou examined heavy episodic or binge drinking among all American adults ages 18–29 in a large national survey completed in 2001–02. [40] Table 2-3 presents data comparing heavy episodic drinking among past-year drinkers: 56.1 percent of college students but 53.1 percent of noncollege-going adults reported any episodic drinking. Overall differences between college and noncollege-going adults were small. By contrast (consistent with Gfroerer's evidence), place of residence was more important: "[R]ates were highest for campus students living on and off campus, next highest for those not in college who were living independently and lowest for individuals living with parents, regardless of student status." [41]

CONCLUSION

Writing in 1970 about the 1950s and 1960s, the sociologist Robert Straus, coauthor of the pioneering 1953 report on college drinking, reflected on the changes he had observed:

During the period since the publication of *Drinking in College*, the meaning of being a college student has changed in a number of ways. Most colleges have greatly increased their enrollment. Many new colleges have been created to meet the rapidly rising demand for higher education. Without academic traditions, these new schools often resemble a business enterprise more than an educational institution. At older, more prestigeful colleges, pressures on faculty to engage in research, consultation, and service have imposed seriously on the time and interest which professors devote to students and on their commitment to teaching. Massive research institutes and skyscraper dormitories are replacing the "halls of ivy." College athletics are becoming increasingly professional. The colleges no longer represent the termination of preparation for a life career, but are just an interlude in a continuing process of education.... All of these factors have been associated with a decrease in the special significance of college life and in the respect accorded by students to college faculty, teens, and counselors who, like parents, find that their influence on the attitudes, values, and behavior of students is waning.[42]

Then, as now, the meaning of being a college student was in flux, with almost all of the changes Straus noted sounding much like those experienced since 1970. But not all: I have omitted from the above quote sentences that talk about the "trend toward earlier marriage" and "a movement of student self-assertion." In those respects, the sixties really were different.

In addition to the changes listed above, Straus noted "the problem of drinking by young people has been complicated by an increase in the use of automobiles by students while in college and by the greatly increased freedom from college imposed sanctions which the automobile has provided."[43] Straus also claimed that

It has also been suggested that pressures associated with the rapidity and nature of recent social change have intensified the need which many young people feel to assert their independence, to reject inconsistent and restrictive authority, or to seek ways of coping with the stresses of uncertainty, frustration, disillusionment, and groping for self identity. Theoretically, all these factors might be expected to have led to an increase in the frequency and quantity of alcohol use by college students and in the incidence of social complications and potential problem drinking. There is no evidence to support or refute such a theory. However, in spite of the grim picture of pressures which impinge on today's college youth, there are some reasons for optimism with respect to college drinking per se.[44]

Reframing college drinking as a social problem involved looking much more critically at what has ensued since Straus wrote in 1970. Whether one agrees with Straus about the "grim picture" of pressures on youth, higher education has been under considerable stress as it continues to grow and change, and student life has hardly been placid and calm. Over the past half-century or more (since 1953), the data show a modest rise in the prevalence of college drinking and especially binge or heavy episodic drinking, but little change has occurred in the past few decades. College students drink differently than their noncollege-going peers, less than those in the military and more than civilians not in college. But the gap between college and noncollege drinking is not large and probably reflects differences in the type of living arrangements as much as anything else. By itself, the college-noncollege gap cannot explain the rise of college drinking as a social problem.

College students drink more than their age-mates who don't attend college, but the difference turns out to be smaller than widely believed. Rates of binge drinking are higher among college students, however, than among their noncollege-going peers. This may reflect the unique environment of the contemporary American campus, the different characteristics of those who go to college and those who don't, or some combination of how colleges both "collect" and "create" problem drinking.

The modest long-term rise in college drinking does not explain why college drinking was reframed as a social problem for higher education. No sudden rise in problematic drinking can account for the considerable rise in mass media and newspaper stories about college drinking or the research and intervention activities that were directed at the issue since 1990. The extensive arguments made about the harm drinking caused to students and those in proximity to them were at least part of the reason for the issue's rise as a social problem as was the argument that going to college was a major factor in bringing about harm. The next chapter takes up the question of the correlates and consequences of college drinking.

NOTES

1. *Chronicle of Higher Education*, August 31, 2007, p. 4.
2. Barnett (1932); Straus & Bacon (1953); Blane & Hewitt (1977); Saltz & Elandt (1986).
3. Eigen (1991: 26).
4. Straus & Bacon (1953: 121).
5. Straus & Bacon (1953: 123).
6. Eigen (1991: 3).
7. Eigen (1991: 4).
8. Eigen (1991: 75).
9. Wechsler, Dowdall, Davenport, & Rimm (1995).
10. Wechsler & Austin (1998).
11. For researchers, see Dowdall & Wechsler (2002) and O'Malley & Johnston (2002). For policy, see the Healthy People 2010 goal of reducing binge drinking at

http://www.healthypeople.gov/document/html/objectives/26–11.htm, accessed January 20, 2008.

12. Dufour (1999).

13. Foss, Marchetti, Holladay, & Scholla (1999); Dowdall & Wechsler (2002).

14. http://www.higheredcenter.org/press-releases/001020.html, accessed January 19, 2008. This Note to the Field: On "binge drinking" was last updated in 2000.

15. http://www.higheredcenter.org/press/hunter.html, accessed January 19, 2008.

16. http://www.higheredcenter.org/press/op-ed.html, accessed January 19, 2007.

17. http://www.jsad.com/jsad/static/binge.html, accessed January 18, 2008.

18. http://pubs.niaaa.nih.gov/publications/Newsletter/winter2004/Newsletter_Number3.pdf, accessed January 18, 2008.

19. See the exchange between Robert Chapman and Robert Saltz on the Alcohol and Other Drug Listserv, sponsored by the AOD Knowledge Community of NASPA, January 17, 2008.

20. For example, in January 2008, Minnesota Public Radio presented its listeners with a multipart series on binge drinking. See http://minnesota.publicradio.org/display/web/2008/01/16/midmorning2/, accessed January 19, 2008.

21. On the use of national data bases and surveys to estimate college drinking, see Meilman, Cashin, McKillip, & Presley (1998); Dowdall & Wechsler (2002); O'Malley & Johnston (2002); Dawson, Grant, Stinson, & Chou (2004).

22. The others are the Core Institute at Southern Illinois University, the University of Michigan's Monitoring the Future Study, the Center for Disease Control and Prevention's National College Health Risk Behavior Survey, and the U.S. Surgeon General's "Healthy People 2010." See Dowdall & Wechsler (2002); Meilman, Cashin, McKillip, & Presley (1998); Douglas, Collins, Warren, Kann, Gold, Clayton, Ross, & Kolbe. (1997).

23. O'Malley & Johnston (2002).

24. Wechsler, Davenport, Dowdall, Moeykens, & Castillo (1994).

25. Dowdall & Wechsler (2002).

26. Wechsler, Dowdall, Maenner, Gledhill-Hoyt, & Lee (1998).

27. Dowdall, Crawford, & Wechsler (1998); Crawford, Dowdall, & Wechsler (1999).

28. Wechsler, Kuo, Lee, & Dowdall (2000).

29. Saltz & Elandt (1986: 129–132).

30. O'Malley & Johnston (2002).

31. Walters & Baer (2006: 7).

32. Cook (2007: 191).

33. Wechsler, Lee, Kuo, Seibring, Nelson, & Lee (2002).

34. http://www.acha-ncha.org/data_highlights.html, accessed December 28, 2007. American College Health Association. American College Health Association–National College Health Assessment (ACHA-NCHA) Web Summary. Updated August 2007.

35. Straus & Bacon (1953).

36. Wechsler, Kuo, Lee, & Dowdall (2000).
37. O'Malley & Johnston (2002).
38. Cook (2007: 191).
39. Gfroerer, Greenblatt, & Wright (1997).
40. Dawson, Grant, Stinson, & Chou (2004).
41. Dawson, Grant, Stinson, & Chou (2004: 481).
42. Straus (1970: 41).
43. Straus (1970: 42).
44. Straus (1970: 43).

CHAPTER 3

The Impact of College Drinking

That college students drink, and that some drink heavily, has been widely known for decades. Aside from the lived experiences of millions of Americans, a series of reports confirm that observation. The pioneering 1953 national study, *Drinking in College*, presented ample evidence of widespread drinking.[1] Similarly, the 1970 volume *The Domesticated Drug* collected the work of social scientists and public health experts on college drinking.[2] The lead federal research agency on alcoholism, the National Institute on Alcohol Abuse and Alcoholism (NIAAA), addressed the issue in its 1976 monograph, *The Whole College Catalog about Drinking*.[3] Independent researchers such as Ruth Engs and David Hanson published data about the links between campus crime and alcohol use during the 1980s.[4]

But it wasn't until the 1990s that research began to produce considerable systematic evidence of the correlates and consequences of college drinking. This evidence was in turn critical for reframing college drinking as a significant public health problem. Among the most important was a 1994 publication in the *Journal of the American Medical Association* (JAMA). Its senior author, Henry Wechsler, was an experienced researcher who had studied such topics as the minimum drinking-age laws and binge drinking in Massachusetts colleges. In the JAMA paper, Wechsler (and his coauthors, including myself) reported on a survey of more than 17,000 college students randomly selected from a scientific sample of 140 colleges and universities, the first (and thus far, the only) large-scale study of college student alcohol use employing this type of college sample.

We have already discussed the JAMA paper's findings about the prevalence of drinking and other substance use. By claiming that 44 percent of college students were binge drinkers, the paper established that heavy episodic drinking was common. But perhaps even more important, the paper presented evidence about "the health and behavioral consequences of binge drinking," including the harm that this type of drinking was associated with for both the individual drinker and for those in his or her immediate environment (termed "secondhand binge effects"). Companion papers appeared soon after in the *American Journal of Public Health* (AJPH) reporting on a gender-specific definition of binge drinking as well as on the personal correlates of college drinking.

Together, the JAMA and AJPH papers presented data that supported reframing college drinking as a social problem, with a shift away from a narrowly individualistic concern with a few "alcoholic" students toward a focus on a widespread and potentially dangerous form of alcohol abuse tied to the college population and its environment. In this chapter, we examine some of the personal and environmental correlates of heavy episodic or binge drinking. Some of these correlates (such as precollege drinking and gender) shed light on why some students abuse alcohol while others who share exactly the same environment drink moderately or not at all. Other correlates help us to understand the impact college drinking has on the health and well-being of both drinking and nondrinking students.

WHAT SHAPES COLLEGE DRINKING?

Why do college students drink the way they do?[5] While no single definitive answer exists, we know an increasing amount about the factors that shape drinking behavior.[6] Table 3-1 presents some of the most important issues, grouped into those that precede college and those that occur during college.[7]

Of those factors preceding college, recent research has examined genetic issues, with one recent study suggesting that college students who binge may have different genetic components than those who don't.[8] Another study concluded, "Exposure to a college environment acts as an environmental moderator, supporting the hypothesis that the magnitude of genetic influence on certain aspects of alcohol consumption is greater in environments where drinking behaviors are more likely to be promoted."[9]

More proximate factors play a role in college drinking, such as the level of high school drinking and parental drinking. For the individual student, age

Table 3-1.
Factors Shaping College Drinking

Before College	*During College*
Family Factors: • Genetics • Parental drinking behavior • Social class • Race or ethnicity • Religion	Individual Factors: • Age of drinking onset • High school drinking • Drug or tobacco use • Gender • Race
Public Policy: • National laws • State laws • Enforcement of minimum drinking age • Local community ordinances	College Environment: • Peer norms • Residential system • Fraternity/Sorority life • Athletics • Academics • Community Service • Religious involvement
Alcohol Environment: • Price of alcohol • Advertising • Marketing practices • Outlet density • Hours of sale	Alcohol Environment On Campus: • Dry or wet campus • Availability • Price • Alcohol policy
Social/Institutional Structures: • Neighborhood • Middle and high school • Church, synagogue, mosque • Subcultures	Alcohol Environment Off Campus: • Retail price • Outlet density and proximity • Advertising • Marketing

Source: Adapted from Dowdall & Wechsler (2002).

of drinking onset has been identified as an important factor in alcohol abuse and dependence; the earlier the onset, the higher the risk of later problems with alcohol.[10] Public policy shapes precollege drinking, including the minimum legal drinking age of 21 and its enforcement: students who live in states with effective alcohol control policies or who attend schools with few alcohol outlets nearby drink less than their peers.[11] The overall alcohol environment shapes the level of drinking in a community, with the cost of alcohol, its promotion through advertising and marketing, and its availability all playing a role. Finally, subcultures of drug and alcohol use within high schools or neighborhoods exert some influence as well.

In middle and late adolescence, alcohol use increases partly as a function of new freedoms but decreases as new responsibilities (such as work, relationships or marriage, and beginning a family) are assumed.[12] Young people may be affected by the advertising of alcohol beverages and their appearance in the mass media.[13]

Drinking during adolescence plays a central role in shaping later college drinking. The NIAAA issued an "alcohol alert" on why adolescents use alcohol.[14] The conclusions of the report deserve scrutiny:

> As children move from adolescence to young adulthood, they encounter dramatic physical, emotional, and lifestyle changes. Developmental transitions, such as puberty and increasing independence, have been associated with alcohol use. So in a sense, just being an adolescent may be a key risk factor not only for starting to drink but also for drinking dangerously.
>
> *Risk-Taking*—Research shows the brain keeps developing well into the twenties, during which time it continues to establish important communication connections and further refines its function.... Developmental changes also offer a possible physiological explanation for why teens act so impulsively, often not recognizing that their actions—such as drinking—have consequences.
>
> *Expectancies*—How people view alcohol and its effects also influences their drinking behavior, including whether they begin to drink and how much. An adolescent who expects drinking to be a pleasurable experience is more likely to drink than one who does not.... As would be expected, adolescents who drink the most also place the greatest emphasis on the positive and arousing effects of alcohol.
>
> *Sensitivity and Tolerance to Alcohol*—Differences between the adult brain and the brain of the maturing adolescent also may help to explain why many young drinkers are able to consume much larger amounts of alcohol than adults ... before experiencing the negative consequences of drinking, such as drowsiness, lack of coordination, and withdrawal/hangover effects....This unusual tolerance may help to explain the high rates of binge drinking among young adults. At the same time, adolescents appear to be particularly sensitive to the positive effects of drinking, such as feeling more at ease in social situations, and young people may drink more than adults because of these positive social experiences ...
>
> *Personality Characteristics and Psychiatric Comorbidity*—Children who begin to drink at a very early age (before age 12) often share similar personality characteristics that may make them more likely to start drinking. Young people who are disruptive, hyperactive, and aggressive—often referred to as having conduct problems or being antisocial—as well as those who are depressed, withdrawn, or anxious, may be at greatest risk for alcohol problems ...
>
> *Hereditary Factors*—Some of the behavioral and physiological factors that converge to increase or decrease a person's risk for alcohol problems, including tolerance to alcohol's effects, may be directly linked to genetics. For example, being a child of an alcoholic or having several alcoholic family members places a person at greater risk for alcohol problems ...

Environmental Aspects—Pinpointing a genetic contribution will not tell the whole story, however, as drinking behavior reflects a complex interplay between inherited and environmental factors, the implications of which are only beginning to be explored in adolescents.... Environmental factors, such as the influence of parents and peers, also play a role in alcohol use. For example, parents who drink more and who view drinking favorably may have children who drink more, and an adolescent girl with an older or adult boyfriend is more likely to use alcohol and other drugs and to engage in delinquent behaviors.[15]

PRECOLLEGE TRAITS PREDICT HEAVY COLLEGE DRINKING

The psychologists Kenneth Sher and Patricia Rutledge examined how well precollege traits predicted heavy drinking in the first semester of college in a large study conducted among entering freshmen to a large Midwest university in 2002. They argue that their research

[D]emonstrates exceptionally strong prospective prediction of heavy drinking across [the transition to college] ... heavy drinking in first-semester, first-time college students is strongly associated with precollege heavy drinking. Thus, collegiate drinking, at least in the first semester, represents a systematic escalation of an ongoing behavior established prior to college as opposed to chaotic, unpredictable change practices (e.g., a "developmental disturbance;"...) precipitated by the transition to college and a host of related transitions inherent in the college transition (e.g., the "leaving home" transition). Thus, although there are many good reasons to focus on "college drinking" as a national health problem ... we need to view early college drinking as embedded in the context of ongoing adolescent development and not viewed as a highly discontinuous phenomena ... it is noteworthy that other college predictors have the ability to provide statistically unique prediction over and above precollege drinking. Specifically, these other predictors are having heavier drinking peers, smoking cigarettes and using other substances, valuing college partying, having a Catholic or other Christian religious affiliation, being less religious, being male, being more able to obtain alcohol, and being less interested in attending college to gain knowledge. The picture that emerges from these correlates is that future collegiate heavy drinkers are more heavily involved in substance use in general (not just alcohol) during high school, are more involved in a social network that provides both facilitative norms and increased access to alcohol and are less likely to report involvement of religious observances and activities.[16]

FACTORS IN COLLEGE DRINKING

Table 3-1 includes a variety of factors that shape college drinking. Some of the factors are personal qualities of students—for example, men still drink more than women, though the gender gap appears to be closing; other personal factors such as high school bingeing, current drug or alcohol use, and attaching little importance to religion in college raise the likelihood of college binge drinking.[17]

Other factors deal with the college environment. Students who misperceive the amount of drinking on a campus may drink more than those who accurately perceive the norms.[18] Students who are part of the social worlds of athletics or fraternities and sororities drink more, while students who think religion should be an important part of their college lives or who regularly perform community service drink less. The alcohol environment on and off campus plays an important role, with the cost, availability, and promotion of alcohol products shaping how much drinking takes place.

Table 3-1 hardly exhausts the factors that shape college drinking, but it does support the important argument that what may seem like a purely individual choice (to drink, or to binge drink) is shaped by many factors, some of them considerably upstream from the behavior of an individual college student. Research about college drinking and interventions to change college drinking need to consider this broader view by "widening the lens and sharpening the focus" on all of these precollege and college factors.[19]

Some of the most important personal correlates of binge drinking are presented in table 3-2. The data come from the first year of the Harvard School of Public Health College Alcohol Study and are based on questionnaires completed at 140 colleges and universities in 1993. Each item is a trait or attitude (e.g., "fraternity residence") that raises the risk of binge drinking by a certain amount (e.g., 4.08) compared with its opposite (e.g., "doesn't live in a fraternity"). So a student who lives in a fraternity is 4.08 times more likely to binge drink than one who doesn't live in a fraternity. This list of 18 correlates of binge drinking was created after analyzing 33 plausible correlates of binge drinking. The list of 18 represents those correlates that remained statistically significant even when all the other factors were taken into account.[20]

Commitment to a lifestyle emphasizing parties, using other substances such as tobacco and marijuana, bingeing in high school, having parents who use alcohol, and having two or more sex partners in the last month all emerged as important predictors of binge drinking. College living arrangements such as fraternity or sorority residence or living with a roommate, believing in the importance of athletics, and spending a lot of time socializing and less studying also predict bingeing. Table 3-2 presents cross-sectional data, so it isn't possible to say with certainty that these are causes of binge drinking, but the data at least suggest that student choices play an important role in college drinking, even with the power of the social context of college.

Table 3-2.

Correlates of College Student Binge Drinking with Indicator of Strength of Prediction (conditional odds ratio, N = 15,592)

Item	Odds Ratio
Age less than 24 years	1.53
Race is white	2.37
Sex is male	1.19
Binged in high school	2.84
Parent was not an abstainer	1.55
Parties are very important or important	3.40
Religion is not very important	2.40
Athletics are very important or important	1.47
Community service is not very important	1.26
Fraternity residence	4.08
Has five or more close friends	1.36
Grade point average is B or less	1.29
Lives in coed dormitory	1.12
Has used marijuana in last month	2.96
Uses cigarettes on a typical day	2.58
Has two or more sex partners in a month	1.66
Hours socializing with friends are more that 2	1.36
Studying	1.15

Source: Wechsler, Dowdall, Davenport, & Castillo (1995).

A large sample of college students responding to a questionnaire from the Core Institute said they thought alcohol had the following effects (percentage agreeing in parentheses):[21]

- Breaks the ice (70 percent)
- Enhances social activity (69 percent)
- Gives people something to do (66 percent)
- Gives people something to talk about (59 percent)
- Allows people to have more fun (55 percent)
- Facilitates a connection with peers (54 percent)
- Facilitates male bonding (53 percent)
- Facilitates sexual opportunities (49 percent)
- Facilitates female bonding (41 percent)

- Makes it easier to deal with stress (35 percent)
- Makes women sexier (21 percent)
- Makes food taste better (14 percent)
- Makes men sexier (12 percent)
- Makes me sexier (12 percent)

In the eyes of college students, drinking solves some issues in establishing themselves in a new social environment, easing the transition from high school and adolescent roles to college and adult ones.[22] These attitudes probably reflect various external and internal factors, including previous positive experience with alcohol, sentiments held by many Americans, as well as the culture transmitted to newcomers on many college campuses. These inferences probably also reflect the impact of alcohol advertising on this age group, even if the ads are supposedly targeted at slightly older adults.[23] Given such positive attitudes about alcohol, along with ease of access to alcohol, widespread use isn't surprising.

The environment appears to be a powerful force shaping college drinking. For those under 21, the campus and its surrounding communities provide easy access to alcohol.

> Underage students drink less often but have more drinks per occasion, are more likely to drink in private settings (off-campus, dormitory, and fraternity parties), and pay less per drink than do of-age students. Correlates of underage binge drinking include residence in a fraternity or sorority…, very easy access to alcohol…, obtaining drinks at lower prices…, and drinking beer.[24]

Data collected from 17,051 students at 32 colleges and universities from 2000 to 2004 suggest how both personal traits and choices combine with environmental features to shape college drinking.[25] The researchers found that a variety of student-level factors (much like those reported earlier) played a role in predicting indicators of college drinking (such as the number of drinks when partying, the mean number of days one got drunk in the last month, and the 30-day frequency of alcohol use). Almost all of the following variables predicted higher levels of those drinking indicators:

- Male
- White race (versus other)
- Hispanic (versus non-Hispanic)
- Age 20 years or over
- Upperclassman (versus freshman)

- Full-time student status
- Live with roommates (versus alone or with family)
- Doesn't live in dorm
- Participation in fraternity/sorority activities more than six hours per week
- Varsity athletic participation less than six hours per week
- Lower grade point average
- Level of high school drinking (none to problem)
- Attitude toward drinking (0–4, not good to okay to get drunk)

Almost all of the findings are strongly consistent with the earlier Harvard College Alcohol Study results on 140 colleges in 1993. What is striking is the addition of two campus-level variables about student exposure to alcohol that also predict the drinking variables. Both measure alcohol outlet densities for on-premise (e.g., restaurants and bars) and off-premise (e.g., grocery and convenience stores) within one, two, and three miles from each campus (per 1,000 students). The authors note that "[t]hese findings suggest campus-level factors many have a significant influence on individual-level processes involved in problem drinking . . . [and] suggest contextual factors like campus alcohol outlet density are at least as important as some individual measures."[26]

New technologies and practices play a role in college drinking as well, though the exact role is far from clearly determined. Anecdotal evidence suggests that social networking software like Facebook and MySpace can help spread the word about parties or bring together students with common interests in heavy partying. Observation of Facebook groups at one high-binge campus shows many student photographs at alcohol-related events, striking poses that borrow from the club life, or with the ubiquitous red Dixie® cups at the ready. On the other hand, the same technologies are now being used by student life staff to spread the word about prevention services, and at least one vendor of prevention software, Alcohol.Edu, has begun to develop social networking software for a "silent majority" who use alcohol moderately or not at all.

The expectation that college will involve alcohol consumption, combined with easy availability, access, and low cost, make alcohol use by a majority of students and alcohol abuse by a substantial minority likely. But "likely" does not have to mean "inevitable," and the more we know about why students drink or abuse alcohol, the more we may be able to change the current picture. In a concluding chapter, we will examine more closely the argument that college drinking is part of a college culture.

CONSEQUENCES OF COLLEGE DRINKING

The consequences of drinking vary greatly from person to person. This variation poses some of the greatest challenges for prevention programs, because messages about the consequences of drinking rarely capture this diversity of outcomes. Simply reciting statistics about overall harm of alcohol abuse does little to convince an individual that his or her personal drinking habits are dangerous—and in fact, for a particular individual, they may not be dangerous.

As figure 3-1 demonstrates, many students have adopted a drinking style that centers on frequent or intense alcohol consumption. When the Harvard researchers asked about their activities during the month before the survey, a large minority (44 percent) of students told them they binged, and often drank with the intention of getting drunk. Depending on the survey year, between 20 and 33 percent of students said they had been drunk three or more times in the previous month, and a slightly smaller percentage drank on 10 or more days over the course of the month.

Men were somewhat more likely than women to respond positively to these items, though the gap was not great. Over the long term, the changes in women's drinking behaviors have been quite large, but even today the gap remains between the genders.

For some students, drinking is not associated with any immediate negative outcomes. But heavy episodic or binge drinking raises the risk of alcohol-related problems, as the data in figure 3-2 indicate. Bingers are more likely than nonbingers to get behind in school work, get into trouble with campus or community police, have unprotected or unplanned sex, or face other alcohol-related problems. Occasional binge drinkers have a higher risk of these

Figure 3-1.
Student Alcohol Use, 1999

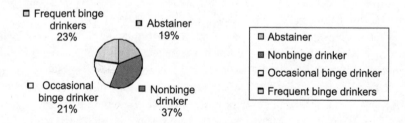

Source: Author; adapted from Wechsler, Lee, Kuo, & Lee (2000).

Figure 3-2.
Problems by Drinking Type, 1999

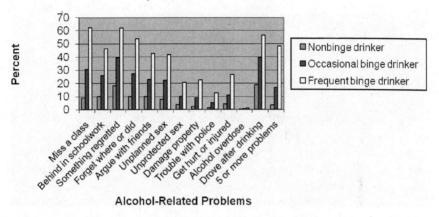

Source: Author; adapted from Wechsler, Lee, Kuo, & Lee (2000).

problems than do nonbingeing drinkers, and frequent binge drinkers have the highest risk of all.

There is a strong, positive correlation between the frequency of binge drinking and alcohol-related health and other problems reported by students. With regard to the more serious alcohol-related problems, the frequent binge drinkers were 7 to 10 times more likely than the nonbinge drinkers to get into trouble with campus police, damage property or get injured, not use protection when having sex, or engage in unplanned sexual activity. Men and women report similar incidence for most of the problems. Among the frequent binge drinkers, however, 35 percent of the men and 9 percent of the women report damaging property and 16 percent of the men and 6 percent of the women report getting into trouble with the campus police.[27]

There is a positive relationship between binge drinking and driving under the influence of alcohol, and a large proportion of the student population reported driving after drinking alcohol. Binge drinkers reported significantly higher frequencies of dangerous driving behaviors than nonbinge drinkers. The 1999 Harvard study reported driving after drinking by one in five nonbingeing students, two in five of the occasional binge drinkers, and almost three in five of the frequent binge drinkers.[28] As many as 2.8 million college students ages 18–24 drove under the influence of alcohol in 2001.[29]

About one-half of the frequent binge drinkers (47 percent in 1993 and 52 percent in 1997) reported having experienced, since the beginning of the school year, five or more of a possible 12 alcohol-related problems (e.g., omitting hangover and including driving after drinking), compared with 14 percent of infrequent binge drinkers and 3 percent of nonbinge drinkers. Frequent binge drinkers were 20 (1997) to 25 (1993) times more likely than nonbinge drinkers to experience five or more of these problems.[30]

ACADEMIC COSTS

Both anecdotal and scientific evidence suggest that student drinking is tied to poor academic outcomes such as missing a class, getting behind in school work, and receiving low grades.[31] Royce Singleton examined academic performance and drinking at a liberal arts college, assembling considerable survey and college record data over four consecutive semesters.[32] His data show that even when controlling for major factors, such as gender, partying, parent income, academic class, and Scholastic Aptitude Test (SAT) score, alcohol consumption remained a statistically significant factor on grade point average (GPA). Much less is known about what may be the greatest academic cost associated with college drinking—dropping out or failing to graduate on time.

SECONDHAND EFFECTS

Almost a third of the Harvard study's colleges have a majority of students who binge. These binge drinkers not only put themselves at risk, but also create problems for their nonbingeing fellow students. Nonbingeing students on high-binge campuses were up to three times as likely to report being bothered by the drinking-related behaviors of other students than non-bingeing students at lower-binge campuses. These problems include being pushed, hit or assaulted, and experiencing an unwanted sexual advance.[33]

Secondary or secondhand binge effects—that is, effects on others around the drinker—were examined by the Harvard researchers. They examined the percentage of nonbingeing students who experienced secondary binge effects, which include eight types of problems caused by other students' drinking. Figure 3-3 shows that these secondary effects range from being insulted or humiliated, to having studying or sleep interrupted, to being a victim of sexual assault. Students at middle- and high-binge-level schools were more likely than students at lower-binge-level schools to experience such secondary problems as a result of the drinking behaviors of others. Specifically, students at the highest-binge-level schools were three times as

Figure 3-3.
Secondhand Binge Effects, 1999

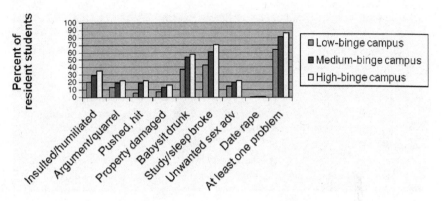

Source: Author; adapted from Wechsler, Lee, Kuo, & Lee (2000).

likely to experience at least one of these eight problems than students at lower-binge-level schools.[34]

ALCOHOL DEPENDENCE AND ABUSE

Some binge drinkers—and many frequent binge drinkers—appear to match the clinical definitions of having a problem with alcohol, and thus should be receiving treatment. But many of these students deny they have a problem, and haven't sought treatment.

The epidemiologist Deborah Dawson and her colleagues analyzed data from a large national survey, the 2001–02 National Epidemiologic Survey on Alcohol and Related Conditions (NESARC) for adults ages 18–29.[35] The NESARC includes questionnaire items that indicate whether a person meets the criteria for having an alcohol use disorder. Table 3-3 presents the psychiatric criteria for alcohol abuse and alcohol dependence. College students were found to have slightly higher rates of both disorders. The data show that 7.8 percent of all college students (and 10.3 percent of past-year college student drinkers) meet the abuse criteria, while 10.9 percent of all students and 14.5 percent of drinkers meet the dependence criteria. In all, 18.7 percent of all students and 24.7 percent of college drinkers meet the criteria for either alcohol abuse or dependence.

Table 3-3.
DSM-IV-TR (Diagnostic and Statistical Manual): Diagnostic Criteria for
Alcohol Abuse and Dependence

ALCOHOL ABUSE

(A) A maladaptive pattern of drinking, leading to clinically significant impairment
or distress, as manifested by at least one of the following occurring within a 12-
month period:

Recurrent use of alcohol resulting in a failure to fulfill major role obligations at
work, school, or home (e.g., repeated absences or poor work performance related
to alcohol use; alcohol-related absences, suspensions, or expulsions from school;
neglect of children or household)

Recurrent alcohol use in situations in which it is physically hazardous (e.g., driving an automobile or operating a machine when impaired by alcohol use)

Recurrent alcohol-related legal problems (e.g., arrests for alcohol-related disorderly conduct)

Continued alcohol use despite having persistent or recurrent social or interpersonal problems caused or exacerbated by the effects of alcohol (e.g., arguments
with spouse about consequences of intoxication)

(B) Never met criteria for alcohol dependence.

ALCOHOL DEPENDENCE

(A) A maladaptive pattern of drinking, leading to clinically significant impairment
or distress, as manifested by three or more of the following occurring at any
time in the same 12-month period:

Need for markedly increased amounts of alcohol to achieve intoxication or
desired effect; or markedly diminished effect with continued use of the same
amount of alcohol

The characteristic withdrawal syndrome for alcohol; or drinking (or using a
closely related substance) to relieve or avoid withdrawal symptoms

Drinking in larger amounts or over a longer period than intended

Persistent desire or one or more unsuccessful efforts to cut down or control
drinking

Important social, occupational, or recreational activities given up or reduced
because of drinking

A great deal of time spent in activities necessary to obtain, to use, or to recover
from the effects of drinking

Continued drinking despite knowledge of having a persistent or recurrent physical
or psychological problem that is likely to be caused or exacerbated by drinking

(B) No duration criterion separately specified, but several dependence criteria must
occur repeatedly as specified by duration qualifiers associated with criteria (e.g.,
"persistent," "continued").

Sources: U.S. Department of Health and Human Services (2007: appendix B), adapted from
American Psychiatric Association (2000).

These are not simple findings, however, because it is unclear how the disorders develop, how many precede going to college, and what impact (if any) the college environment has on their progression. But demonstrating this powerful connection between college drinking and serious psychiatric disorder should make it clear that college drinking is not a harmless rite of passage.

FATALITIES

Reframing college drinking as a social problem involves illuminating some of the darkest areas of college life, such as student fatalities involving alcohol. The stunning headlines about alcohol-related deaths at institutions across the country make this an issue of intense public interest. However, the enumeration of several dozen deaths each year in newspaper headlines hardly constitutes a definitive assessment of the extent of the problem.

USA Today gathered data on 857 deaths to college students in the years from 2000 to 2005, finally examining 620 deaths involving four-year college students, occurring within or related to the college community or campus, and taking place while classes were in session.[36] The reporters made use of a number of sources to compile these data and noted how difficult it was to gather the information.

By contrast, the epidemiologist Ralph Hingson prepared several estimates of the number of college students of traditional college age (18–24 years) who experience alcohol-related deaths, constituting the best estimate of the most serious outcomes of college drinking.[37] Hingson estimated more than 1,400 student deaths in 1998, and more than 1,700 deaths in 2001, an increase of 6 percent over the period. Many of the deaths, perhaps 80 percent, were due to alcohol-related car crashes, many of which probably occurred off campus and some of which occurred during summer and other vacations.

So, 1,700 alcohol-related deaths in a single year were estimated by Hingson, whereas 620 deaths of any kind were found for five years in the public news and other sources used by *USA Today*. Most college student deaths are probably not reported in the media. This glaring gap in data collection reflects the fact that American death certificates do not routinely report whether the deceased was a college student. Public attention usually focuses on student deaths that occur on campus during the academic year, with less known about deaths under other circumstances.

Alcohol abuse also raises the risk of suicide among young people, and alcohol is involved in two-thirds of college student suicides. The increase in the minimum legal drinking age during the 1980s is estimated to have saved 125 lives from suicide per year among youths ages 18 to 20 years.[38]

HARD AND SOFT COSTS

From the facts above, it is obvious that the costs of college binge drinking must be substantial, but no precise estimates exist. Estimates are available, however, of the related problem of the costs of underage drinking. Note that underage drinking includes a far larger population than college binge drinking: the large number of Americans of traditional college age who don't go to college as well as those of high school age or younger are included in the former but not the latter.

Far from being trivial, the annual overall cost of alcohol use by those under 21 was estimated at more than $58 billion dollars in 1999. One estimate, prepared for the U.S. Department of Justice, Office of Juvenile Justice and Delinquency Prevention, used current health and criminal justice data to arrive at these broad components:[39]

- Violent crime: $35 billion
- Traffic crashes: $18 billion
- Suicide attempts: $1.5 billion
- Treatment: $1 billion
- Drowning: $0.5 billion
- Fetal alcohol syndrome: $0.5 billion
- Burns: $0.3 billion
- Alcohol poisonings: $0.3 billion

What colleges end up paying for college drinking is difficult, perhaps impossible, to estimate. Dividing the costs into hard (actual dollars) and soft (loss of reputation, institutional focus) helps us to begin an accounting for the entire bill. Many of the hard costs find their way into charges for room and board for residential students, and into student affairs and public safety costs passed on in higher tuition bills for all students. Some fraction of community police and public safety costs in communities with college campuses also go to covering the costs of college drinking. As for the soft costs, those are even harder to estimate: some part of the reputation and public regard that higher education has developed must be affected by the negative view of college drinking, although to some this view may make college more attractive. On the other hand, the local alcohol outlets and the industry that supports them sell a significant amount of product to students both of and below legal age.

SNAPSHOT OF HEALTH CONSEQUENCES

The evidence reviewed so far shows that heavy episodic or binge drinking is associated with a much higher risk of negative health and behavioral outcomes. To bring home how many students are actually affected by college drinking, Ralph Hingson and his colleagues used these and similar data to make estimates of the magnitude of alcohol-related morbidity (illness) and mortality (death) among college students of traditional college age (18–24), producing the following "snapshot":

> The consequences of excessive and underage drinking affect virtually all college campuses, college communities, and college students, whether they choose to drink or not.

- **Death**: 1,700 college students between the ages of 18 and 24 die each year from alcohol-related unintentional injuries, including motor vehicle crashes.
- **Injury**: 599,000 students between the ages of 18 and 24 are unintentionally injured under the influence of alcohol.
- **Assault**: More than 696,000 students between the ages of 18 and 24 are assaulted by another student who has been drinking.
- **Sexual Abuse**: More than 97,000 students between the ages of 18 and 24 are victims of alcohol-related sexual assault or date rape.
- **Unsafe Sex**: 400,000 students between the ages of 18 and 24 had unprotected sex and more than 100,000 students between the ages of 18 and 24 report having been too intoxicated to know if they consented to having sex.
- **Academic Problems**: About 25 percent of college students report academic consequences of their drinking including missing class, falling behind, doing poorly on exams or papers, and receiving lower grades overall.
- **Health Problems/Suicide Attempts**: More than 150,000 students develop an alcohol-related health problem … and between 1.2 and 1.5 percent of students indicate that they tried to commit suicide within the past year due to drinking or drug use.

- **Drunk Driving**: 2.1 million students between the ages of 18 and 24 drove under the influence of alcohol last year.

- **Vandalism**: About 11 percent of college student drinkers report that they have damaged property while under the influence of alcohol.

- **Property Damage**: More than 25 percent of administrators from schools with relatively low drinking levels and over 50 percent from schools with high drinking levels say their campuses have a "moderate" or "major" problem with alcohol-related property damage.

- **Police Involvement**: About 5 percent of 4-year college students are involved with the police or campus security as a result of their drinking ... and an estimated 110,000 students between the ages of 18 and 24 are arrested for an alcohol-related violation such as public drunkenness or driving under the influence.

- **Alcohol Abuse and Dependence**: 31 percent of college students met criteria for a diagnosis of alcohol abuse and 6 percent for a diagnosis of alcohol dependence in the past 12 months, according to questionnaire-based self-reports about their drinking.[40]

This snapshot may well be an underestimate of the current health and behavioral consequences of college drinking. It does not take into account such issues as suicide. Nor does it attempt to deal with the problems of mixing alcohol with other substances, such as prescription drugs, thought to be on the rise among young populations.[41] It points to academic problems, but it does not attempt to estimate the impact alcohol abuse might have on not completing college.

The snapshot does not try to assess the long-term consequences of heavy college alcohol use. There is some evidence that abusing alcohol in college increases the risk of long-term problems with alcohol.[42] But other evidence shows that having graduated from college is associated with lower risk of having an alcohol use disorder 10 years after graduation from high school.[43]

A CULTURE OF COLLEGE DRINKING

Many people now think that college drinking is best understood as part of a deeply entrenched culture. A turning point was the 2002 publication of a special Task Force on college drinking assembled by the NIAAA. The NIAAA report was called, *A Call to Action: Changing the Culture of College Drinking*. Accompanying it was a special issue of the *Journal of Studies on Alcohol* titled, "College Drinking: What It Is and What to Do About It."

We will examine critically how much the concept of a culture of college drinking helps or hinders our ability to respond. We will add another point to the argument: in addition to a culture of college drinking, there is also a culture of how to respond to college drinking.

Like the NIAAA Task Force, many observers of contemporary college students assume that college students share a common culture (either with all other college students or at least those at the specific college of attendance). Sharing that culture may mean college students have a distinctive point of view or frame of reference built around values such as openness, and a social life built around "friendly fun," self-realization, and development of an individual identity. Some argue that college students share social norms that define how much alcohol is being used by their peers, often including the misperception that many drink more heavily than is actually the case.

The evidence reviewed above might suggest rethinking the notion of a culture of college drinking. College students attend a single university at a time. They often face choices of different types of living arrangements and subcultures within the same institution. Choosing to live in fraternity or sorority housing, becoming an athlete or part of an athletic-centered world, or placing great emphasis on partying and social life raises or lowers the odds of having an alcohol-centered experience in college.

Colleges differ enormously in how much drinking and binge drinking actually goes on, and discussing a culture of college drinking illuminates such great variation. By contrast, one-third of the colleges in the Harvard School of Public Health College Alcohol Study were identified as high-binge campuses, where more than half of the students were binge drinkers. At such high-binge schools, it makes sense to invoke the notion of a culture of college drinking. As a later chapter discusses, some data exist to allow one to identify such colleges or to choose others that have less drinking.

The NIAAA Task Force was without doubt the largest effort ever assembled to look at the question of college drinking. Taken as a whole, a remarkably detailed picture of college drinking was painted. At the very end, the concept of culture was introduced to label the effort, although few of the supporting documents refer to culture. This gap between the overall title of the report and its underlying support materials deserves further analysis.

CONCLUSION

Reframing college drinking changed the issue from a personal trouble of an individual alcoholic or habitual drunk to a public issue involving an entire population at risk. Reframing also shifted the focus from harmless though perhaps embarrassing consequences for the individual drinker to serious and even deadly consequences for both the drinker and those in the immediate environment.

The iconic images of *Animal House* (1978) could not be more misleading about college drinking. Heavy college drinking turns out not to be the innocent rite of passage celebrated in popular culture. Instead, such drinking exposes students to a much higher risk of a range of health and behavioral problems, and also raises the risk for those in the drinker's immediate environment. Discovered by independent scholars, these negative correlates of college drinking underscore widely publicized estimates made for the NIAAA College Drinking Task Force. A huge gap between reported deaths linked to college drinking and a persuasive estimate by an experienced researcher exist, so that mass media report somewhere below 100 deaths per year, while the epidemiolgocal estimate is at least 1,700. Similarly, only a small fraction of the rapes tied to alcohol are reported to the police or made known in the mass media.

Why should students who have been educated about the risks of drinking often end up drinking excessively? Researchers have discovered a relatively stable set of family, personal, and college factors that raise the risk of drinking and excessive drinking. Prior high school drinking by itself is one of the most important predictors of freshman drinking. Within the college scene, powerful subcultures centered around partying, fraternity or sorority life, and athletics shape drinking. Reframing college drinking now points to a deeply entrenched culture shaping student alcohol consumption.

NOTES

1. Straus & Bacon (1953).
2. Maddox & Society for the Study of Social Problems (1970).
3. NIAAA (1976).
4. Engs & Hanson (1994).
5. For an insightful discussion of answers to the question, "why?" see Tilly (2006).
6. For a recent review of natural and social science research about alcohol use and abuse, see NIAAA (2000). For comprehensive reviews of the literature about college student drinking, see Goldman, Boyd, & Faden (2002).
7. Dowdall & Wechsler (2002); see also Wechsler & Wuethrich (2002).
8. Herman, Philbeck, Vasilopoulos, & Depetrillo (2003).
9. Timberlake et al. (2007).
10. NIAAA (2000).
11. Dowdall (2006).
12. Martin (1995). For an overview of the impact of the media on youth alcohol use, visit http://camy.org/, accessed January 19, 2007.

13. Martin (1995).

14. http://pubs.niaaa.nih.gov/publications/AA67/AA67.htm, accessed January 19, 2007.

15. *Ibid.*

16. Sher & Rutledge (2007: 831).

17. Wechsler, Dowdall, Davenport, & Castillo (1995).

18. Perkins (2003).

19. Dowdall & Wechsler (2002).

20. In other words, these are the results of a multiple logistic regression analysis in which whether a student binge drinks or not is the dependent variable. A prior analysis of 33 correlates showed these 18 to be statistically significant, and then the 18 were used to predict binge drinking. See Wechsler, Dowdall, Davenport, & Castillo (1995).

21. Presley, Leichliter, & Meilman (1998).

22. Clydesdale (2007).

23. Federal Trade Commission (1999). Ehrenberg & Hacker (1997); see http://camy.org/, accessed January 19, 2007.

24. Wechsler, Kuo, Lee, & Dowdall (2000: 24).

25. Scribner, Mason, Theall, Simonsen, Schneider, Towvim, & DeJong (2008).

26. Scribner, Mason, Theall, Simonsen, Schneider, Towvim, & DeJong (2008: 118–119).

27. Wechsler, Davenport, Dowdall, Moeykens, & Castillo (1994).

28. Wechsler, Lee, Kuo, & Lee (2000).

29. Hingson, Heeren, Winter, & Wechsler (2005).

30. Wechsler, Dowdall, Maenner, Gledhill-Hoyt, & Lee (1998).

31. Perkins (2002).

32. Singleton (2007).

33. Wechsler, Dowdall, Maenner, Gledhill-Hoyt, & Lee (1998).

34. Wechsler, Dowdall, Maenner, Gledhill-Hoyt, & Lee (1998).

35. Dawson, Grant, Stinson, & Chou (2004).

36. Robert Davis and Anthony DeBarros, "In college, [the] first year is by far the riskiest" (*USA TODAY*, January 25, 2006).

37. Hingson, Heeren, Zakocs, Kopstein, & Wechsler (2002); Hingson, Heeren, Winter, & Wechsler (2005).

38. Birckmayer (1999).

39. Pacific Institute for Research and Evaluation (1999).

40. Source: http://www.collegedrinkingprevention.gov/StatsSummaries/snapshot.aspx, accessed February 23, 2008. See also Hingson et al. (2002) and Hingson et al. (2005).

41. CASA (2007).

42. Fillmore (1974), Vaillant (1996), and Jennison (2004).

43. Harford, Yi, & Hilton (2006).

CHAPTER 4

The "Dark Figure" of Alcohol-Related Campus Crime: The Gap Between Reported Incidents and Victimization

A major theme in the development of college drinking as a social problem inside higher education has been the argument that students, college faculty and staff, and the general public simply don't know the real problems associated with excessive alcohol consumption. This argument has been made particularly strongly about crime. This is partly because many college crimes were not reported to the authorities or, if they were, historically had not been reported to the public. Even today, when colleges are required to report some categories of crime, few people outside the campus security office know the full story. Faced with crime, some colleges still prefer to "dodge a bullet" if they can, rather than "teach a lesson" by explaining what happened to a broader public. Many Americans minimize the connection between alcohol and crime, because alcohol is a legal substance and integrated into daily life.

At issue is the "dark figure" of campus crime. There is a gap (and in the case of some crimes like sexual assault, a huge gap) between the number of crimes reported to the police and the number of actual crimes committed. This gap is made wider by the role of alcohol in campus crime. This gap also reflects variations among campuses in reporting practices. The publication of a handbook about crime reporting by the U.S. Department of Education may reduce the variability in how college crimes are reported.[1] The watchdog group, Security on Campus, Inc., has begun to offer training programs in campus crime reporting, also likely to lessen its variation.

This chapter describes alcohol-related crime among college students. Most of the violations reported by campus police involve alcohol, and alcohol violations have increased over the past decade, a time when other kinds of crime in the broader society have been falling. The consequences of college drinking include alcohol-related problems such as assault and other forms of violence. Intoxicated rape, among the most serious consequences of drinking on campus, is discussed briefly, but because of its unique character it is addressed more fully in a separate chapter. Having established a powerful correlation between alcohol and crime, a section then explores whether alcohol is a cause of violence. If colleges want to reduce campus crime, do they need to focus on reducing alcohol abuse? The conclusion explores implications for those trying to understand or contain campus crime.

CAMPUS CRIME

A generation ago, colleges and universities were often perceived as safe, virtually crime-free "ivory towers." Episodes of college crime were rarely mentioned in newspapers, though evidence suggests that there was a large gap between reality and reporting.[2] The isolated incidents of mass violence, like a shooting spree leaving 13 dead at the University of Texas in 1966, were stunning exceptions to the image of the college campus as an exceptional place in its serenity and safety.[3]

The image of safety, lax reporting practices, and to some degree how universities deal with crime were "changed forever with the brutal rape and murder of Lehigh University freshman Jeanne Ann Clery in the early morning hours of April 5, 1986."[4] Another Lehigh student entered Clery's dormitory room after passing through a series of doors propped open or left unlocked. The university had been aware of these security problems but had never warned its students about any imminent danger to them. Jeanne's death spurred her parents, Connie and Howard Clery, and their family to create a watchdog agency, Security on Campus Inc. (disclosure: I am currently a board member). This effort eventually led to the passage of a federal law, the Crime Awareness and Campus Security Act of 1990. It was renamed the Jeanne Clery Disclosure of Campus Security Policy and Campus Crime Statistics Act in 1998, and is now known as the Clery Act.

The Clery Act has substantially increased both the quality and quantity of information available to the public about college crime. It requires colleges and universities (1) to prepare and publish an annual security report that presents crime statistics and policy; (2) to disclose timely information in a public crime log and issue warnings about threats; and (3) to protect the rights of sexual assault accusers and accused.[5] The crime statistics are presented separately for those events that occur on campus, in residential facilities on campus, in noncampus buildings, or on public property. Reported crime data are available on the Internet in an easy-to-use form for thousands of individual campuses.[6]

Security on Campus, Inc. (S.O.C.) has emerged as the foremost critic of how colleges and universities respond to crime.[7] It has succeeded in helping pass federal legislation that mandates crime reporting and it has pushed for improvement in the quality of the data available to the public.[8] It maintains an Internet Web site that monitors crime and crime prevention activities on college campuses, and it has a rich set of reference materials about college crime, including news stories and educational videos. S.O.C. maintains a toll-free number (1-888-251-7959) and has helped students and others to file complaints about the Clery Act or to offer counsel for those victimized by crime. It has led in efforts to help colleges comply with the Clery Act by offering workshops around the country.[9]

Two prominent criminologists who are experts on campus crime, Bonnie Fisher and John Sloan, point out some of the Clery Act's limitations. The Clery Act requires data about crimes that have been reported to campus officials or to local law enforcement authorities. So, just like crime data published in the United States by the Federal Bureau of Investigation in its *Uniform Crime Reports*, the Clery Act does not deal with unreported incidents of crime. For college populations, the gap between reported and unreported crime (the "dark figure" of crime) is large: as many as 47 percent of robberies, 52 percent of aggravated assaults, 75 percent of burglaries, and 95 percent of rapes involving college students were not reported to the police.[10] Several of the most common crimes committed against college students, such as personal larceny without contact/theft, vandalism, simple assault, or stalking, are not required to be reported by the Act. Several of these crimes are thought to have strong connections to alcohol abuse, although firm data are absent. Moreover, Clery Act alcohol violations do not include public drunkenness, underage drinking, or driving under the influence, and thus they represent only some of the alcohol-related crime. Fisher and Sloan conclude, "the important point here is that publicly reported post-secondary crime statistics (mandated by *Clery*) most likely significantly underreport the 'true' amount of campus crime."[11]

In spite of these gaps, the Clery Act has led to a veritable explosion in the amount of knowledge about campus crime. An indicator of how public knowledge about campus crime has changed since before the Act can be found on the Web site of the Higher Education Center for the Prevention of Alcohol and Other Drugs and Violence. In a recent and typical week, a report on "Alcohol, Other Drug, and Violence-Related Incidents" presented the following stories, all published previously in news media across the country.[12]

A University of Colorado student apologized to a Boulder County judge Thursday for barging into women's dorm rooms in Stearns East while tripping on psilocybin mushrooms.

An alleged acquaintance rape was reported to the [Loyola Marymount University] Department of Public Safety (DPS) on Thursday, Oct. 4 at 7:35 A.M.

Eastern Michigan University public safety officials say the 17-year-old female who accused an 18-year-old student of molesting her last week has now admitted the two had dated and had an off-and-on intimate relationship since they met this semester.

Bainbridge College has issued a campus alert advisory regarding a threat of a shooting on the Bainbridge College campus. This incident has caused Bainbridge College administrators to post an emergency safety message on their Web site.

241 students have been referred to [Southern Methodist University's] judicial affairs office for alcohol- or drug-related offenses so far this school year, compared with 206 referrals over the same period last year.

Eight Panhellenic sororities were sanctioned and five are on social probation after [Towson University] discovered alcohol was involved in recruitment activities related to Bid Day, held Sept. 16.

A Syracuse University student was allegedly attacked and threatened with a pair of scissors at her South Campus apartment on Sunday night, police said.

A Stephen F. Austin [State University] freshman treated for alcohol poisoning following an off-campus party has died, police said.

On the morning of Sept. 24, a [Chabot College] student parked his 1995 Lexus SC400 in Parking Lot G. The student got out of his car and was walking to class when two men approached him. One of the men pointed a gun at the student and demanded his car keys.

A University of Wyoming fraternity has been sanctioned because several students were dangerously intoxicated at a fraternity event, the university announced Thursday.

Many of these stories probably would not have been reported in the press without the Clery Act. These news stories show that, just like other

Americans, college students are at risk of crime victimization (being the victim of a crime), including violent crimes such as rape. College students studying or living on campus are exposed to a unique set of both risk and protective factors. Arguably highest among the risks is the greater use of alcohol and other drugs on or near the campus than in the broader society.[13] But there are also protective factors—colleges often provide extensive security and public safety services beyond those available in the communities that surround them, and often offer programs to educate students about the risks of substance use.

ALCOHOL AND CAMPUS CRIME

What role does alcohol play in college crime? A review of published studies concluded that alcohol was involved in two-thirds of college student suicides, in 90 percent of campus rapes, and in 95 percent of violent crime on campus.[14] These findings support the view of college presidents that alcohol abuse is the number one student life problem on campus.[15] Alcohol abuse contributes to almost half of motor vehicle fatalities, the most important cause of death among young people.[16] Alcohol plays an important but complex role in campus crime. Many of the college crime incidents reported to the police are alcohol related, and many if not most of the serious crimes on college campuses involve alcohol. Students who abuse alcohol are more likely to be victims of crime than nonusers or nonbingeing users. That many college students abuse alcohol is well known, but its impact on other aspects of college life is more controversial. The role that alcohol plays in campus crime deserves reexamination. Does student alcohol use drive most of campus crime, or is it merely one of a number of factors, and perhaps a minor one at that, that plays a limited role? Should preventing alcohol abuse be seen as a way to prevent campus crime?

A series of sensational accounts of student deaths and rapes focuses attention on the relationship between alcohol and campus crime and poses an urgent question. In this section, we explore that relationship, arguing that alcohol-related incidents have become the most common kind of crime activity on American college campuses.

College students are at risk of crime victimization, ranging from larceny to violent events such as rape, but students' risks are lower than those of the general public. During the period 1995–2002, rates of violent victimization of Americans ages 18–24 fell for both college students (a decrease of 54 percent) and for nonstudents (a decrease of 45 percent), part of a broad decline in violent crime during these years.[17] The same data show that college students ages 18–24 experience lower rates of violent crime such as robbery, aggravated assault, and simple assault (except for rape/assault) than do nonstudents. The glaring exception is rape, experienced by both students and nonstudents at the same rate.

For college students, studying or living on a college campus brings a unique set of both risk and protective factors.[18] Highest among the risks is the greater use of alcohol and other drugs than among noncollege-going youth. National Crime Victimization Survey (NCVS) data on violent victimizations of college students show that roughly 4 in 10 offenders were perceived to be using alcohol or drugs, whether the crime was violent crime (41 percent), rape/sexual assault (40 percent), aggravated assault (44 percent), or simple assault (42 percent); only robbery (25 percent) had lower rates of perceived drug and alcohol use by the perpetrator.[19]

It is widely assumed in criminology that substance use plays an important role in crime, especially violent crime, in the broader society, and that it is involved in much if not most campus crime. An extensive study of campus crime based on a survey of more than 3,000 college students found that recreational drug use and a lifestyle with high levels of partying were the main predictors of a college student being the victim of a violent crime.[20] Rape and sexual assault victimization rates were higher on campus than off campus. The main predictor of being a victim of violent crime was participating in a lifestyle with high levels of partying on campus at night as well as taking recreational drugs regularly.[21]

Crimes associated with alcohol and drug use are the most prevalent crimes on college campuses today. Alcohol use and abuse is by far the most prevalent form of substance use by college students, but some drug use is also widespread; one in every four college students is a current-year user of marijuana.[22] Subgroups of students such as intercollegiate athletes are at higher risk of both alcohol abuse and drug use.[23]

Substance use is a particularly strategic issue for those concerned with college crime for two reasons. First, drugs are illegal for all students and alcohol is illegal for those under 21, so substance use is of immediate importance to campus police and other college administrative personnel; they place alcohol and drug use at or near the top of the list of problems with which they must deal. Second, substance use increases the risk of criminal victimization on campus, as it does in the broader society, suggesting that the role of campus police and security in restricting access to alcohol and other drugs will play a role in lessening crime. Crimes associated with alcohol and drug use are the most prevalent serious crimes on college campuses today. Since alcohol is overwhelmingly the substance of choice on college campuses, it make sense to focus attention on alcohol use and abuse, including binge drinking. On college campuses as in the broader society, heavy episodic or binge drinking poses a danger of serious safety, health, and other consequences for both the alcohol abuser and others in the immediate environment. Alcohol contributes to the leading causes of accidental death, such as motor vehicle crashes and falls. Alcohol abuse contributes to almost half of motor vehicle fatalities, the most important cause of death among young Americans.[24] On college campuses, alcohol-related crime involves underage drinking, driving under the influence, public intoxication, and a variety of criminal acts ranging from theft to violence.

The *Chronicle of Higher Education* regularly reports data about campus crime gathered as part of the requirements of the Clery Act by the U.S. Department of Education (2005).[25] Alcohol arrests have increased at American colleges for 12 years running. Liquor law violations rose from 108,846 reported in 1999 to 161,974 in 2003, an increase of 49 percent.[26] This may reflect both rising amounts of alcohol-related crime and increased attention to alcohol issues by college security officials. In any case, alcohol arrests or liquor law violations are far more numerous than other kinds of reported crime. For the period 2001–2003, the U.S. Department of Education reported 84 murders and manslaughters, 7,941 forcible/nonforcible sex offenses, 566 hate crimes, and 514,568 liquor law violation arrests or disciplines.[27]

These Clery Act data are subject to the limitations discussed earlier. To get a more complete picture of crime and especially violent crime, data from the NCVS were compiled for the years 1995–2004 for college students and nonstudents separately.[28] College students have lower rates of violent crime victimization than nonstudents, with the single exception of rape and sexual assault for which both groups have equal chances of victimization. Overall, rates of victimization for both students and nonstudents fell significantly, mostly because of a decline in the most common kind of violent victimization, simple assault.

CONSEQUENCES OF COLLEGE DRINKING

College drinking is often viewed as a harmless rite of passage, but the Harvard School of Public Health College Alcohol Study and other studies point to a darker reality. The National Institute on Alcohol Abuse and Alcoholism's (NIAAA) Task Force on College Drinking commissioned extensive new studies of the issue.[29] The NIAAA'Task Force report summarized the outcomes associated with college drinking, including 1,400–1,700 deaths; 500,000 injuries; 400,000 students having unprotected sex and more than 100,000 having sex without consent; more than 150,000 reporting an alcohol-related health problem and 1.5 percent attempting suicide; and 31 percent meeting the criteria for a diagnosis of alcohol abuse and 6 percent for a diagnosis of alcohol dependence in the past 12 months.[30]

Of particular importance for present purposes are the numbers associated with crime perpetration and victimization:

- Assault: 600,000 assaulted by another student who has been drinking
- Sexual abuse: 70,000 victims of sexual assault or date rape
- Drunk driving: 2.1 million drove under the influence of alcohol
- Vandalism: 11 percent report damaging property while under the influence
- Property damage: 50 percent of administrators at schools with high binge levels report "moderate" or "major" alcohol-related damage
- Police involvement: 110,000 students arrested for an alcohol-related violation

Crime victimization on college campuses is often linked to alcohol consumption. Table 4-1 presents College Alcohol Study data on alcohol-related problems, including ties between alcohol abuse and campus crime victimization. A significant minority of American college students report serious alcohol-related problems.

The data in table 4-1 show clearly that many alcohol-related problems do not come to the attention of campus or community police. Relatively few students (6.5 percent in the last survey year) get into trouble with campus or community policy as the result of their own drinking. By contrast, almost a third (29 percent) report driving after drinking, and over a quarter (26.8 percent) forgot where they were or what they had done. Roughly 1 in 10 students damaged property or got hurt or injured. The "dark figure" of campus crime is clearly significant from these data—much more troubling behavior takes place than comes to the attention of the police.

Data on crime perpetration show a similar pattern. Whether an offender is perceived to be under the influence of alcohol or drugs depends on whether a criminal incident was on or off campus; 27 percent of violent crime victims thought the offender was using drugs or alcohol when the incident was on campus, contrasted with 42 percent when the incident was off campus.[31] The

Table 4-1.
Alcohol-Related Problems Among College Students, 1993–2001

Problem	1993	1997	1999	2001
Forgot where you were or what you did	24.7	27.4	27.1	26.8
Argued with friends	19.6	24.0	22.5	22.9
Damaged property	9.3	11.7	10.8	10.7
Got into trouble with campus or local police	4.6	6.4	5.8	6.5
Got hurt or injured	9.3	12.0	12.4	12.8
Required medical treatment for an overdose	0.5	0.6	0.6	0.8
Drove after drinking alcohol	26.6	29.5	28.8	29.0
Had five or more different alcohol-related problems	16.6	20.8	19.9	20.3

Source: Pastore & Maguire (2003) at http://www.albany.edu/sourcebook, accessed March 3, 2006.

same data show that on-campus violence is relatively infrequent, 17 times less frequent than off-campus violence.

Another large survey of college students sheds additional light on the question of alcohol-related victimization—the use of alcohol by the victims of crime.[32] Table 4-2 presents Core survey data for 1993 through 2002 showing that many students experienced threats of physical violence (9.6 percent), ethnic or racial harassment (5.7 percent), actual physical violence (4.7 percent), forced sexual touching or fondling (5.0 percent), or theft involving force or threat of force (47.9 percent). Many students reported

Table 4-2.
Students Reporting Victimization and Prior Substance Use

	Report being victim	Consumed drugs or alcohol beforehand
Threats of physical violence	9.6	34.2
Ethnic or racial harassment	5.7	13.5
Actual physical violence	4.7	67.3
Forced sexual touching or fondling	5.0	74.0
Theft involving force or threat of force	1.9	47.9

Source: Pastore & Maguire (2003) at http://www.albany.edu/sourcebook, accessed March 3, 2006.

that they had consumed alcohol or drugs before the incident. Except for ethnic or racial harassment, the risk of victimization is powerfully linked with prior alcohol use by the victim. To be sure, no one but the perpetrator of a crime is responsible for that crime, and these data should not be used to "blame the victim." But the data clearly suggest how alcohol use is associated with a higher likelihood of victimization.

At any one college, the alcohol-crime relationship may look quite different from what is portrayed by these national figures. Given the huge variation in the frequency and amount of drinking by students at different campuses, individual institutions might show a great deal of crime activity (some or much of it alcohol related) or almost none. For example, consider the published incidents of crime at one Philadelphia institution in the fall semester of 2007. At Saint Joseph's University, with about 4,200 undergraduates and a reputation for extensive drinking, the campus newspaper (*The Hawk*) published the following items for a single week:[33]

On Campus

Vandalism, Boland Hall, 11/3/2007. Residence Life observed a student and a guest damage art work on display outside of Boland Hall. The student was also cited by Lower Merion Police for underage drinking.

Vandalism, McShain Hall, 11/3/2007. Residence Life reported furniture was damaged.

Alcohol Poisoning, McShain Hall, 11/4/2007. Student was taken to Lankenau Hospital by Narberth Ambulance. Student was also cited by Lower Merion Police.

Burglary, Campion, 11/4/2007. Two students forced open a roll gate and took items from the cafeteria.

Vandalism, Merion Gardens, 11/5/2007. Student reported damage to his room.

Assault, LaFarge Hall, 11/5/2007. A guest was assaulted by a student.

Theft, Claver House, 11/7/2006. Student reported that her wallet was taken from her sweat shirt which she had left in the building.

Alcohol Incident, Lancaster Court, Weymouth, 11/7/2007. Residence Life observed a student passing beer through a window.

Off Campus

Aggravated Assault, 5313 Wynnefield Avenue, 11/4/2007. Student reported that he was punched in the face at a party. The student was transported to Lankenau Hospital and received six stitches.

Alcohol Party, 5313 Wynnefield Avenue, 11/4/2007. Public Safety observed empty beer bottles, empty beer kegs and numerous plastic cups. Underage students were present at the party. The occupants of the residence were identified.

Alcohol Party, 5630 Overbrook Avenue, 11/8/2007. Public Safety and Philadelphia Police observed numerous cans and cases of beer and numerous plastic cups containing beer. Underage students were present at the party. The occupants of the residence were identified.

Vandalism, 6396 Sherwood Road, 11/8/2007. Student reported that the air was let out of two tires on his car.

Many of the incidents appear alcohol-related, with several the direct result of enforcing the university's alcohol policies.

Alcohol is associated with a wide range of problems among college students and certainly with a wide range of criminal behaviors and victimizations. The next chapter examines one of the most serious, rape and sexual assault, treated separately because of the complexity of the crimes and their relationship to alcohol use by both perpetrator and victim. But for now, the question of whether alcohol is a causal factor in violence will be assessed.

IS ALCOHOL A CAUSE OF VIOLENCE?

The data presented so far make a strong case for a powerful correlation between alcohol and crime among individual college students and among campuses. But do the data prove causation? The question is not merely of academic concern. If the two are causally linked, then strong evidence would support the thesis that preventing crime on campus depends in part on somehow lowering the rate of alcohol abuse. If they are not causally linked, reigning in binge drinking might have no effect on crime rates.

The question of whether alcohol is a cause of violence provokes considerable controversy, at least in part because it may inadvertently shift attention away from the issue of the criminal responsibility of the perpetrator. It is also controversial because of the difficulty of establishing causality in matters of human behavior. Some observers claim that alcohol and drug use and criminal events are closely, even causally, linked, whereas others argue that there is almost no relationship or "less than meets the eye."[34]

To prove causality, three pieces of evidence are needed. First, time order needs to be established: changes in alcohol use must precede changes in crime. Second, alcohol and crime have to be demonstrated to co-occur or to be correlated. Finally, rival causal factors must be eliminated: in other words, the possibility that some third factor brings about both alcohol use and crime has to be removed.

The data presented earlier make a powerful case for correlation, but whether alcohol and crime are causally related on college campuses or among college students has yet to be proven definitively. However, the fact that this same correlation has been found among noncollege populations strengthens the case for the causal link in the college setting.[35] Abbey provides a helpful discussion of how alcohol might be associated with sexual assault among college students.[36] Establishing time order would help understand this relationship. For example, instead of alcohol consumption causing sexual assault, the reverse could be true—that is, if men consume alcohol before perpetrating sexual assault to provide an excuse for their criminal behavior. Finally, eliminating rival causal hypotheses would increase confidence in the alcohol-rape causal connection. For example, some third factor such as peer group norms that promote heavy drinking and the perpetration of sexual assault might explain the correlation, rather than a causal link. A definitive answer to these questions cannot be presented.[37] For similar reasons, considerable controversy exists in the broader scientific literature about whether alcohol and violence are causally linked.[38] NCVS data show that college students are more likely to be the victims of violent crime off campus than on campus, and that these crimes are more likely to occur during the evening or at night—times and places when heavy drinking is more likely to occur, perhaps increasing the correlation between alcohol and violence.[39]

If alcohol plays a causal role in much if not most of the violence among college students, then preventing alcohol abuse becomes part of the way to lower crime among students. The next section examines what is known about preventing college alcohol abuse.

PREVENTING BINGE DRINKING AND ALCOHOL-RELATED CRIME

Studying college alcohol use and crime is important in its own right, but many people hope to figure out ways to reduce the amount of college crime. A reasonable working assumption is that some substantial part of college crime is brought about by the high rates of alcohol abuse among college students. Put another way, it will be difficult to make much progress against certain kinds of college crime—particularly violence against women, fighting, and vandalism—unless something is first done to lower the rates of alcohol abuse. Purely educational efforts (used alone) against both violence and alcohol abuse have been demonstrated to fail.[40] What is needed is fresh thought that explores the link between alcohol and violence. On a theoretical level, Abbey has presented some important ideas about how alcohol and sexual violence might be connected.[41] On a practical level, Langford offers suggestions about how administrators and activists can attack the roots of much campus crime.[42]

DRUG USE

Like alcohol, drug use also is a significant concern on campus and is associated with college drinking. Illicit drugs and their prevalence of use vary greatly within and among campuses.[43] Age is an especially significant factor in drug use, so it makes sense to confine the analysis to the 83 percent of the students who were under age 24 when the Harvard College Alcohol Study was conducted. The Harvard researchers reported that the prevalence of use was highest for marijuana (24.8 percent), followed by psychedelic drugs other than LSD (4.7 percent), LSD (4.4 percent), amphetamines (3.6 percent), opiates (3.2 percent), tranquilizers (1.9 percent), cocaine (1.9 percent), barbituates (1.3 percent), crack (0.4 percent), and heroin (0.1 percent). Marijuana use exceeds the use of all other drugs combined; thus alcohol and marijuana are the substances of choice for college students.

Binge drinking is itself a risk factor for other substance use and abuse, and vice versa. For example, students who binge drink are much more likely to use cigarettes.[44] Less well understood is the abuse of licit drugs obtained through prescription and then abused by individual student or others in his or her environment. Recent reports of student deaths involving the mixture of several licit and illicit drugs and alcohol are of concern.

The National Center on Addiction and Substance Abuse at Columbia University (known as CASA) reanalyzed data from the National Survey on Drug Abuse and Health. The CASA researchers concluded that

> 69.0 percent or 5.4 million full-time college students reported drinking, abusing controlled prescription drugs, using illicit drugs or smoking in the past month; 49.4 percent, or 3.8 million, reported binge drinking, abusing controlled prescription drugs or using licit drugs in the past month. Almost one-half of those who are current drinkers (45 percent or 2.3 million) engaged in two or more other forms of substance use (binge drinking, prescription drug abuse, illicit drug use or smoking).[45]

HOW ONE CAMPUS RESPONDS TO CRIME

To get a fuller picture of the relationship between alcohol and college crime, this section offers a glimpse at how one campus responds to crime. The institution chosen, the University of Pennsylvania, is hardly typical. As one of the eight Ivy League universities, Penn is at the very top of American campuses in faculty research productivity, academic quality, student selectivity, and resources. Sometimes called "the social Ivy," it has a reputation for a more vibrant social scene, a more active fraternity and sorority life, and arguably heavier alcohol use than its peers. Its campus sits close to the center of Philadelphia, known for its many bars, clubs, and restaurants. The campus is surrounded by neighborhoods with high rates of crime.

Penn is also atypical in its public safety programs, recently receiving an award from the nonprofit organization S.O.C. for "demonstrating the highest commitment to ... safety by implementing a highly effective solution to the problem of campus crime." S.O.C.'s founder and president, Connie Clery, presented the award to Penn, saying that "[b]y providing [24/7] monitored surveillance with an extensive network of campus security cameras, and by maintaining a caring and committed sworn police force patrolling not only the campus but also the surrounding police district, you have set a noteworthy example for universities nationwide."[46]

Maureen Rush, vice president for public safety at the University of Pennsylvania, has had to address the public safety needs of this large urban university.

> One of the things that we [did was to] make rules for monitoring the parties, registering the parties, having the TIPS (Training for Intervention Procedures) training for bartenders and paying full-time staff to be monitors who go in and out of the [student] houses. If we drive alcohol off the campus it is going to cause more deaths [and] more violence and as it turned out that did not happen. We did not have any more problems on campus. In fact, we were at the same time doing enforcement levels that many places weren't doing, because we have the police patrolling the majority of off-campus living areas where students live. We were, at the same time doing on-campuses enforcement. We were doing off campus as well. We [used to] shut down the party at the fraternity house at 2 am and the years before they would wander out ... into the neighborhood and they would go in groups. But then they would get picked off, and girls and boys would come out solo, drunk and not knowing where they are at. They were coming out at 4 or 5 o'clock in the morning. So we started doing enhancements of our patrols out there and at 2 o'clock we started to shut those parties down as well so there was no more overflow coming off the porch and screaming and yelling and people screaming in the neighborhood about boys and people doing obscene things like urinating [and] vomiting.... We [worked] with the different control enforcement agents to go in and do some undercover things.... We worked with beer distributors about making sure that they check ID.... So it was a full court press. Our student conduct office worked with putting together a new web mediation program. Neighborhood adults were really upset with the way the kids were acting up there.[47]

Campus crime data are required by the Clery Act to be reported and then published. Are these data of any help to students or parents thinking of choosing a college? Rush responded,

I don't think so and let me tell you why. Back in the 90s . . . we would have hundreds and hundreds of alcohol arrests and citations listed in Clery [Act reports] between us [the University of Pennsylvania] and the Pennsylvania Liquor Control Board. . . . Years later, you know, [we'd have fewer]. So did we just have an artificial number then or now? Well, now it is for real, but it is because of a lot of work.

If somebody has a high number, it does not necessarily mean that it is a bad place. It means they are enforcing it more. It is like reports of rape, you know, when you have a lot of education and you have access points where they can come in and people are going to report more. So . . . when parents are looking at a school for their kids . . . you have to look at the whole picture. The Clery Act report is one truth, but it is not the end all. When you look at Clery you are looking at on or off campus continuous, but the reality is our issues for robbery and things like that are not on campus. So whether [these off-campus crimes] are for you or for Temple [another Philadelphia university] or any of these schools [isn't always clear]. . . . More and more students are not living on campus, so as a parent you need to really research the community that the kids live in. What is the crime rate like? What is the bar scene like? Is there enforcement in state, city, and local areas? It is the bigger picture.

An experienced law enforcement professional like Rush has a complex view of alcohol abuse. Instead of using the language of cause-and-effect preferred by social scientists like criminologists, Rush approaches alcohol in terms of a larger context:

I think alcohol is one of the major [factors in] bad things happening to good people, people acting differently than they would on a good day. It is not having a couple of beers, it is the whole "I am going out to get drunk tonight" and "I am going to let off steam and I am going to do stupid shit, but it is OK because I am drunk." We ask them the next day why did you do that? Why did you pour beer over someone's head knowing they were going to knock your head off? . . . [W]e all do stupid things when we are young and alcohol is probably involved there too. . . . What parents should worry about is, especially off campus, when students live in multi-dwelling houses. . . . You are going to introduce alcohol, introduce matches, cigarettes, introduce candles and parties are started were people are careless. The next thing you know a cigarette is left in the sofa that blows up at 4 am when everybody is asleep. That is the kind of stuff I worry about. I think, ultimately, we have enough police on the street that we will see someone who is impaired and we take care of them. We get them home safely.

Rush talks to the question of how campus police can play a role in ensuring the safety of students, some or many of whom use alcohol unwisely and thereby raise the risks of harm. She advises students venturing off campus to consider calling for "walking escorts" who will be at their side. As universities expand, those police play an expanded role in safety and security. Penn has become heavily involved in leasing its properties to a wide variety of merchants, bars, and restaurants, increasing pedestrian and vehicular traffic into its campus and surrounding neighborhoods.

> I think that a lot of universities resemble the Penn model in that they are bringing in properties and retail establishments with restaurants and bars.... Penn for example, in the 90s, wanted a super market and diner that was open 24–7, a bowling alley, and a movie theater and we have all that here now. So, with that comes more maintenance.... Our job isn't as simple. I could go work on a campus that is a square block and I won't be worried about retail theft from property development. I would not be worried about all the bars and the liquor licenses; that would be the municipal court's problem. There are still universities or colleges that do that today. You walk past the street; you are not our problem anymore. The reality is you are our problem and whether you believe it or not, it is going to impact the community. So, [we patrol] into the neighborhood as far as 43rd Street; we worked with the rape and victim unit in the early 90s because our kids lived out there. We developed the campus ... and we have to do the same thing, we have to offer the same security. We could help tell our cops "don't worry about the 7-11 [a convenience store], don't worry about Urban Outfitters [a clothing store].... Not our problem. Where is the moral compass of what we are trying to do here? ... We look at this whole area as our security package. So, from 30th to 23rd [Streets], Market [Street] to Baltimore [Avenue] ... everything that happens in there is our business and matters to us. So our retail [development] is driven by what kind of problems will this place bring or what kind of value will it bring, and we are part of that decision as well. We have consulted with our real-estate offices on that. If we are having a problem with the bar, we are not shy about using any force that we can. If we own it, we have a big force, if we don't own it we work with the state or DA's [District Attorney's] office.... At Penn, our model is enforcement and we have the education on and off campus. We have the research ... looking to see where we can do more of the social norm training. We have the peer education part.... We have the task force in general, which again has like 35 to 40 people at the table from all across the university and all different environments to hear the alcohol stories. Are we doing OK? Do we have underground issues? Do we have a lot more sexual assault? All that is discussed. We work closely with student health in the hospital for the kids that come in off the road to keep an eye on them as well.

CONCLUSION

Alcohol and crime are powerfully linked. Data show that individual college students who report binge drinking are much more likely to be either the victims or the perpetrators of crime. Campuses with high rates of binge drinking also experience relatively higher rates of crime victimization. At a time when society-wide rates of crime have fallen significantly, campus alcohol-related crimes such as rape have not fallen as much, probably reflecting the largely unchanged rate of alcohol abuse among college students.

Changing the culture of alcohol use on college campuses will not be easy, and commitment to change should be realistic and assume the necessity of long-term efforts. But there is a glimmer of hope. By better understanding the alcohol-crime connection, colleges can begin to develop and implement interventions that will lower both the rates of binge drinking and the rates of crime. Some crime on campus has little to do with binge drinking, so one should not cast alcohol abuse reduction in the role of panacea. Nonetheless, environmental interventions offer evidence of successfully reducing both alcohol abuse and its consequences, including college student crime victimization.

NOTES

1. U.S. Department of Education (2005).

2. For example, there is a large literature about the gap between the reality and reporting of rape and sexual assault, with early research by Kanin (1957) appearing in scholarly journals well before the issue reached broader publics (Warshaw 1988).

3. By contrast, the worst episode of campus violence, in which 31 people were killed by a lone gunman on the campus of Virginia Tech, appears as only the most horrific of crimes that occur with some frequency at colleges across the country. See Thomas Frank, "Campus security flaws a pattern in slayings," *USA TODAY*, June 12, 2007.

4. Carter & Bath (2007).

5. Carter & Bath (2007).

6. S.O.C. has compiled past and current data at http://www.securityoncampus. org/crimestats/index.html (accessed November 28, 2007). The S.O.C. site has a link to the main U.S. Department of Education Web site: http://www.ope.ed.gov/ security/Search.asp (accessed November 28, 2007).

7. Author's interviews with S.O.C. leaders Catherine Bath and S. Daniel Carter. See the S.O.C. Web site at http://www.securityoncampus.org/ (accessed November 28, 2007).

8. Author's interview with S. Daniel Carter.

9. I attended a two-day workshop offered by S.O.C. in Philadelphia in June 2007.

10. Fisher & Sloan (2007: 9).

11. Fisher & Sloan (2007: 9).

12. Email received from the HEC/News email service, Higher Education Center for Alcohol and Other Drug and Violence Prevention, October 12, 2007.

13. Johnston, O'Malley, & Bachman (1986).

14. CASA (1994).

15. Carnegie Foundation, cited in Wechsler, Davenport, Dowdall, Moeykens, & Castillo (1994).

16. Robert Wood Johnson Foundation (2001).

17. Baum & Klaus (2005); see also Hart (2003).

18. Fisher & Sloan (1995).

19. Baum & Klaus (2005); see also Hart (2003).

20. Fisher, Sloan, Cullen, & Lu (1998).

21. However, alcohol use (defined as the likelihood of regularly drinking three or more alcoholic beverages during the year) was not a statistically significant predictor of experiencing a violent victimization or a theft victimization.

22. Bell, Wechsler, & Johnston (1997).

23. Wechsler, Davenport, Dowdall, Grossman, & Zanakos (1997).

24. Robert Wood Johnson Foundation (2001).

25. Hoover (2005). The Department of Education Web site, http://www.ope.ed. gov/security/index.asp, presents data on reported campus crime and alcohol and drug violations at thousands of college campuses across the country.

26. It is difficult to compare Clery Act data over time because of changes in definitions and requirements. The data on liquor law violations were taken from http://www.securityoncampus.org/crimestats/index htm, accessed June 1, 2006.

27. See the Department of Education Web site at http://ed.gov/admins/lead/safety/crime/criminaloffenses/index.html, accessed September 1, 2008.

28. Baum & Klaus (2005).

29. Readers interested in an extensive discussion should go to its Web site, www.collegedrinkingprevention.gov, which contains its final report, a special supplement of *Journal of Studies on Alcohol*, and a series of reports about the question.

30. NIAAA (2002a); see also Hingson, Heeren, Winter, & Wechsler (2005).

31. Baum & Klaus (2005).

32. Unlike the Harvard College Alcohol Study data cited earlier, data collected by the Core Institute at Southern Illinois University are not based on a representative sample of colleges and universities, but only on those institutions that choose to participate in the survey. Frequently the survey is not given to a representative sample of students at each school, but distributed in classes whose instructors choose to do so. Nonetheless, the Core data are collected at a large number of institutions across the country with an impressive number of student participants; in 2004, for example, the Core surveys had 68,000 undergraduate respondents at 133 colleges and universities.

34. *The Hawk* online edition, "Incidents of Crime, November 2, 2007, through November 8, 2007" (http://www.sjuhawknews.com, accessed November 20, 2007).

34. For the argument that substance use is causally related to crime, see Abbey (1991, 2002); for the argument of little or no relationship, see Collins (1989) and Martin (1992, 1993).

35. Greenfield (1998).

36. Abbey (2002; see also 1991).

37. Abbey (2002).

38. NIAAA (2000: chapter 1).

39. Baum & Klaus (2005; see also Hart (2003).

40. Bachar & Koss (2001); NIAAA (2002).

41. Abbey (1991, 2002).

42. Langford (2005).

43. Bell, Wechsler, & Johnston (1997).

44. For the data on tobacco, see Emmons, Wechsler, Dowdall, & Abraham (1998); for marijuana data, see Bell, Wechlser, & Johnston (1997).

45. CASA (2007: 27).

46. http://www.securityoncampus.org/update/v03n07.html, accessed October 12, 2007.

47. Author's interview with Maureen Rush (2007).

CHAPTER 5

Work Hard, Play Hard: College Drinking, Social Life, and Sex

Reframing college drinking as a social problem focuses our attention on the role of drinking in social life and especially sexual behavior. Popular culture such as *Animal House* and its many descendants portray drinking as a central part of college life. The phrase "work hard, play hard" and its many variants heard on campuses across the county tie alcohol use to the academic life as a just reward for hard work in the classroom or laboratory. At its best, in this view, college drinking is a harmless rite of passage.

Reframing that positive or harmless image highlights the negative side of alcohol-fueled social life. College drinking was reframed to show both the (primary) harm to the individual drinker as well as the (secondary) impact on those in the immediate environment. Estimates of between 1,400 and 1,700 deaths, most from automobile crashes, gave one kind of body count of harm to the individual drinker, inarguable in its terrible costs to those involved. But reframing college drinking also draws attention to another kind of cost, much more intimately involved in pursuit of "friendly fun" as the major theme of nonacademic college life.[1]

This chapter explores the links between college drinking and social life and sexuality. What do students expect to have happen in college? How much does the current dominant sexual script, described by the phrase "hooking up," depend on widespread alcohol use? Although most college women don't experience rape, nonconsensual drunken sex, or "party rape," many women do. What are the consequences? The Duke lacrosse case, the most notorious recent incident of alleged party rape, remains the most important image of problems that arise when college drinking, social life, and sex mix. What lessons can be learned from it?

WHAT STUDENTS EXPECT FROM COLLEGE

What students want out of college is visible to some degree in the college guides they use to choose among thousands of institutions. Two popular guides—the *Princeton Review* and the *Fiske Guide*—show just how important social life is for the college-going student.[2] The *Princeton Review*—unrelated to the Ivy League university but instead the product of a college preparatory company—presents two pages of data and opinion about each of the 361 colleges and universities it reviews. The single largest category of its "Students Say" section is about academics, but the next two sections—"Life" and "Student Body" when taken together usually exceed academic content in amount of coverage. "Life" usually includes a sentence or two about alcohol and its availability. (Other sections take up admissions and financial aid information.) Clearly, social life is a central part of how students choose colleges, at least as judged by what the editors of this successful college guide think its readers want.

The *Fiske Guide* presents a much more detailed assessment of academics at the more than 300 institutions it reviews. Each institution is described in a detailed narrative which usually mentions the level of drinking, the availability of bars and other outlets, and, for many schools, comments about efforts by the administration to deal with alcohol issues. Twenty items of information are included in a sidebar, among them a ranking of academics (the graphic is from 1 to 5 hands holding a pen), social (1 to 5 telephones), and quality of life (1 to 5 stars). Other pieces of information describe enrollment, financial aid and expenses, graduation rates, and the strongest academic programs.

At least as judged by the editors of these two successful college guides, social life (including using alcohol) is at least an important, and for some the most important, factor in choosing a college. But its importance varies greatly across the millions of American college students. Entering college freshmen, asked about their last year in high school, responded to a question about how much time they spent "socializing with friends."[3] Almost half (47.5 percent) had spent more than 11 hours a week socializing, and

17 percent had spent more than 20 hours per week. By contrast, a quarter of these students (25.9 percent) had spent less than five hours socializing. It is important to balance the media stereotypes of college students who endlessly party with the reality that a quarter of college students spend little time with their friends.

HOOKING UP: SEX, SOCIABILITY, AND ALCOHOL

Data from the Harvard School of Public Health College Alcohol Study show a strong correlation between a party-centered lifestyle and drinking. Students who said that parties were a very important or important part of college life were more than five times more likely to be binge drinkers than those who placed less importance on parties, the strongest single individual correlate of binge drinking in the entire study.[4] Another national survey led two researchers to conclude, "[c]ollege students say the number one fun-time activity for them is drinking."[5]

We've already reviewed national data that show a remarkably stable picture, both over time and across the country: about two in five college students engage in heavy episodic or binge drinking, and about one in five had three or more episodes of such drinking in a two-week period. Not surprisingly, other social activities, including sex, take place when students have been drinking.

Heavy drinking by both men and women has become part of "hooking up," a sexual script widely practiced on college campuses, as a recent study by sociologist Kathleen Bogle explains.[6] Binge drinking facilitates hooking up, and hooking up meshes with heavy alcohol consumption. Among affluent college students in particular, hooking up and heavy drinking are often part of a partying-centered subculture.[7] Bogle writes,

> It is important to understand why alcohol plays such a major role in the hookup script. According to the college students I spoke to, alcohol makes initiating sexual encounters easier by setting a tone of "kicking back," "letting loose," or "partying...." At bars and parties, college students may be in an environment where they can meet potential hookup partners, but the alcohol helps facilitate the interaction between potential interested parties. Without alcohol as a social lubricant, the series of nonverbal cues (e.g., eye contact, body language, etc.) used to determine if a potential partner is interested in a hookup could be rather nerve racking. College students also firmly believe that alcohol lowers their inhibitions and makes them want to hook up.[8]

Bogle points out that if alcohol facilitates hooking up, then the reverse is also true: hooking up provides a powerful incentive for college drinking. The

sexual and drinking scripts support one another, fusing together two powerful themes in contemporary college life. Bogle told me,

> If students weren't able to get access to alcohol for the weekend . . . what would
> happen? [The students she interviewed] say it woudn't happen: this speaks to
> how the social scene requires alcohol. [Students] want to have relationships
> with people, and alcohol is needed to do that. I interviewed nondrinkers and
> those who weren't big drinkers, and they don't have relationships. . . . Drinking
> is now so normative on some college campuses that you have to explain your-
> self if you don't drink.[9]

College drinking varies greatly according to the particulars of specific settings. Sociologist David Grazian paints a vivid portrait of affluent University
of Pennsylvania students in his rich ethnography *On the Make: The Hustle of
Urban Nightlife.*[10] His Penn students use the clubs, bars, and restaurants of
downtown Philadelphia ("Center City") as the settings for their nocturnal
prowls for sex and status, with alcohol freely available as the lubricant:

> In the company of their friends and classmates, college students explore elabo-
> rate codes of fashion, appearance, and personal grooming; engage in rituals of
> confidence-building; employ tactics of deception intended to trick nightlife
> gatekeepers and unwitting bystanders; strategically avoid risky confrontations
> with overbearing competitors; playfully flirt with desirable members of the op-
> posite gender; and cautiously defend themselves against unwanted advances,
> aggressive come-ons, and other forms of sexual harassment. For these young
> thrill-seekers, the consumption of urban nightlife requires engaging in sporting
> rituals designed to take advantage of the anonymity of urban life while defend-
> ing themselves from the occasional dangers that accompany public interactions
> with strangers. For better or worse, in today's age of elongated adolescence,
> these moments make up the experience of emerging adulthood, a developmen-
> tal stage that for some may seemingly last through one's thirties and beyond.[11]

Alcohol (and equally importantly, the clubs and bars in which it is served)
are woven through nights on the make. Actual sexual encounters with desir-
able strangers happen much less frequently than hoped, probably adding to
the amount of drinking.

Narratives of college life often include descriptions of the interplay
between alcohol and sex. In Koren Zailckas's bestselling memoir *Smashed:
Story of a Drunken Girlhood*, partying and socializing from the earliest days
of high school usually included some drinking, often some heavy drinking.[12]
By the time Zailckas reaches Syracuse University, her drinking has advanced
considerably, and almost all of her social life is alcohol-infused. Some readers of the book would reach the conclusion that she had advanced into
actual alcoholism by her freshman year, but she argues otherwise; and since

she (like most college students) is never screened or interviewed by a clinician, it's difficult to say.

By her sophomore year of college, Zailckas is going out four or more nights a week and drinking heavily. Most college women aren't virgins, she reports, and then adds,

> Still, through all the weekend parties where I've sipped vodka straight-up and gone wandering through strange bedrooms, whacking into door frames, and bumming cigarettes from boys, I know I've stayed as chaste as an unscooped sugar bowl. That certainty lasts until two days before winter finals, when I open one eye after the soundest sleep of my life.[13]

She wakes up naked in bed with someone she barely knows.

> If this were a movie, this would be the point where I would lean over and ask Skip what happened. He would say, "We just passed out is all." And then we would both hide our heads under our pillows, and cringe at the close call that nearly spoiled our friendship.

But of course this wasn't a film but real life, and Zailckas grabs her clothes to leave. "I have never felt so lost ... I'll never know how I got there. I'll never know what intersections I crossed along the way."[14]

The Harvard College Alcohol Study asked students whether, since the beginning of the school year (in surveys done during the spring semester), their drinking resulted in the problem of "[forgetting] where you were or what you did." Between 24 and 27 percent responded positively.[15] Answers to single survey questions certainly can't provide conclusive evidence, but they suggest that a sizable minority of college students experience "blackouts," during which time the kind of sexual experience Zailckas reports can happen. Another piece of evidence: about 20 percent of the College Alcohol Study respondents said they had engaged in unplanned sex. One veteran public safety official at a southern state university told me that unplanned sex is often less-than-fully-consensual sex, with alcohol playing a major role.

A COLLEGE RAPE: KATHY AND JOE

To understand better how alcohol and sexuality can interact to produce rape, I interviewed a student at a private university in the east about an experience she had with a fellow student; the episode happened during the summer while she and a girlfriend were camping at the New Jersey shore. (All names have been changed):

Basically, I was friends with [Joe] for maybe half a year. We had hung out a couple of times, in groups of people, never anything very romantic between us. And eventually we began, we like got a little bit closer at parties, and then I was in right outside of [a beach town] staying at a campground with my friend, and he lives [nearby].... And he had called me the week before and [said] we should hang out.... And then he ends up calling me late Saturday night. My friend Sarah and I had built a campfire and we sat around playing cards. We had like two glasses of wine.

And he called, and he was like, yeah, I was out at the bar all night and I'm pretty drunk, I don't think I'll be able to drive, and I was like oh, if any of your friends can drive, come on over. He called me maybe twenty minutes later, and said that he was right outside the campground, he had driven from his house. So he came over, and the three of us were hanging out, and things were getting like a little bit flirtatious between us. And Karen wound up going to bed. We had an RV and a tent at the campsite.... And I was saying like goodbye to him in his car. We started kissing. And then he was like, "Hey, do you want to go into the tent?" And I was like alright, and so, sort of making out and stuff, and then before I knew, he was inside of me.

And I was like oh no, I really don't want to do this, I can't do this. I can't. Let's not do this please, and he wouldn't stop. And at that point I was very small. I weighed maybe 100 pounds and he was well over 200. And he was on top of me and I was basically pinned up against the side of the tent. And I felt like my entire body was completely frozen. Because I said like I can't do this, you know, please stop, and he wasn't listening. And he was just mumbling incoherently to me, and that basically went on, it was over. He got dressed, said goodbye and left.

And I was in such a state of personal shock, I didn't know what to do, I just went inside and curled up in bed next to my friend, and didn't sleep all night. I got up (it had to be seven o'clock in the morning) and did the stereotypical, after-school-special, a steaming hot shower. No idea of what just happened, I mean obviously I knew what happened but couldn't possibly understand how it happened and why it happened. And so I didn't say anything to anyone for maybe two weeks until I finally ... told a couple of my friends, and they were like, "You were raped!"

I didn't tell Sarah for months.... When I finally told her what happened, she told me that she knew that something was wrong. But we've been friends since we were born, and she respected the fact that I would tell her what had happened in my own time. And so she didn't pry at all. But, I felt so bad because I knew that she would feel guilty for what had happened ... because she was right there. And you know in my mind it was really hard to accept the fact that I had been raped by someone, let alone someone that I was good friends with, and it took a lot of time for all of that to sink in. For months I couldn't even use the word.

And I was very close to a lot of his guy friends, I had even dated one of them for a month, and they wound up finding out. And of course everyone was, "Oh my God I can't believe this happened to you, I can't believe he did this to you." Later it was like, "you were sort of like asking for it, you sort of brought it on yourself." And of course that was my own reservation ... I was afraid that something happened in a dark alley by someone I didn't know, I didn't have an idea of how that could really be rape. And that was something that took me a really long time to come to terms with ...

[Interviewer: "There was never any question when you woke up the next morning that you were not going to head for a hospital or call a cop?"]

No.

A couple days later, he had sent me a text message. And it said, "I'm sorry about what happened, I didn't mean to make you do something that you didn't want to do, and I would really appreciate it if you didn't tell anyone about this." Especially because he said he was still in love with his ex-girlfriend ... and he didn't want anyone to find out. And I think that is what started the ball rolling in my head, that it was something really horrible that had happened, because he was guilty, he felt guilty about it, and he apologized.

When school began in the fall, Kathy had transferred (as planned) to another institution, but she called the director of public security at her old college who helped her fill out a report of the alleged rape; she also called several faculty members. A formal hearing was conducted by the college's chief judicial officer who ruled that a rape had in fact happened. Joe was told that he would be suspended for the rest of the academic year and would be banned from the campus. He appealed the sentence, claiming it was too harsh, in part because he was drunk when the incident happened. An appeals board decided in his favor, dropping the full-year academic suspension; instead, he could continue his classes but had to leave the campus as soon as the last class ended each day.

Kathy appealed to the college's vice president for student affairs, who decided in Joe's favor, leaving him with a campus activities ban but no academic suspension. Two months elapsed before Kathy, accompanied by two faculty, one of them the leader of rape prevention on the campus, the other Kathy's freshman-year faculty advisor, went to appeal the suspension. Kathy sat between the two faculty members, opposite the vice president of student affairs and the college's president. Kathy recounted her experience in calm and measured terms, and the vice president confirmed those parts of the story about the series of hearings, the original sanction, and then Joe's successful appeal to have the sanction lowered. The president expressed his sympathy for Kathy, and said that he'd reflect on what he heard and then get back to her with his final judgment.

A month later Kathy received word that the college president would not intervene, and so the judgment stood.

Several months later, the judicial officer had a conversation with Joe's ex-girlfriend, who said that Joe had had several other similar sexual encounters with other young women, saying in each case that the sex happened because he was drunk.

The highly experienced judicial hearing officer was correct in judging that Joe had raped Kathy. It is possible, even likely, that the reversal of his initial sanction left an experienced rapist sitting in classes with college women who will give him the benefit of the doubt and even the presumption of inno-cence. His sanction required him to leave campus immediately after class but left open many approaches to hooking up with other students, including instant messaging, emails, and phone calls. His broad friendship network allows access to dozens of other college women.

What does this one story of the college rape have to say more generally? Unlike most college rapes, the woman in this one wasn't drunk enough so that she couldn't give consent, though her judgment may have been a bit impaired.

The man's story is another matter. He later claimed to have been drunk, but he also acknowledged his culpability. He told the victim, with a room-mate friend listening to the conversation, that he could get into a lot of trou-ble. But he used his drunken state to argue successfully that his punishment of a year's suspension was too harsh.

Alcohol is used as a weapon in many rapes, probably far more frequently than other so-called date rape drugs. It is also used, as it was in Joe's case, to mitigate, minimize, or trivialize drunken rapes that may have some degree of conscious perpetration.

A large national survey of sexual victimization among college women found that, during a six-month reference period, 1.7 percent of the respondents reported experiencing a completed rape, and 1.1 percent an attempted rape.[16] Four factors were significant predictors of these and other sexual victimiza-tions: frequently drinking enough alcohol to get drunk, being single, having already experienced a sexual victimization before the beginning of the current school year, and living on campus (for on-campus victimization). This evi-dence supports the conclusion that alcohol abuse by college women raises the risk of sexual victimization.[17] It is crucial not to "blame the victim," since rape is a violent crime, but it is also important to point out how the victim may unwittingly raise the risk of victimization through substance use.

INTOXICATED RAPE

Arguably one of the most serious forms of alcohol-related crime on cam-pus is rape, so this section presents data on the extent of rape, including intoxicated rape. Like other forms of violence, rape has been implicated as an outcome of alcohol consumption in many settings. The number of reports of rape on college campuses is clearly the small tip of a large iceberg. For a number of reasons, women who have been raped don't usually report their victimizations to the campus or community police.

A Department of Justice–sponsored study estimated that the chances of a woman being raped during her undergraduate studies was between one in four and one in five.[18] Koss and colleagues found that more than 15 percent of college women had experienced a completed rape, and another 12 percent an attempted rape, since age 14.[19] Abbey reviewed research reporting similar prevalence rates, and noted that alcohol-related sexual assault was a common problem, with alcohol associated with more than half of college sexual assaults on women.[20] After reviewing the alcohol-sexual assault research, Abbey argued that alcohol increased the likelihood of sexual assault through several related pathways. She concluded that "beliefs about alcohol, deficits in higher order cognitive processing and motor impairments induced by alcohol and peer group norms that encourage heavy drinking and forced sex."[21]

Using data from the 1997, 1999, and 2001 College Alcohol Study surveys of 119 colleges, my colleagues and I assessed the correlates of rape while intoxicated across a large national cross-section of more than 25,000 women at four-year colleges, to our knowledge the largest survey assembled on this topic.[22] Questions that conformed to the legal definition of rape in many states were included to indicted *rape while forced* ("Since the beginning of the school year, have you ever had sexual intercourse against your wishes because someone used force?"); *rape while threatened* ("Apart from question 1, since the beginning of the school year, have you had sexual intercourse against your wishes because someone threatened to harm you?"); and *rape while intoxicated* ("Apart from questions 1 and 2, since the beginning of the school year, have you had sexual intercourse when you were so intoxicated that you were unable to consent?"). The possible responses ("0 times, 1 time, 2 times, 3 or more times") were dichotomized into "yes" or "no."

Table 5-1 presents the prevalence of these types of rape based on asking women during the spring semester whether they had sex without consent "since the beginning of the school year," a period on average of about seven months. Roughly 1 in 20 college women had been raped in that short time period, with 72 percent of those raped experiencing rape while intoxicated, the most frequent form of rape. Except for rape by threat, there were no significant differences across the three surveys.

Women who went to colleges with medium and high binge drinking rates had more than a 1.5-fold increased chance of being raped while intoxicated than those from institutions with lower binge drinking rates. Other factors

Table 5-1.

Prevalence of Rape Since the Beginning of the School Year (percent)

	Year			
	All years	1997	1999	2001
Type	(N=23,980)	(N=8,567)	(N=8,425)	(N=6,988)
Intoxicated	3.4	3.6	3.4	3.2
Forced	1.9	2.1	1.8	1.7
Threatened	0.4	0.5	0.3	0.3
Any type of rape	4.7	5.1	4.5	4.3

Source: Mohler-Kuo, Dowdall, Koss, & Wechsler (2004).

that raised the risk of rape included being under 21 years old, being white, residing in sorority houses, using illicit drugs, and having been a binge drinker in college. These findings have important implications for prevention programs:

> College prevention programs must give increased attention to educating male students that one of the first questions they must ask themselves before initiating sex with a woman is whether she is capable of giving consent.... College men must be educated for their own protection that intoxication is a stop sign for sex. College women need to be warned not only about the vulnerability created by heavy drinking, but also about the extra dangers imposed in situations where many other people are drinking heavily. The person who commits rape is, of course, responsible in both the legal and the moral sense, and we must view rape from that perspective. For purposes of prevention, however, identifying the factors that place women at increased vulnerability to rape is also important.[23]

Alcohol is clearly present in many of the crimes of violence among college students, and in more than 7 of 10 rapes that occur among college women.

ALCOHOL AS A DATE RAPE DRUG

Alcohol's pharmacological properties are a key factor in its role in rape and other nonconsensual sex. Alcohol produces biphasic effects, with initial stimulation followed by sedation. Figure 5-1 presents an image of the impact of rising levels of breath alcohol concentration on the central nervous system. Initially at modest or moderate levels of consumption, alcohol produces relaxation and then disinhibition. Rapid drinking of alcohol as in college

Figure 5-1.
Psychodynamics of Alcohol Use

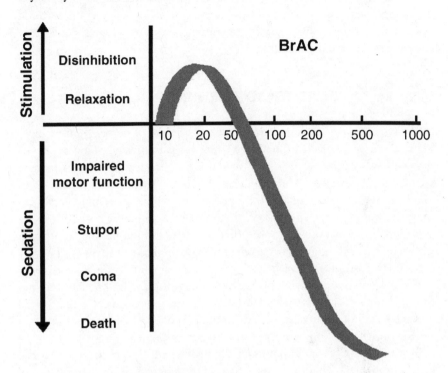

Source: Adapted from NIAAA (2007b: figure 1-9).

binge drinking quickly can produce both forms of stimulation, leading to even heavier and quicker drinking. Women who try to match men drink-for-drink are even more likely to move down the path toward heavier intoxication. Greater consumption produces sedative effects, including impaired motor function and stupor.

Alcohol is also viewed by many as a safe substance, one that they and their friends have used in the past without major negative effects. As a legal substance to those over 21, it has little of the negative images now held about illicit drugs. Its widespread use by college students makes it appear a safe choice, and its initial effect is to make the party shine even more brightly. Its appearance signals that fun is about to happen. Alcohol's public use now happens largely off campus, in locales like off-campus apartments and fraternity houses that have minimal or no adult supervision and where common sources of supply like kegs or open bottles make ingestion of much more than a standard drink likely. College-oriented bars combine music, party atmosphere, and lots of new faces, helping to move drinking along through the night, making each person fit the images of happy party-goers featured in alcohol advertising. By contrast, on-campus dormitory lounges and other common spaces are dry and dull.

"GRAY RAPE," INTOXICATED SEX, PARTY RAPE?

Some part of having sex without consent because of intoxication involves sex between people who are both too drunk to give consent. Some have used the term "gray rape" to discuss drunken sex where the motivation to rape appears to be absent.[24] Unfortunately this term has also been adopted to minimize the estimates of rape on college campuses. For a number of reasons, there is a great gap between the number of women who have experienced nonconsensual sex because of intoxication and the number of women who report that they have been raped.[25] Not the least of these is the difficulty that prosecutors have in gathering evidence about rape when one or both parties have been drinking heavily. U.S. Attorney Pat Meehan told me that this type of rape remains almost beyond prosecution; at a time when resources for public prosecutors are strained, these type of rape cases simply are too difficult for prosecutors to pursue with sufficient energy.[26]

But some part of sex without consent because of intoxication involves the deliberate use of alcohol as a date rape drug designed to get women drunk enough to have nonconsensual sex. A detailed portrait of this type of behavior at a fraternity house has been reported at another elite university much like Duke.[27] A Department of Justice report defines "party rape" as one that "occurs at an off-campus house or on- or off-campus fraternity and involves ... plying a woman with alcohol or targeting an intoxicated woman."[28]

A study of undergraduate life at Rutgers, a major public research university, pointed to the central value of "friendly fun" for understanding that life.[29] A recent study of a similar university helps to understand how party rape is produced by the very same forces that generate "friendly fun." The authors note that "the vast majority of heterosexual encounters at parties are fun and consensual."[30] But their data show how the organization of everyday life for freshmen women facilitates party rape:

> Party rape is accomplished without the use of guns, knives, or fists. It is carried out through the combination of low level forms of coercion—a lot of liquor and persuasion, manipulation of situations so that women cannot leave, and sometimes force (e.g., by blocking a door, or using body weight to make it

difficult for a woman to get up). These forms of coercion are made more effec-tive by organizational arrangements that provide men with control over how partying happenings and by expectations that women let loose and trust their party-mates. This systematic and effective method of extracting nonconsensual sex is largely invisible, which makes it difficult for victims to convince anyo-ne—even themselves—that a crime occurred. Men engage in this behavior with little risk of consequences.[31]

ALCOHOL AND DUKE LACROSSE

On March 13, 2006, Durham, North Carolina, police responded to a com-plaint that a young African American woman hired to strip at a college party had been brutally raped by members of the Duke University lacrosse team. The ensuing media firestorm led to headlines across the entire world: drunk young white men at one of the most privileged universities had attacked a minority woman driven to stripping to support herself through college.

Eventually the truth came out: a rogue prosecutor facing a tough election had withheld crucial evidence from the defense that supported the lacrosse team's innocence of rape. But the episode raised the allegedly heavy drink-ing and partying at Duke to national attention, a key case in reframing col-lege drinking as a social problem.

The reactions at Duke to the stripper party incident shed light on alcohol use by the lacrosse team and the broader Duke undergraduate student body. Several weeks after the incident, Duke's president asked James E. Coleman, a professor in the School of Law, to chair an ad hoc committee to review la-crosse team member conduct. Because the criminal investigation was still going forward, the committee didn't consider questions about "the alleged criminal conduct."[32]

Finding the team members to have been "academically and athletically re-sponsible students" with no disciplinary problems with their professors, the ad hoc committee concluded,

> Paradoxically, in contrast to their exemplary academic and athletic perform-ance, a large number of the members of the team have been socially irrespon-sible when under the influence of alcohol. They have repeatedly violated the law against underage drinking. They have drunk alcohol excessively. They have disturbed their neighbors with loud music and noise, both on-campus and off-campus. They have publicly urinated both on-campus and off. They have shown disrespect for property. Both the number of team members impli-cated in this behavior and the number of alcohol-related incidents involving them have been excessive compared to other Duke athletic teams. Neverthe-less, their conduct has not been different in character than the conduct of the

typical Duke student who abuses alcohol. Their reported conduct has not involved fighting, sexual assault or harassment, or racist behavior. Moreover, even the people who have complained about their alcohol-related misconduct often add that the students are respectful and appear genuinely remorseful when they are not drinking.[33]

Most of the incidents of team member misconduct involved alcohol, including underage possession and public urination, and one incident involving 10 students playing a drinking game in a dorm room while hosting a high school recruit.[34]

A Durham police captain reported that

[L]acrosse players did not represent a special or unique problem in District 2; in fact, none of the houses rented by lacrosse players was among the worst of those whose loud parties attracted hundreds of disorderly Duke students on weekends. Although lacrosse players rented a large house at 1206 W. Markham, Captain Sarvis said it was not among the top 10 houses about which neighbors complained the most. Nor did lacrosse players as a group stand out as the worst student offenders. Captain Sarvis said the fraternity-affiliated houses presented a greater challenge to police than any of the houses rented by athletes.[35]

The ad hoc committee found that Duke student affairs administrators were aware of "the irresponsible conduct of lacrosse players associated with drinking." But, except for the Office of Judicial Affairs, none were alarmed by the conduct, and none communicated with Coach Pressler.[36] The Committee concluded that Duke's process for dealing with "non-academic and non-suspendable athlete misconduct (and student misconduct generally) is hampered by an approach that is informal to the point of being casual. The result is a process that is arbitrary and often ineffective."[37]

For present purposes, the most important finding of the ad hoc committee centers on Duke's stance toward alcohol:

The University's ability to deal fully with the problem of alcohol is undermined by its own ambivalence toward drinking and the conduct it spawns.
Alcohol is the single greatest factor involved in the unacceptable behavior of Duke students in general and members of the lacrosse team specifically, both on- and off-campus. Drunkenness is the cause of behaviors that represent a serious nuisance to the community and a source of significant personal danger for the student. The University's alcohol policy is reasonable, but it is inconsistently enforced and only ineffectually disciplined. The University's ambivalence is most obviously manifested in the University's tolerance of egregious violations of its own policies at events such as Tailgate and Last Day of Classes, as outlined in the Report of the Committee to investigate the Judicial

Procedure. While the alcohol related misconduct by members of the lacrosse team is deplorable, the University is, by its lack of leadership in this area of deep concern, implicated in the alcohol excesses of lacrosse players and of Duke students more generally.[38]

The ad hoc committee came up with four recommendations. The first three focused on athletics, whereas the fourth recommendation sought a new approach to alcohol issues:

1. Continuance of the Men's Lacrosse Team with appropriate oversight
2. Code of conduct for athletes
3. Need for Improved Communication between Student Affairs and Athletics
4. Need for a Clearly Articulated and Enforced Alcohol Policy

The university's own apparent ambiguity regarding underage alcohol consumption conveys inconsistent messages and confuses expectations regarding alcohol. Duke University has fostered a number of problems among its undergraduates, including lacrosse players, by its ambivalent policies toward underage and over-consumption of alcohol at Duke. This problem needs serious review and remediation within the University.[39]

THE DUKE ALCOHOL SCENE

In the recent past, Duke had acquired a reputation as a major party school, with Greek life, big time athletics, and a supportive campus culture for alcohol abuse. Observers within the Duke community confirmed that reality matched reputation. In the mid-1990s, while Duke was shifting toward a much more restrictive alcohol policy on its campus, its alumni magazine reported that the university had a binge drinking rate slightly higher than the national average.[40] Duke's Dean of the Chapel William Willimon had issued a widely noted report, "Work Hard, Play Hard," that captured the prevailing Duke ethic of the 1990s.[41]

Duke's current national reputation as a party school, though one with strong academics, appears in several college guides. For example, the *Princeton Review's* 2007 *The Best 361 Colleges*, published before the lacrosse incident, describes Duke as "the fun younger brother of the aging Ivies," quoting a student who claims the campus has "top-ten academics, a beautiful campus, wonderful climate, a fun social scene."[42] Noting that Duke has "lots of beer drinking," the guide goes on to comment, "Duke has a party scene, or rather, several (centered on the Greek houses, dorms, and off-campus apartments)," although this may be changing, as "strict alcohol policies are pushing a lot of weekend activity off campus." Duke balances academics with "cultivating sociable, friendly people who will be able to succeed in all future life situations."

The *Fiske Guide to Colleges 2007*, published after the first stories about Duke lacrosse, mentions Duke's policy requiring freshmen to live on the dry East Campus as a way of "insulating them from the wilder aspects of Duke's social scene, which attracted national attention for a scandal involving off-campus behavior of members of the lacrosse team."[43] *Fiske* reports a freshman as saying, "alcohol, it seems, is quite easy to find."[44] It also notes how Greek life has been pushed off campus and how town-gown relationships (those between the nonacademic and academic people) are strained. *Fiske* gives Duke the highest rating for its academics, but slightly lower ones for "social" and "quality of life."

What was the reality of alcohol use at Duke at the time of the stripper party? Some evidence suggests that if anything, Duke was apparently making some progress in dealing with alcohol issues. A profile of Duke published in 2001 noted,

> Data collected at Duke have shown that changes are occurring in desired directions. Emergency room admissions data have shown decreases in alcohol-related accidents and alcohol overdoses. Core Surveys have been conducted at Duke every two years; survey results have shown that the binge drinking rate has decreased, although Duke is still slightly above the national norm. The negative consequences of drinking assessed by the Core Survey have also decreased, and the incidence of negative consequences at Duke is below national norms.[45]

The 1999 death of Duke student Raheem Bath as the result of a night of heavy drinking leading to aspirational pneumonia was a milestone for the university. Policies were changed, but the problems continued. By 2003, Duke's student newspaper would report: "Last year, 47 students were transported to the hospital for alcohol-related incidents, down from 2000–2001's high of 57, including 38 students hospitalized in fall 2000. Alcohol policy violations also remained roughly the same as in fall 2001."[46]

More recent data also hint at a slightly different reality than Duke's party school image:

> It turns out that Duke isn't really the party school everyone seems to think. According to the American College Health Association National College Health Assessment, Duke students believe that the use of drugs and alcohol

on campus is more prevalent than it actually is. The study—which is conducted at Duke every two years—was last reported in Fall 2006. The results revealed fairly large discrepancies between what students perceive and what students actually do. At Duke, 15.5 percent of students reported never drinking alcohol, though students predicted that only 2.3 percent of the student body were nondrinkers. Although the perceived percentage of alcohol use, at 70.8 percent, is on par with what is actually consumed, 74.6 percent, the perceived prevalence of starting heavy drinking upon coming to Duke is not accurate.[47]

A more comprehensive view of Duke's alcohol scene was presented in reaction to the stripper party incident. Duke launched an extensive review of its undergraduate campus culture by the Campus Culture Initiative (CCI) Steering Committee.[48] While the results of the review were necessarily controversial, it suggests how one set of Duke students and faculty viewed campus alcohol issues:

> Alcohol issues are not one single problem, but rather a series of three, interrelated problems that are viewed in multiple ways: "bad behavior," "impaired health," and "lost weekends." All three tend to involve heavy drinking—drunkenness—rather than drinking *per se*. With regard to bad behavior, drinking is a factor in much of the serious misbehavior, assault, property damage, injury, unwanted sex, and neighborhood disruption involving undergraduates. Drinking also creates a substantial legal liability to the University and is a significant risk to Duke's reputation. In terms of impaired health, a large minority of undergraduates engage in heavy drinking on a regular basis, putting their academic performance and their health at risk. Recent biomedical research on adolescent brain development underscores that heavy drinking can cause brain damage. The immediate threat is that students will be injured while drunk. Overdose appears to be a particular problem for first-year students: 37 were transported to the Emergency Room last year, and there were 7 transports of first-year students just during orientation week this year. The risk of another alcohol-related death in the Duke community is very real. Furthermore, several dozen students are seen in CAPS every year with serious symptoms of alcoholism, and far more than that will graduate with a heavy-drinking habit. Alcohol use also complicates other mental health problems and heightens impulsive behavior, both contributing to and creating high risk in vulnerable students. Beyond bad behavior and impaired health is the problem of alcohol-induced lost weekends; much weekend social life at Duke is organized around getting drunk, an activity that is alluring for many students, but ultimately unsatisfying. Where, how, and with whom Duke students socialize are important influences on campus culture.[49]

The CCI Report presented data comparing Duke undergraduates with peers at comparable institutions:

> Duke students report higher levels of drinking in college and more frequent binge drinking (three or more occasions of 5 or more drinks in the last 2 weeks)

than their peers at comparable institutions. It is, however, Duke students in Greek letter organizations, not independents, who set Duke apart from its comparison schools. (For example, in the 2003 survey, binge drinking was reported by 43% of Duke fraternity members and 29% of sorority members compared to 14% non-fraternity and 8% non-sorority members.)[50]

The report also showed Duke students studying less and partying more than at the other schools.

The CCI Report noted the difficulty of dealing with these issues, including not enough capacity to treat clinically those with alcohol problems and inadequate monitoring of trends in use. The CCI reported the following recommendations about alcohol, designed "to promote a more responsible approach to the culture of campus drinking:"

1. Re-orient social life on campus to reduce the centrality of alcohol and enable more non-alcohol events and venues

2. Establish attractive venues for controlled distribution of alcohol for students of age, including a large space able to accommodate 300–400 people

3. Clarify alcohol regulations and enforce these regulations consistently. Specifically, target disorderly and disrespectful behavior and dangerous drinking

4. Increase staffing and resources for the oversight of policies and practices and for alcohol/substance abuse prevention and treatment services

5. Implement an evidence-based approach, based upon public health principles, to alcohol policy, initiatives, and accountability.[51]

The present Duke alcohol scene, like many other colleges across the country, appears to have some percentage of students heavily engaged in binge dinking, with a majority of students either occasionally or never bingeing. But its image has now become the thing of "sex and scandal," to borrow the title of a widely read *Rolling Stone* profile: Duke's undergraduate image, unfair or not, is a sum of "Lacrosse players, sorority girls and the booze-fueled culture of the never-ending hookup on the nation's most embattled campus."[52]

A Duke student observed,

Indeed, our current policy's most unfortunate consequence is that it consistently allows a small minority of students, on the order of 15 to 20 percent, to ruin things for the rest of us; their involvement in things like baby oil-wrestling matches sullies the good name of all Duke students, especially those of us who have never found it necessary to urinate publicly.[53]

LESSONS LEARNED FROM THE DUKE LACROSSE CASE

What lessons can be learned from the Duke lacrosse case about college drinking? In one sense, none: the case is a "false positive": no rape happened, and any discussion of the role alcohol played in the case obviously can't explain what didn't happen. But the case opened up discussion of alcohol problems at Duke, and may raise more general questions about the role of alcohol in current undergraduate life.

Reports of the alleged rape by the Duke lacrosse team members frequently mentioned drinking and underage drinking, drug use by the alleged victim, and a "culture of excess" that marked some part of Duke undergraduate life. Some members of the team were under 21, and so plans to go to a bar or strip club were shelved; the party the team attended had been moved to a private house off campus because of a university crackdown on on-campus drinking. Reactions to the alleged rape included investigation into the conduct of the lacrosse team members and a critical assessment of Duke's culture, both raising the issue of alcohol abuse as a common problem at the university.

Duke has some of the institutional characteristics that make it likely to exhibit a culture of heavy college drinking. Big-time athletics, active Greek life, and a reputation for vibrant social life are often associated with that culture. But its own data show that most Duke students don't frequently binge drink, and even the lurid and sensational reporting after the stripper party indicates that only a minority of its students were part of the "Duke 500."[54] As some measure of how the alcohol issues raised by the stripper party were eclipsed by the furor over prosecutorial misconduct, a Duke alumni magazine "one year later" story did not even mention student drinking.[55] Media stories about the stripper party also have dropped the student drinking theme.[56]

In the end, the Duke lacrosse rape case proved to be an example of egregious prosecutorial misconduct, since the lacrosse team members were innocent of rape. It appears that the students involved did some heavy drinking, including playing drinking games, some underage drinking, and voicing crude racist insults. Hiring a stripper may not be in the best of taste but violates no laws. And what the students drank isn't that far from what many others at their institution consume, even though many Duke students (like college students more generally) use alcohol moderately or not at all.

So in this one case, the underage and immoderate drinking ends up being linked to boorish and immature behavior, apparently commonplace (though not the norm) at Duke. A minority of Duke's students apparently live in a

subculture in which heavy drinking, hooking up, Greek life, and involvement in athletics mark their behavior off from other students. This same
subculture exists at many other colleges and universities and has been linked
with a higher risk of intoxicated rape. Because of the media attention surrounding the stripper party, the Duke drinking subculture has been the subject of intense scrutiny.[57] That this describes a minority of Duke students is
easy to forget. Whatever the reality of Duke undergraduate life, its image as
the *Animal House* of the twenty-first century has been presented as "Dupont
University" in Tom Wolfe's novel, *I Am Charlotte Simmons*.[58]

Extensive public health evidence has shown that heavy episodic or binge
drinking is associated with a host of health and behavioral consequences,
including intoxicated or party rape. As one scholar of college sexuality
observed,

> Regardless of the outcome of the criminal investigation, it was clear that mem-
> bers of [the Duke lacrosse team] were engaging in heavy alcohol consumption
> and creating a sex-charged atmosphere by hiring two exotic dancers. It is this
> type of behavior that has concerned many scholars who have studied binge
> drinking, fraternity life, and rape.[59]

There is little evidence that college drinking has changed much across the
country (if anything, it may have increased and intensified), and so one
assumes that some of its correlates or consequences will continue—1,700
deaths, and 1 in 20 women raped, almost three-quarters because they are
too intoxicated to give consent.

It is too early to assess the lasting consequences of the Duke episode (as
reports circulate of continuing legal actions by the team members). The episode focused attention on how a culture that mixes alcohol, sex, and sports at
an elite university, and raises both the risk of serious and criminal outcomes
as well as troubling questions about alcohol use yet to be answered effectively
by higher education. But raising the risk is not the same thing as certainty:
no rape happened at the Duke stripper party, though thousands do at colleges across the country, most of them because of too much alcohol.

CONCLUSION

Alcohol, sex, and social life are joined together in both popular culture
and in everyday college student behavior. One part of college culture drives
the others, and so it is difficult for many college students to imagine life
without the other. That popular culture tends to exaggerate the level of
drinking and sex matches the misperceptions that many students hold of

how their peers behave: most college students don't drink dangerously or heavily, most don't engage in frequent sex with anonymous partners, and most college women aren't the victims of intoxicated or other forms of rape. That having been said, two in five binge drink, about a quarter drink so heavily that they forget what they did, and 1 in 20 college women has non-consensual sex, mostly because of intoxication.

Enough problematic or troubled behavior happens to a substantial minority of college students that one might ask whether anything can be done to make college life more temperate. The next chapter takes up the question of how higher education has responded to college drinking, and what forms of prevention might work.

NOTES

1. Moffatt (1989) uses the phrase "friendly fun" to discuss undergraduate culture.

2. *Princeton Review* (2007); Fiske (2006).

3. Pryor, Higher Education Research Institute, & Cooperative Institutional Research Program (2007: 57).

4. Wechsler, Dowdall, Davenport, & Castillo (1995).

5. Levine, Cureton, & Levine (1998: 103).

6. Bogle (2008).

7. For a detailed picture of that subculture at another elite university with a mixture of athletics, parties, and fraternities, see Grazian (2008).

8. Bogle (2008: 63).

9. Interview with Kathleen Bogle.

10. Grazian (2008).

11. Grazian (2008: 226–227).

12. Zailckas (2005).

13. Zailckas (2005: 212).

14. Zailckas (2005: 215).

15. Wechsler & Wuethrich (2002).

16. Fisher & Cullen (1999).

17. See also that presented by Schwartz & Pitts (1995); and Wechsler, Lee, Kuo, & Lee (2000).

18. Fisher, Cullen, & Turner (2000).

19. Koss, Gidycz, & Wisniewski (1987).

20. Abbey (2002).

21. Abbey (2002: 125).

22. Mohler-Kuo, Dowdall, Koss, & Wechsler (2004).

23. Mohler-Kuo et al. (2004: 43).

24. Stepp (2007).

25. See the papers in Part II of Fisher & Sloan (2007).

26. Interview with Patrick Meehan (2007).

27. Sanday (1990).

28. Sampson (2002).

29. Moffatt (1989).

30. Armstrong, Hamilton, & Sweeney (2006).

31. Armstrong, Hamilton, & Sweeney (2006: 492).

32. http://news.duke.edu/mmedia/pdf/lacrossereport.pdf, accessed February 25, 2008.

33. *Ibid.*, 6–7.

34. *Ibid.*, 7–8.

35. *Ibid.*, 13.

36. *Ibid.*, 17.

37. *Ibid.*, 22.

38. *Ibid.*, 24, emphasis in original.

39. *Ibid.*, 25.

40. http://www.dukemagazine.duke.edu/alumni/dm11/moderate.html#top, accessed February 20, 2008. Duke's current alcohol policy can be found at http://judicial.studentaffairs.duke.edu/policies/policy_list/alcohol.html, accessed February 29, 2008.

41. See also Willimon & Naylor (1995).

42. *Princeton Review* (2006: 200).

43. Fiske (2006: 215).

44. Fiske (2006: 216).

45. http://www.higheredcenter.org/casestudies/duke-a.html, accessed February 29, 2008.

46. Lees (2003).

47. Zhao (2007).

48. http://news.duke.edu/reports/ccireport.pdf, accessed February 20, 2008.

49. *Ibid.*, 19.

50. *Ibid.*, 19.

51. *Ibid.*, 21.

52. Reitman (2006).

53. Butler (2006).

54. Reitman (2006).

55. Bliwise (2007).

56. Aldridge (2008).

57. Reitman (2006).

58. Wolfe (2004).

59. Bogle (2008: 162).

CHAPTER 6

Public Alcohol Policy and College Drinking

Whether or not a college student drinks seems to be a fundamentally personal and private act. Most of the attempts by colleges to shape student drinking begin with that assumption, attempting to address the decisions students make by calling attention to the personal drinking decisions made by other individuals or seeking to protect the student individually. So why should anyone concerned about college drinking be concerned about public policy about alcohol? Isn't policy a distant and abstract issue, far away from what happens daily on college campuses, and what individuals choose to do?

This chapter argues that public alcohol policy is one of the important factors shaping college drinking. Alcohol policies shape how alcohol is produced, distributed, marketed, and sold; what can be done about college drinking; and even the discourse about college prevention programs. Recent evidence supports the argument that upstream factors like policy may be as important—or even more important—than downstream efforts to prevent or control drinking by individual students.

PUBLIC POLICY ABOUT ALCOHOL

We can define alcohol policies as "authoritative decisions made by governments through laws, rules, and regulations . . . that pertain to the relation between alcohol, health, and social welfare."[1] The focus of this chapter will be on public alcohol policies (i.e., those of governments) rather than private policies (i.e., by universities), though we will also note how public policies can often shape private policies, as well as individual behavior.

Alcohol is no ordinary commodity, to borrow a phrase from a recent international study of alcohol policy.[2] Policies to control alcohol have been used by societies as far back as ancient Greece and Rome. Almost every modern society has elaborate public policies about its production, marketing, sale, and use. This near-universality of public concern reflects the substantial health and other costs associated with alcohol use. In the United States, more than 100,000 people a year die directly as a result of alcohol abuse, a far larger number than die because of illicit drugs.[3] Worldwide, alcohol accounts for 4 percent of the total cost to life and longevity, and while some positive health effects have been discovered, "the detrimental effects of alcohol on disease burden by far outweigh the beneficial effects."[4]

In addition to health issues, alcohol is also associated with both extensive costs and revenues. Costs include the impact on the criminal justice system, the health care system, and the workforce. In 2001, alcohol abuse was estimated to cost American society more than $166 billion dollars.[5] But public policy is also driven by other factors: alcohol is a commodity that generates important tax revenues for governments, and the alcohol industry provides jobs for a large workforce as well as profits for several major related industries (from trucking to restaurants).

Societies have employed many different kinds of alcohol policies, covering production, advertising and marketing, consumption, prevention, and treatment. This chapter will focus on policies in contemporary United States and in particular those that have an impact on college students. But some historical and comparative analysis will sharpen our understanding of the present situation in this country.[6]

THE AMERICAN CONTEXT OF PUBLIC ALCOHOL POLICY

Policies begin with definitions and distinctions. Especially relevant are definitions of alcohol and drugs. Both alcohol and drugs have powerful effects on human behavior, including pharmacological effects, so they are often discussed as "drugs" in everyday speech. But in the United States, they are defined quite differently in law and public policy.

The most important American alcohol policies were shaped by the experience of Prohibition. Concerns about alcohol's impact on society led to the development of a powerful Temperance movement in the late-nineteenth and early twentieth century, propelling many of the states and finally the federal government to prohibit its use. The 18th Amendment to the U.S. Constitution (1919) and the Volstead Act defined the era of Prohibition in the 1920s.[7] While Prohibition cut consumption and some alcohol-related problems, it had unanticipated consequences, including a flourishing black market and rising public unhappiness with its restrictiveness. These led to a backlash that ended in the passage of the 21st Amendment (1933), repealing Prohibition and placing the regulation of alcohol in the hands of the individual states. Much of the recent history of American alcohol policy was colored by the experience of Prohibition.[8] To this day, the alcohol industry looks over its shoulder at the impact public policy can have on its operations, making it an energetic participant in shaping policy.

By contrast with alcohol policy, American drug policy flowed from different sources. Policies about drugs grew out of rising public anger about sales of worthless medicines, fears of drug abuse and addiction and their consequences, and rising international pressure for the formation of an American drug policy. Also in contrast to alcohol, American drug policy has always been formulated at the national level, from the Pure Food and Drug Act of 1906 to the Controlled Substance Act of 1970 and the Anti-Drug Abuse Act of 1988.[9] Drugs are illicit; by contrast, alcohol is legal for those over 21, widely marketed, and much less feared, even though alcohol abuse results in far more deaths and larger costs to society than illegal drugs.[10]

A recent international collaboration of leading scholars about the issue reached the following definition of alcohol policy:

> At its broadest meaning, alcohol policy refers to any measure that affects the market in alcohol, the level and patterning of alcohol consumption, or the occurrence of alcohol-related problems. In this sense, policy can include a whole range of governmental actions that have little to do with alcohol specifically (such as mandating seat-belts in cars), or which have little connection to social and health problems from drinking (such as beer bottle recycling programs).[11]

Alcohol policies are formulated at every level of government, including international, national, state or regional, and local. By contrast, policy about illicit drugs is largely national in scope as defined by the Commerce Clause of the U.S. Constitution and reaffirmed by Supreme Court decisions.

THE ALCOHOL INDUSTRY

The alcohol policy researcher James Mosher provides a useful framework for examining alcohol policy.[12] Alcohol is a legal product widely consumed in the United States, and the industry that profits from its use is a major factor in shaping public policy. The American alcohol industry is huge, with $115 billion in annual sales. The industry is highly concentrated, with a handful of producers such as the two largest beer companies and eight other alcohol companies accounting for 70 percent of all U.S. alcohol sales. Consumption is also concentrated, with most Americans either nonconsumers or light consumers of alcohol; 42 percent of all the alcohol sold is consumed by the heaviest 5 percent of drinkers. Young people are a particularly critical part of the market for alcohol, in part because they consume more than older people and because their use of the product will shape lifelong consumption patterns.

The industry uses its marketing prowess to encourage consumers (including young consumers) to buy its products.[13] The "four P's of marketing" are used to drive up sales:

- *Product:* the industry has introduced new products such as wine coolers, "alcopops," and malt liquor to appeal to younger tastes.
- *Promotion:* vast amounts are spent on promoting alcohol products to younger consumers, with the implicit message that everyone uses them. (For more information about the promotion of alcohol to youth, visit http: camy.org.)
- *Place:* alcohol is widely available, and even more so near college campuses.
- *Price:* alcohol is cheap, and taxation hasn't kept up with inflation. In some communities, beer is cheaper than soft drinks. Young people are price-sensitive, and as alcohol has become relatively cheaper, consumption has increased.

Mosher concludes from this analysis,

> Taken together, these marketing strategies communicate a powerful message about alcohol's role in society. The marketing in college communities is particularly aggressive, promoting alcohol's glamour and attractiveness and making it readily available at low prices, variables that a recent study found to correlate directly with underage college binge drinking.[14]

Mosher claims that a range of environmental prevention programs have been found to be effective in lowering the risk of hazardous drinking by youth. He argues that the alcohol industry has supported social norms and other alcohol education programs, but Mosher views these education programs as substitutes and not supplements to effective environmental programs. The alcohol industry has favored those approaches that shift responsibility for alcohol problems onto the shoulders of individual consumers and away from the industry's products. The industry has even tried to take credit for decreases in alcohol problems, decreases that evidence shows were due to such environmental changes as increasing the minimum drinking age and improving law enforcement of underage drinking. Mosher argues that an important priority of industry education messages is to normalize drinking:

> Cultural acceptance ... is the key to boosting industry sales. This priority reflects the industry's frustration that so many Americans drink so little or not at all, a major impediment to market growth. It also helps explain the industry's enthusiasm for social norms marketing: Ignoring the environmental component, its message blames deviant "irresponsible" drinkers for problems and normalizes college drinking.[15]

The journalist Michael Massing paints a vivid portrait of leaders of the lobbying efforts of the alcohol industry, one of the most effective in Washington and in state capitals as well. Organizations such as the Beer Institute, the Wine Institute, the Distilled Spirits Council of the United States, and the National Beer Wholesalers Association (NBWA) have big staffs and make large contributions to politicians of both parties. They also organize at the grassroots level: the NBWA has members in every congressional district across the country. Individual companies such as Anheuser-Busch also advocate effectively, with a company lobbyist in every state capital.[16]

By contrast, those who advocate alcohol control appear less formidable. Massing terms George Hacker the "undisputed general of the nation's alcohol control forces." As director of the alcohol-policies project of the Center for Science in the Public Interest, Hacker has a staff of seven and is described as "constantly outmaneuvered by the industry."[17] Mothers Against Drunk Driving (MADD) has been a major force behind public policies such as raising the minimum drinking age and advocating for 0.08 blood alcohol concentration (BAC) levels that define driving under the influence.[18] But even MADD has no full-time lobbyist in Washington, and usually calls on volunteers to staff its policy efforts in state capitals. When organized into community coalitions, grassroots activists can have significant influence in efforts to control alcohol. In addition to its focus on drunk driving, MADD has expanded its mission to include combating underage drinking.

Other organizations have attempted to play roles in shaping alcohol policy as well, including foundations that have funded research and policy (such as the Robert Wood Johnson Foundation); community coalitions (such as represented by the Community Anti-Drug Coalitions of America). Security on

Campus has pushed successfully for federal legislation requiring colleges and universities to report crime, including drug and alcohol offenses.

A variety of federal and state agencies are involved in studying the effects of policy. The National Institute on Alcohol Abuse and Alcoholism (NIAAA) has funded much of the research about alcohol and its impact on society, including a special task force on college drinking. Other federal agencies such as the Office of National Drug Control Policy (ONDCP) also affect alcohol policy, though in complex ways: ONDCP has been criticized for neglecting to address alcohol abuse in its well-funded efforts to raise public consciousness about substance abuse. Within higher education, organizations such as the American Council on Education (ACE) have played a major role in shaping how colleges and universities deal with alcohol issues.

Like other public policies, alcohol policies have been created over a long period of time by complex processes that involve many participants. The alcohol industry is a powerful interest group, though by no means a monolithic one. Other interest groups include the media; private sector organizations that try to influence alcohol policy, such as the national and local chapters of MADD; or state-level organizations (e.g., Pennsylvanians Against Underage Drinking).[19] Also at the state level, other kinds of organizations may become involved in public policy debates, including owners of alcohol outlets, employees of state liquor stores, taxpayers groups, and so on.

CONTEMPORARY ISSUES IN PUBLIC ALCOHOL POLICY

While the "drinking age" has long been debated, states have had some kind of age requirement for purchasing alcohol.[20] Because of the 21st Amendment, which ended Prohibition and gave individual states the right to regulate alcohol, individual states determine much of the public policy about alcohol. And although the states often took different paths, they all decided to set minimum purchasing age laws. Most of the states in the period since Prohibition set the age limit at 21. Over the years, and particularly after the voting age fell to 18 during the Vietnam War to match the age of eligibility for the military draft, most states made changes in the minimum age for purchase. The result was hardly uniform; by 1979, 11 states and the District of Columbia had different ages for purchasing beer of more than 3.2 percent alcohol versus beer less than 3.2 percent and requiring purchasers of distilled spirits to be 21 or older. In the same year, 39 states had set a single standard for all alcohol purchases, but it varied from 12 states requiring age 18, 10 setting the age at 19, four at age 20, and the remaining 13 at age 21. (So in almost half the states, a person had to be 21 or older to purchase distilled spirits.) There was wide variation even within the same region. Pennsylvania had a minimum purchase age of 21, whereas bordering states had lower ages: New York and New Jersey set the age at 18, Ohio at 18 for 3.2 percent beer (but 21 for stronger beer and all distilled spirits), Delaware at 20 for all alcohol products, and so on. People under the minimum purchase age in one state could drive across the border to buy alcohol, setting up the inevitable problem of "bloody borders." Along with rising concern about drunk driving deaths, the interstate differences in drinking age led to pressure for a higher and uniform drinking age. President Ronald Reagan, a conservative Republican, signed a bill passed by a Democratic-controlled Congress, which tied a state minimum drinking age of 21 to the availability of federal highway funds. The outcome was one of the few current alcohol policies that does not vary much across the states.[21] States, however, do vary considerably in how vigorously they enforce these policies.[22]

The NIAAA's Alcohol Policy Information System site lists current policies across the 50 states about underage drinking.[23] Data on each state's policies on the following topics are available:

- Underage possession of alcohol
- Underage consumption of alcohol
- Underage purchase of alcohol
- Furnishing alcohol to minors
- Minimum ages for on-premises servers and bartenders
- Minimum ages for off-premises sellers
- False identification for obtaining alcohol
- Blood alcohol concentration limits for drivers under 21
- Keg registration
- Loss of driving privileges for alcohol violations by minors ("use/lose" laws)
- Hosting underage drinking parties: criminal liability

Since important American alcohol policy is formulated at the state level, it is necessary to look at that level to understand many current policy debates.[24]

Most public policies about alcohol are formulated in ways that affect all citizens and communities, and few have been enacted specifically about colleges and universities. Major exceptions include the Clery Act (which mandates the reporting of crimes on college campuses, including alcohol and drug violations) and the regulations of the U.S. Department of Education (EDGAR Code of Federal Regulation Part 86), which require colleges and universities to inform their students and employees about alcohol policies and laws. Because many undergraduate students are under the age of 21, the minimum drinking age laws (MDAL) have an unusually important impact on colleges and universities.

In recent years, alcohol control policies have weakened in the United States, and rates of taxation have as well.[25] A recent review of American alcohol policy notes that the "bar tab" of the costs to society of alcohol abuse is "much larger than it needs to be or should be," and that "beer and liquor have become too cheap and readily available," leading its author to "make the case for revising alcohol-control policy to help right the balance between the two sides of this problematic commodity, conveying as it does such harm and such pleasure."[26] Others argue that the United States also has relatively weak controls on alcohol advertising.

What public policies work? An international group of experts on alcohol-control policies reviewed available research evidence to rate policy-relevant strategies and interventions.[27] The following came out at the top of the list, with all but one providing clear examples of public policy:

- Minimum legal purchase age
- Government monopoly of retail sales
- Restrictions on hours or days of sale
- Outlet density restrictions
- Alcohol taxes
- Sobriety check points
- Lowered BAC limits
- Administrative license suspension
- Graduated licensing for novice drivers
- Brief interventions for hazardous drinkers

PUBLIC ALCOHOL POLICY AND COLLEGE DRINKING

Underage drinking (and drug use) on college campuses became a social problem in part because of federal legislation, the Safe and Drug

Free Schools Act. The Higher Education Center summarizes its requirements:[28]

> At a minimum, each school must distribute to all students and employees annually:
>
> - Standards of conduct that clearly prohibit the unlawful possession, use, or distribution of illicit drugs and alcohol on school property or as part of any school activities
>
> - A description of the applicable legal sanctions under local, State, or Federal law for the unlawful possession or distribution of illicit drugs and alcohol
>
> - A description of the health risks associated with the use of illicit drugs and the abuse of alcohol
>
> - A description of any drug or alcohol counseling, treatment, or rehabilitation or re-entry programs that are available to employees or students
>
> - A clear statement that the institution will impose sanctions on students and employees (consistent with local, State, and Federal law), and a description of those sanctions, up to and including expulsion or termination of employment and referral for prosecution, for violations of the standards of conduct
>
> - The law further requires an institution of higher education to conduct a biennial review of its program to:
>
>   - determine its effectiveness and implement changes if they are needed
>
>   - ensure that the sanctions developed are consistently enforced.

Colleges and universities are required to inform students and employees about local, state, and federal laws; the health risks; any programs available; and that the institution will impose sanctions. The actual contents are not defined, however, and the institution appears to have wide latitude in its biennial review. No sanctions are specified for failure to meet these requirements. The NIAAA's college-drinking prevention Web site includes a page that directs visitors to college-drinking policies of various institutions.[29]

What effects do these college alcohol policies have on actual behavior? The NIAAA's Task Force on College Drinking is a major source of ideas about forces (including public policy) shaping college drinking. Its Panel on Prevention and Treatment discussed prevention in a social ecological framework—that is, it views health-related behaviors such as college drinking as "affected by multiple levels of influence such as intrapersonal (individual) factors, interpersonal (group) processes, institutional factors, community factors, and public policies."[30] The task force notes that most campuses have prevention efforts that are concerned with the first three of these factors, but it finds that "[l]ess attention has been paid to factors in the local community that affect student alcohol use, and calls by campus officials for changes in State and Federal policy remain rare."[31]

The NIAAA Task Force Panel on Prevention and Treatment commissioned comprehensive reviews of existing research to arrive at its recommendations.[32] Under public policy, the NIAAA Panel made the following observations: "Laws designed to decrease alcohol-related harm in the general population have had considerable success. Public policies designed to reduce the commercial availability of alcohol have also shown promise in some areas."[33] Among these laws and policies are the following:

- Minimum legal drinking age
- Lowered BAC limits
- Administrative license revocation
- Increasing the price of alcohol
- Restricting licenses for retail sales of alcohol
- Limiting hours/days of sale
- Reducing the social availability of alcohol

The final report of the NIAAA Task Force reflected the panel's findings. The majority of its "most promising" strategies are public policies that have been found to be effective among general populations, such as the following:

- (2a) Increased enforcement of minimum drinking age laws;
- (2b) Implementation, increased publicity, and enforcement of other laws to reduce alcohol-impaired driving;
- (2c) Restrictions on alcohol retail density;
- (2d) Increased price and excise taxes on alcoholic beverages; and
- (2e) Responsible beverage service policies in social & commercial settings.

Finally, a majority of these "promising" strategies either seek to enforce public policy (e.g., "(3c) Increasing publicity about enforcement of underage drinking laws/eliminating 'mixed' messages") or are forms of university policy.

UNDERAGE DRINKING POLICY

Almost half of American undergraduates are under 21, with 45 percent of the Harvard School of Public Health College Alcohol Study sample of four-year full-time students in 1993 under that age.[34] Therefore public policy that focuses on underage drinking has a major impact on college drinking. Among the most important recent statements about underage drinking policy was formulated by the National Academy of Sciences/Institute of Medicine (NAS/IOM) report on the topic.[35] The report places substantial emphasis on public policy to shape advertising and media messages targeted toward the selling and consumption of alcohol, complying with existing law, and deterring adults from purchasing alcohol for minors.

The NAS/IOM report included the following recommendations:

- A national media effort
- An independent nonprofit foundation
- Strengthened alcohol marketing practices
- Strengthened advertising codes
- Monitored youth exposure to alcohol advertising
- Rating codes for the entertainment industry, film, and music
- Monitored mass media messages
- Strengthened enforcement of the MDALs
- Enforced compliance checks
- Enacted or strengthened dram shop laws (that hold sellers of alcohol products liable for damages) by states
- Implementation of programs by states and localities to deter adults from purchasing alcohol for minors

The NAS/IOM report was followed by other federal efforts to deal with underage drinking, in particular the Interagency Coordinating Committee on the Prevention of Underage Drinking (ICCPUD), which included representatives from several cabinet agencies (Defense, Education, Health and Human Services, Justice, Transportation, Treasury, the Office of National Drug Control Policy, and the Federal Trade Commission).[36] The ICCPUD drafted a detailed plan to prevent underage drinking. The National Alliance to Prevent Underage Drinking (NAPUD), a coalition of six groups seeking a robust national response to underage drinking, found the draft promising but also claimed it was limited:

We appreciate the effort and good intentions that went into preparing the report, and are aware of the political and budgetary constraints that may limit the scope of the plan. Nonetheless, we are extremely disappointed that the draft plan does not move much beyond the status quo in reflecting a real commitment to elevating underage drinking prevention as a national public health priority. We are deeply concerned that the draft document only mentions in passing, then largely ignores, the National Academy of Sciences Institute of Medicine's landmark September 2003 recommendations to Congress for a cost-effective national strategy to prevent and reduce underage drinking. More than a year after release of that report and despite several Congressional directives, we remain troubled by the apparent continued absence of will to address seriously America's number one youth substance use crisis.[37]

Missing from the plan, according to its critics, were benchmarks, means of monitoring progress, a visible role for the Surgeon General, a mention of the Healthy People 2010 goals dealing with alcohol targets, and detailed information about funding across the agencies.

In addition to public efforts to advocate for policy or policy enforcement changes at the national level, there are significant private efforts as well; a few cases will suffice to indicate the nature of recent attempts. For example, two prominent not-for-profit alcohol policy organizations (Join Together and the Marin Institute) have published a list of "Ten Policies That Save Lives."[38] Prominent among them are raising taxes on alcohol products, limiting advertising, and passing more effective laws. Similarly, MADD has promoted a renewed effort to lower alcohol-related car crash deaths with its "Getting MADD All Over Again" campaign.[39] One of its targets is to "reduce underage drinking—the No. 1 youth drug problem—through improving minimum drinking age laws, adopting tougher alcohol advertising standards and increasing enforcement and awareness of laws such as "zero tolerance drinking-driving" and sales to minors."

RECENT FEDERAL LEGISLATION: THE STOP ACT

Since the Safe and Drug Free Schools Act, only one major piece of new federal legislation has affected the college-drinking problem, and even that only bears on those college students who are under 21. Legislation was introduced in both the U.S. Senate and the House that would fund several of the recommendations of the NAS/IOM Report on Underage Drinking. The STOP Act (Sober Truth on Preventing Underage Drinking Act), was sponsored by a bipartisan group of legislators led by Representative Lucille Roybal-Allard and Senators Mike DeWine and Chris Dodd, with support from a broad coalition of groups such as MADD and Community Anti-Drug Coalitions of America (CADCA) and major components of the alcohol industry.[40]

According to the Congressional Reference Service (CRS), the STOP Act "amends the Public Health Service Act with respect to underage drinking. Expresses the sense of Congress with regard to addressing the problem of underage drinking."[41] CRS summarizes its major provisions (emphasis added):

- Requires the Secretary of Health and Human Services to **formally establish and enhance the efforts of the Interagency Coordinating Committee on the Prevention of Underage Drinking** that began operating in 2004. Requires the Committee to guide policy and program development across the federal government with respect to underage drinking. Sets forth reporting requirements.

- Requires the Secretary to **issue an annual report on each state's performance in preventing or reducing underage drinking**. Requires the Secretary to **develop a set of measures** to be used in preparing the report on best practices and to consider including measures on whether a state: (1) has comprehensive anti-underage drinking laws; (2) encourages and conducts comprehensive enforcement efforts to prevent underage access to alcohol at retail outlets; (3) encourages training on the proper selling and serving of alcohol as a condition of employment; (4) has programs or laws to deter adults from purchasing alcohol for minors; and (5) has programs targeted to youths, parents, and caregivers to deter underage drinking.

- Requires the Secretary of Health and Human Services to continue to fund and oversee the production, broadcasting, and evaluation of the **national adult-oriented media public service campaign**, if the Secretary determines that such campaign is effective in achieving the media campaign's measurable objectives. Sets forth reporting requirements.

- Requires the Administrator of the Substance Abuse and Mental Health Services Administration, subject to the availability of appropriations, to **award enhancement grants** to eligible entities to design, test, evaluate, and disseminate effective strategies to maximize the effectiveness of **community-wide approaches** to preventing and reducing underage drinking, if the Administrator determines that the Department of Health and Human Services (HHS) is not currently conducting duplicative activities.

- Requires the Secretary of Education to: (1) **award grants to eligible entities to prevent and reduce the rate of underage alcohol consumption, including binge drinking, among students at institutions of higher education;** and (2) publish achievement indicators for the program.

- Requires the Secretary of Health and Human Services, subject to the availability of appropriations, to **collect data and conduct or support research** that is not duplicative of research currently being conducted or supported by HHS, on underage drinking with respect to: (1) comprehensive community-based programs or strategies and statewide systems to prevent and reduce drinking from early childhood to age 21; (2) obtaining and reporting more precise information on the scope of the underage drinking problem and patterns of underage alcohol consumption; and (3) compiling information on the involvement of alcohol in unnatural deaths of persons age 12 to 20 in the United States.

- Requires the Secretary to carry out activities to: (1) **obtain epidemiological data** within the national or targeted surveys that identify alcohol use and attitudes about alcohol use during pre- and early adolescence, including harm caused to self or others as a result of adolescent alcohol use; and (2) **develop or identify successful clinical treatments** for youth with alcohol problems. Requires such research to meet current federal standards for scientific peer review.

- Authorizes appropriations.

In essence, then, the STOP Act requires state-level data collection, more research, and better epidemiological data, but the act does not touch the many recommendations of the NAS/IOM report about advertising, marketing, or sales of alcohol to minors. How much Congress eventually appropriates for the STOP Act will be a key factor in determining how much of an impact it has on underage drinking or on college drinking.[42]

HOW STATE POLICY SHAPES COLLEGE DRINKING

What effect does state alcohol policy have on college drinking? Much of the research about college drinking does not address this question, because the typical study is based on data gathered at one campus and thus all students are affected by the same policy environment.[43] One study, however, examines students in 40 states. Data from the Harvard School of Public Health College Alcohol Study and from the Center for Disease Control and Prevention's (CDC's) Behavioral Risk Factor Surveillance System suggest that "the state sets the rate" of college binge drinking.[44]

The researchers examined individual student data from surveys taken in 1999 and 2001 at 120 colleges and universities, for a total of 22,453 individuals. The researchers identified those states that had four or more alcohol control laws (including keg registration, illegal per se laws [defining driving with a particular BAC as an offense], restrictions on happy hours, open containers, beer sold in pitchers, and billboards and other advertising). They also compared states that MADD identified as having strong alcohol control law enforcement. States with stronger alcohol control policies had college binge drinking rates of 33 percent, whereas those with weaker policies had rates of 48 percent This finding held up even when the researchers controlled for 17 correlates of individual binge drinking. The college binge drinking rate across the states was strongly correlated with the adult binge drinking rate, another indication that college binge drinking was shaped by the larger policy environment. The results of this study show that state alcohol policy can have an impact on individual student binge drinking and that certain state policies can protect students by reducing abuse.

To give a picture of how states vary in their binge drinking rates and in state policy enforcement, table 6-1 presents data on adult binge drinking and on MADD's rating of the state's underage drinking control efforts. The table also presents the overall letter grade that MADD gave the state in 2002 for its underage drinking and drinking and driving control. MADD noted,

> States scored high in this category if their programs included the following components: comprehensive 21 MDA [minimum drinking age] laws; strong GDL [graduated driver licensing] provisions; strong, ongoing enforcement programs such as compliance checks, meaningful sanctions for selling or providing alcohol to minors, and extensive school-based alcohol education programs; Youth Education Programs.[45]

Half of the letter grade reflected "the rate and trend of alcohol positive youth drivers involved in fatal crashes between 1999 and 2001." Table 6-1 is based on data on the percent of adults (18 and over and those who are 18–20 years old) in 2001 who reported binge drinking (drinking five or more drinks on a single occasion one or more times during the past month).[46] Finally, table 6-1 presents the college binge drinking rates for the 40 states for which the Harvard School of Public Health College Alcohol Study has reported data. The last two columns of data allow a comparison for each state between young adults 18–20 years old, and data for those (of any age, but obviously concentrated in the age-group 18–23) who are full-time undergraduates.

Table 6-1.
State Control of Underage Drinking and Rates of Binge Drinking

STATE	MADD Rating of Underage Control	Adult Binge-Drinking Rate	18–20 Binge-Drinking Rate	College Binge-Drinking Rate
Alabama	C	11.6	15.5	46.0
Alaska	F	18.2	15.6	
Arizona	C	16.8	33.4	48.0
Arkansas	B	11.3	24.6	33.0
California	B	15.5	27.5	34.0
Colorado	D	16.7	36.5	59.0
Connecticut	D	13.8	25.4	54.0
Delaware	C	15.7	22.8	62.0
D.C.	F	14.8	41.2	
Florida	C	12.0	19.2	49.0
Georgia	B	11.9	21.5	32.0
Hawaii	C	10.4	19.2	
Idaho	B	12.8	15.4	34.0
Illinois	D	17.3	24.6	58.0
Indiana	B	13.8	27.5	52.0
Iowa	F	16.2	29.1	51.0
Kansas	B-	14.7	37.2	52.0
Kentucky	B	8.7	15.3	44.0
Louisiana	C	13.8	23.9	48.0
Maine	B	15.4	33.4	
Maryland	D	11.9	17.3	80.0
Massachusetts	F	18.1	38.0	48.0
Michigan	B	18.0	32.5	40.0
Minnesota	B	19.6	41.3	54.0
Mississippi	D	11.8	14.6	
Missouri	F	14.1	36.8	50.0
Montana	F	16.7	33.8	
Nebraska	D	14.6	28.0	
Nevada	C	16.7	11.5	42.0
New Hampshire	F	15.8	27.6	30.0
New Jersey	C	13.5	33.8	39.0
New Mexico	B	15.8	19.6	39.0
New York	B	14.4	35.1	42.0
North Carolina	C	9.8	17.0	34.0
North Dakota	F	23.3	42.4	

(*Continued*)

Table 6-1. (*Continued*)

STATE	MADD Rating of Underage Control	Adult Binge-Drinking Rate	18–20 Binge-Drinking Rate	College Binge-Drinking Rate
Ohio	B	16.2	24.7	51.0
Oklahoma	B	11.0	13.1	9.0
Oregon	B	14.7	27.0	23.0
Pennsylvania	C	15.6	31.7	54.0
Rhode Island	D	15.1	31.4	53.0
South Carolina	D	12.3	19.4	60.0
South Dakota	D	18.5	26.7	
Tennessee	D	6.8	10.4	38.0
Texas	D	15.1	26.5	42.0
Utah	B	9.7	10.3	0.0
Vermont	A-	15.7	30.7	53.0
Virginia	C	14.3	31.3	48.0
Washington	C+	14.9	26.5	53.0
West Virginia	D	9.4	26.1	
Wisconsin	D	25.7	35.6	65.0
Wyoming	C-	16.0	23.0	

Source: MADD (2002); NIAAA (2003); Nelson, Naimi, Brewer, & Wechsler (2005). *Note*: MADD = Mothers Against Drunk Driving.

Table 6-1 suggests two conclusions. First, states vary greatly in the degree to which they address underage drinking. Second, states vary considerably in how much adults, young adults, or college students binge drink. The adult and college student rates are strongly correlated, implying that how states vary in shaping alcohol consumption also affects college student behavior.

HOW PUBLIC POLICY SHAPES COLLEGE PREVENTION

Public policies affect college-based policies and prevention activities. The Drug-Free Schools and Campuses Act (EDGAR 34 Code of Federal Regulation Part 86) requires colleges to carry out certain activities, including attempting to explain and enforce public policy. The Clery Act requires that campuses report about crime, including drug and alcohol violations. Other federal laws, such as Family Educational Rights and Policy Act (FERPA), shape how colleges may report drug and alcohol violations to parents.[47] Any important policy initiative directed at underage drinkers will have an impact on college-drinking prevention discussions.

CONCLUSION

Public policy has shaped college drinking and also its construction as a social problem within higher education. As concern about the problem rose during the past decades, some part of the discussion of college drinking began to address public alcohol policy questions, especially about whether the minimum legal drinking age should be changed and how effective (or for its critics, ineffective) the MDALs have been. Much less attention has been paid to the question of whether such public policies as the Clery Act (about crime reporting, including alcohol violations) or the Safe and Drug Free Schools Act (requiring colleges to have alcohol policies) are effective. Finally, there has been little discussion about how other public policies (not specifically about alcohol) have shaped college drinking, such as those that encourage college attendance or support dormitory construction, even though these policies probably play a role as well.

The reality of college life raises severe challenges to the enforcement of the MDALs and other public alcohol policies by combining underage and above-age students and placing all students in proximity to retail alcohol outlets or fraternities. The next chapter discusses what can be done by college or political authorities.

NOTES

1. Babor (2003: 6).
2. Babor (2003).
3. Robert Wood Johnson Foundation (2001).
4. Babor (2003, 71–73).
5. Robert Wood Johnson Foundation (2001).
6. Greenfield's "Alcohol Policy" (available at http://www.rsoa.org/lectures/09/09.pdf, accessed on June 29, 2005) presents an overview of preventive alcohol policies in the United States, while Sewel (2002) discusses changing European views on policy. Detailed information about public policy in the United States can be found on a special Web site maintained by the lead federal agency about alcohol, the NIAAA (see http://alcoholpolicy.niaaa.nih.gov/, accessed on July 25, 2005).
7. The first paragraph of the 18th Amendment reads, "Section 1. After one year from the ratification of this article the manufacture, sale, or transportation of

intoxicating liquors within, the importation thereof into, or the exportation thereof from the United States and all territory subject to the jurisdiction thereof for beverage purposes is hereby prohibited." The 21st Amendment's first paragraph states, "Section 1. The eighteenth article of amendment to the Constitution of the United States is hereby repealed" (http://www.law.cornell.edu/constitution/constitution.table.html#amendments, accessed December 13, 2007).

8. Moore & Gerstein (1981).

9. For a comprehensive but readable narrative of drug and alcohol policy development, see Faupel, Horowitz, & Weaver (2003).

10. Walsh (1990).

11. Babor (2003: 225).

12. Mosher (2002).

13. Mosher (2002).

14. Mosher (2002). For more information about how the environment shapes underage college binge drinking, see Wechsler, Kuo, Lee, & Dowdall (2000).

15. Mosher (2002: 9).

16. Massing (1998).

17. For information about the CSPI Alcohol Policies Project, see http://www.cspinet.org/booze/pdbooze.htm, accessed July 29, 2005.

18. Reinarman (1988).

19. For policy and policy groups for each state, see http://www.jointogether.org/, accessed December 13, 2007.

20. For a review of the minimum drinking age laws in the nineteenth and twentieth centuries, see Wechsler & Sands (1980).

21. For a review of current state policies, see the APIS Web site (http://www.alcoholpolicy.niaaa.nih.gov/, accessed November 25, 2007).

22. See MADD (2002) for an attempt to rate the states on this question.

23. See http://www.alcoholpolicy.niaaa.nih.gov/, accessed November 25, 2008.

24. To take one example, Pennsylvania state legislature held public hearings in 2005 about underage drinking. Representatives from the liquor industry and from organizations such as the state chapter of MADD and Pennsylvanians Against Underage Drinking (PAUD) testified at hearings held across the state. The liquor industry has sought in the past to reduce taxes on its products and to loosen restrictions on sales. A representative of the state's tavern owners argued for increased penalties for minors who try to break the law and cracking down on fake identification users. At the same time as the hearing, the tavern owners were engaged in an effort to allow increased Sunday sales of beer by their licensees. The chairperson and executive director of MADD's state chapter presented testimony in support of HB 959, enhancing sanctions to adults who provide alcohol to minors resulting in death or injury. MADD's other priorities in Pennsylvania include increased penalties for transporting a child while driving under the influence (DUI), keg registration, automatic license suspension and vehicle seizure at time of DUI arrest, and increased tax on beer. I testified at the hearings as a

MADD volunteer and presented some of the key findings of the NIAAA Task Force on College Drinking. A leader from PAUD also spoke, representing a group that advocates for environmental policies, such as allowing compliance checks for underage youth, tagging beer kegs, retaining the state system of liquor sales, seeking liquor code revisions, and using age verification scanners.

25. Babor (2003: 227).

26. Cook (2007: xi).

27. Babor (2003: 270).

28. http://www.edc.org/hec/dfsca/minrequi.htm, accessed June 29, 2005.

29. http://www.collegedrinkingprevention.gov/policies/default.aspx, accessed December 13, 2007.

30. NIAAA (2002b: 3).

31. I noted that research about college drinking is similarly focused on the individual college student, with much less attention given to such factors as public policy, which may play a role in shaping drinking (Dowdall & Wechsler 2002).

32. Approaches that touch on public policy were often discussed in research that dealt with college-age youth but have the potential to affect college students.

33. NIAAA (2002b: 7).

34. Wechsler, Davenport, Dowdall, Moeykens, & Castillo (1994).

35. Bonnie & O'Connell (2003).

36. http://www.samhsa.gov/samhsa_news/VolumeXIII_6/article9.htm, accessed December 7, 2007.

37. National Alliance to Prevent Underage Drinking, letter of January 19, 2005, to Charles C. Curie, administrator, Substance Abuse and Mental Health Services Administration, http://camy.org/washington/files/samhsaletter.pdf, accessed December 7, 2007.

38. JTO/Marin Institute's Ten Policies That Save Lives:

1. Increase alcohol prices through taxes, particularly on beer.

2. Limit alcohol advertising and promotional activities that target youth.

3. Adopt laws to prevent alcohol-related deaths among young people.

4. Require equal insurance coverage for drug and alcohol treatment.

5. Support the development of effective medications for addiction treatment.

6. Make screening for alcohol and drug problems routine.

7. Give higher payments to providers who get better results.

8. Require effective treatment and supervised aftercare programs.

9. Repeal policies that prevent ex-offenders from participating in society.

10. Support the work of community coalitions.

(http://www.marininstitute.org/alcohol_policy/jto.htm, accessed on June 29, 2005).

39. http://www.madd.org/news/0,1056,4395,00.html, accessed on June 29, 2005.

40. The alcohol industry supported the bill in its final form. Author's interview with Sue Thau, 2007. The following passage from a press release from Representative Roybal-Allard shows the breadth of support: "The measure is endorsed by many public health and alcohol beverage industry groups, including: Mothers Against Drunk Driving (MADD); the Community Anti-Drug Coalitions of America (CADCA); the American Medical Association; the Center for Science in the Public Interest; the American Public Health Association; the National Beer Wholesalers Association; the Beer Institute; the Wine and Spirits Wholesalers of America; the Wine Institute; the Distilled Spirits Council of the United States; the Century Council; and the Brewers Association" (http://www.house.gov/roybal-allard/press/2006/pr061220.html, accessed December 13, 2007).

41. http://thomas.loc.gov/cgi-bin/bdquery/z?d109:HR00864:@@@D&summ2=m&, accessed November 7, 2007.

42. Author's interview with Beth DeRicco, 2007.

43. Nelson, Naimi, Brewer, & Wechsler (2005).

44. Nelson, Naimi, Brewer, & Wechsler (2005).

45. MADD (2002: 17).

46. NIAAA (2003: table 2).

47. http://www.ed.gov/policy/gen/guid/fpco/ferpa/index.html, accessed November 9, 2007.

CHAPTER 7

The College Response: Reframing Prevention

Reframing college drinking as a social problem transformed what had been seen as a harmless rite of passage into a major public health threat to students. This in turn implied that colleges or other organizations would attempt to lower student alcohol consumption and the risk of alcohol-related health and behavioral problems. Such activities as preventing alcohol use, restricting the supply of alcohol, inducing students to drink less or drink less dangerously, intervening in ongoing drinking patterns, or treating full-blown alcohol use disorders have all been fielded during the past few decades. To simplify the discussion, the term "prevention" will be used to cover all of these activities, following today's usage in the field of college drinking field. We will concentrate our discussion on prevention issues in the strict sense, but end with some comments on intervention and treatment as well.

Thousands of American colleges and universities have done a lot to influence drinking behavior. Some part (perhaps a very small part) of what they did was the product of formal prevention programs, but there is nothing approaching a full history or catalog of those efforts. A larger part of what colleges did to influence student behavior was the unintended or unrecognized consequence of how colleges operate, particularly what they do intentionally or unintentionally to influence student nonacademic life.

Richard Lucey is a key administrator of the U.S. Department of Education postsecondary substance abuse office; his views are particularly helpful in understanding how college prevention activities evolved. In the 1960s and 1970s, providing students with information about the negative consequences of substance use was in vogue, but knowledge alone was judged ineffective as a prevention strategy.[1] The early 1980s saw the rise of the "alternatives model," attempting to provide alternative activities to substance use, again without results. By the mid-1980s, a "social competency model" argued that better decision-making skills were needed, but again evaluation proved this approach ineffective. Three similar models emerged in the late 1980s and 1990s: the "social environment," "public health," and "risk and protection" models, three variations on a theme of changing parts of the social environment. Two other recent models are the "responsible drinking" and "social norms" approaches.

From an organizational perspective, the entrance of two federal agencies into the college drinking prevention field was critical. The National Institute of Alcohol Abuse and Alcoholism (NIAAA), established in 1970 as the nation's primary research agency about alcohol, began to address college drinking through publications and research. The U.S. Department of Education funded programs at individual schools, a network of colleges, and finally through the Higher Education Center for the Prevention of Alcohol and Other Drug Abuse (the title would later be expanded to include "Violence" as well).

An image of prevention in the 1970s is presented in *The Whole College Catalog about Drinking: A Guide to Alcohol Abuse Prevention*, a 130-page monograph published in 1976 by the NIAAA. The report, the first the newly formed NIAAA issued about college drinking, was its only lengthy assessment of the issue until its 2002 Task Force report. In 1973–74, NIAAA had conducted "University 50 + 12," visiting a college or university in each of the 50 states plus 12 minority institutions, concluding, "Most colleges visited saw alcohol abuse as a serious problem on the campus in terms of drunkenness and the ... damage or injury that resulted."[2] About 15 percent of the colleges visited had programs in alcohol education or abuse prevention, with others looking for ideas, and so the *Whole College Catalog* was created. (The name was adapted from the bestselling *Whole Earth Catalog*, a repository of countercultural ideas and practices.)

Heavy drinking and drunkenness were widespread, with 65.6 percent of students at one university (Massachusetts) saying they had been drunk in the past month. Many schools offered alcohol-free activities, though they proved unsuccessful. "Many of the people interviewed substantiated the thesis that there had been a switch from other drugs to alcohol over the last few years and that there had been an increase in alcohol use and abuse."[3] To counter this trend, the *Whole College Catalog* suggested gathering information, engaging in needs assessment and planning, implementing a program, and then evaluating the program to check whether it worked. A long list of strategies, both personal and environmental, was presented, including various kinds of education efforts as well as attempts to change the cultural meaning of drinking. Recent prevention projects at 18 universities were described in detail.

The 1980s saw changes in the minimum drinking age, with all states raising the legal age to 21, and in the increased involvement of government in encouraging college-drinking prevention activities. The 1986 "Anti Drug Abuse Act" included the "Drug Free Schools and Communities Act." Institutions of higher education were required "to establish, implement, and expand programs of drug abuse education and prevention (including rehabilitation referral) for students enrolled in college. As a result, the U.S. Department of Education became responsible for awarding grants to colleges developing drug and alcohol programs."[4] The Department, through its Fund for the Improvement of Postsecondary Education (FIPSE, usually pronounced "fip-see"), had funded more than 130 institutions by 1989.

The Department of Education also helped establish the Network of Colleges and Universities Committed to the Elimination of Drug and Alcohol Abuse. "The Network was created to collect and disseminate research and practice-based knowledge about successful programs, to provide a forum and mechanism for continuing communications and collaboration among institutions of higher education, and to identify areas and problems for further research and development."[5] Founded in 1987 and initially established through the consulting firm Abt Associates, the Network developed a set of standards that shaped the growth of the college alcohol field for decades to come and became one of the most important sources shaping professional identity and development among those working in the field.[6]

Privately funded organizations also were influential in shaping the college alcohol prevention field. Among the earliest was BACCHUS (an acronym for Boosting Alcohol Consciousness Concerning the Health of University Students), founded in 1975.[7] It was joined in 1985 by a sister organization focused on fraternity and sorority members, GAMMA (Greeks Advocating Mature Management of Alcohol). The two organizations came to be known in the 1990s as the BACCHUS and GAMMA Peer Education Network, and in 2005 as the BACCHUS Network.

By 1989, 32 organizations "concerned with drugs and alcohol on campus" were identified in an appendix to a college guide about alcohol policies.[8] Among the most important was the Inter-Association Task Force on Alcohol and Other Substance Abuse Issues (IATF).[9] Along with BACCHUS and

GAMMA, IATF led the effort to create campus responses to heavy drinking by using peer educators to transmit an antiabuse message to other students. The IATF also created National Collegiate Alcohol Awareness Week. (I was unable to locate an independent public evaluation of these programs.)

In the early 1990s, the alcohol industry entered the growing field of college alcohol prevention. In 1991, large distillers founded the Century Council, which launched several widely used programs such as "Alcohol 101" to educate students about college drinking.[10] Based on the work of David Anderson, a leading figure in the prevention field, the Century Council helped publish and distribute *Promising Practices*, a program guide, CD, and later Web site that described notable programs at more than 600 colleges and universities. The Council also published the CD "Alcohol 101," widely used in college prevention programs and known for such innovations as a virtual bar; students could estimate their blood alcohol concentrations after making some choices about the amount, timing, and type of drinks consumed.

Other segments of the alcohol industry provided funding to social norms activities. For example, a *Wall Street Journal* story reported that big brewers such as Anheuser-Busch (A-B) had been supporting social norms marketing projects at prominent universities such as Virginia and Georgetown.[11] A-B would later fund a National Social Norms Resource Center at the University of Virginia.[12] The industry also supported other private efforts, including projects by scholars such as David Anderson (in his College Alcohol Study, begun in 1979) to study drinking and college responses to it.[13]

The result of all these efforts was the institutionalization of college drinking as a social problem, based on an expansion in the number of colleges involved in prevention, the recruitment of a cadre of specialists to staff the programs, and a proliferation of models that shaped college prevention. Many more voices joined the argument that college drinking wasn't a harmless rite of passage, but was a major public health problem. Perhaps as important, it was reframed as a social problem, one that could be solved by college action.

THE HIGHER EDUCATION CENTER

During the 1980s, the U.S. Department of Education gave grants to hundreds of colleges to establish alcohol and drug prevention programs through FIPSE. The FIPSE program led to the widespread establishment of alcohol programs, usually a mixture of education about the dangers of abuse combined with counseling to those seeking treatment. (The 1993 Harvard School of Public Health College Alcohol Study data found no correlation between FIPSE program development and a college's binge drinking rates.)[14]

In part replacing the old FIPSE program, the Higher Education Center for Alcohol and Other Drug Prevention provides a source of advice for college administrators. The Higher Education Center, a nongovernmental organization, is funded by a contract from the U.S. Department of Education. The Higher Education Center has been an advocate for environmental strategies against drug and alcohol use. This approach presents the argument that educational efforts warning about the harm of drug and alcohol use have a limited if any impact on student behavior. Instead, prevention must begin with a broad effort to change the total environment through the development of task forces, campus-community coalitions, and statewide groups of colleges. The Center's Web site also provides a large number of publications about various topics, such as the extent of drug and alcohol use by college students; how to measure or estimate use; the consequences of use and abuse; and prevention, intervention, and treatment. The Center has provided technical assistance to individual colleges, organized a national annual meeting (another outgrowth of FIPSE), and published in print and on the Web a series of bulletins and monographs about alcohol abuse. (No evaluations or audits of the Center's operations are publically available.)

The Higher Education Center presents the old and new approaches to thinking about prevention:

> Stated simply, traditional approaches to prevention have tacitly accepted the world as it is and then tried to teach students as individuals how to resist its temptations. In contrast, with the environmental management approach, there is a coordinated effort to change the world—that is, the campus and community environment—in order to produce a large-scale impact on the entire campus population, including students, faculty, staff, and administrators.[15]

The Center's current mission is presented on its Web site:

> The Higher Education Center's purpose is to help college and community leaders develop, implement, and evaluate programs and policies to reduce student problems related to alcohol and other drug use and interpersonal violence. The Center favors a comprehensive approach to prevention. Central to this approach is a mix of environmental management strategies to address the institutional, community, and public policy factors that contribute to these problems. The Center supports the development of a prevention infrastructure, primarily by facilitating the work of statewide prevention initiatives and

campus-community coalitions. The Center provides trainings, technical assistance, and publications to support these efforts. The Center also promotes innovative program development to improve student education, campus-based media campaigns (including social norms campaigns), early intervention, treatment, and recovery strategies, and enforcement.[16]

The Higher Education Center has played a central role in the development of the college drinking field. Its origins in the 1990s imprinted it with some of the characteristics of the college prevention field at the time. Social norms marketing was rising in visibility and importance, and seemed to show that dramatic improvements were possible even as the older approaches (like trying to scare students with horror stories, a form of "health terrorism") appeared not to be working. Evaluation seemed to be necessary to figure out "what works and why," the phrase used in one of its early publications about this strategy.[17]

But above all was the imperative of growing the prevention field's infrastructure, so that most if not all colleges and universities had programs in place to deal with college drinking. Social norms marketing had a number of advantages: it was perceived to be cheap, effective, and popular with students.

In 1987, the first U.S. Department of Education's "National Meeting on Alcohol and Other Drug Prevention in Higher Education" attracted 182 attendees; by 1994, 1,200 came to the meeting. The Department's expert on prevention, Ronald B. Buckman, explained how central institutionalization was to the growth of the field:

> Our vision of comprehensive, institution-wide prevention programs that are institutionalized into higher education is prospering. Our concept of "proactive prevention" is beginning to be understood and implemented. We have refined the operationalization of proactive prevention to mean prevention that focuses on changing expectations of appropriate behaviors relating to drug and alcohol use. (This is accomplished by creating a new critical mass of individuals, through working with, giving permission to and empowering students, staff and faculty, who would rather live in a drug free environment.) This means working with the assets that campus members bring with them rather than focusing on their deficits.

Some of the most common responses to the problem of college drinking have been educational in nature. For example, during the 1980s the U.S. Department of Education sponsored programs at hundreds of colleges and universities through grants from FIPSE. Many of these efforts spread the word among college students that alcohol abuse or binge drinking was harmful, much as the Drug Abuse Resistance Education (DARE) program attempted to inform a younger population about drug abuse. The FIPSE program also led to the development of offices for drug and alcohol education or counseling at many schools, many of which continue to this day. Their work has included offering education programs at freshmen orientation, encouraging faculty to include alcohol and drug information in their courses (sometimes called "curriculum infusion"), and fostering the development of "wellness" programs and health-oriented messages on campus.

NEW ORGANIZATIONS JOIN THE COLLEGE DRINKING FIELD

The 1990s added several new components to the college prevention field. The Robert Wood Johnson Foundation began to fund several projects that followed a different agenda and emphasized environmental issues and alcohol control efforts. The Harvard School of Public Health College Alcohol Study, directed by Henry Wechsler, published a series of reports based on the first national scientific sampling of colleges and students in its surveys of 1993, 1997, 1999, and 2001.[18] The reports included the widely cited *Journal of the American Medical Association* paper, "Health and Behavioral Consequences of Binge Drinking in College" (discussed at length earlier in this book), as well as more than 80 other publications. Wechsler proved to be adept at attracting media attention to college binge drinking. He also criticized both the earlier FIPSE programs as well as the Higher Education Center's promotion of social norms marketing, adding to the growing tension within the field.

Robert Wood Johnson also funded other efforts. One of the most successful was the Center for Alcohol Marketing to Youth, which conducted research and aided interventions in dealing with this issue.[19] Joseph Califano, a former cabinet secretary in the Carter administration, founded CASA (The National Center on Addiction and Substance Abuse at Columbia University).[20] One of its first reports targeted college drinking, arguing that it had to be reframed as a serious health issue.[21] CASA continued to address the problem, including in a 2007 article, "Wasting the Best and the Brightest."[22]

THE NIAAA TASK FORCE

NIAAA had funded research about college drinking, and how to respond to it, and had issued an alert about the problem of college drinking in 1995. The NIAAA's Director, Enoch Gordis, wrote about the problem:

It is clear that an overwhelming number of college students, many of whom are below the minimum drinking age, use alcohol and that the pattern of binge drinking is widespread among our college campuses. Binge drinking is of particular concern, not only because of its risks to the drinker but because of the problems it causes for those around the drinker. Research on the extent of the problem is detailed and persuasive. Unfortunately, comparatively little evidence exists about which interventions would be successful if applied widely and at an acceptable cost. Not only must future research inform us on effective interventions, but other questions must be answered that involve both science and social policy. For example, proscribing alcohol on campus may drive students onto the highway with risk of crashes. Risk of this complication might differ between urban and rural schools. Restrictions on advertising are not only of unknown impact but raise issues of rights of expression because many students are 21 or older. Even when these questions are answered, within any campus administration, faculty and alumni may differ on the degree to which schools are obligated to act as surrogate parents and on which measures are acceptable. We have much to learn.[23]

NIAAA also had sponsored research about college drinking, including about interventions such as BASICS (Brief Alcohol Screening and Intervention for College Students), targeted at changing the behavior of individual students.[24] A series of student deaths, and continued and perhaps increased student drinking, led to increased attention to college drinking as a social problem. This in turn led during the last years of the Clinton administration to the decision by NIAAA to assemble a task force on college drinking. After two years of wide-ranging and intense work, the NIAAA Task Force published its report, a major step in reframing the problem and its possible solutions.

THE CULTURE OF COLLEGE DRINKING

To better understand college drinking and its correlates and consequences, recent research about college drinking has tended to frame the problem in environmental and cultural terms. The NIAAA report also argued persuasively to reframe college drinking as a *culture*, not merely something that can be understood in terms of individual pathology or personal troubles.

The tradition of drinking has developed into a kind of culture—beliefs and customs—entrenched in every level of college students' environments. Customs handed down through generations of college drinkers reinforce students' expectation that alcohol is a necessary ingredient for social success. These beliefs and the expectations they engender exert a powerful influence over students' behavior toward alcohol.

Customs that promote college drinking also are embedded in numerous levels of students' environments. The walls of college sports arenas carry advertisements from alcohol industry sponsors. Alumni carry on that alcohol tradition, perhaps less flamboyantly than during their college years, at sports events and alumni social functions. Communities permit establishments near campus to serve/sell alcohol, and these establishments depend on the college clientele for their financial success.

Students derive their expectations of alcohol from their environment and from each other, as they face the insecurity of establishing themselves in a new social milieu. Environmental and peer influences combine to create a culture of drinking. This culture actively promotes drinking, or passively promotes it, through tolerance, or even tacit approval, of college drinking as a rite of passage.[25]

Perhaps the most innovative part of the report is its framework for assessing what interventions have worked against excessive college drinking. The Task Force brought together leading experts on the college alcohol problem and on interventions that seek to moderate it. The Task Force argued "that to achieve a change in culture, schools must intervene at three levels: at the individual-student level, at the level of the entire student body, and at the community level. Research conducted to date strongly supports this three-level approach."[26]

A particularly important set of findings from the NIAAA report concern what has been found to work, or shows promise of working, in lowering the risk of college drinking. The NIAAA report divides these strategies into four tiers, based on how much evidence supports their efficacy, according to a review by a panel of experts of published studies about prevention. The NIAAA Task Force reviewed what it deemed to be "creditable research" to compile these tiers of strategies, identifying those that were effective among college students (e.g., offering brief motivational enhancement interventions in student health centers or emergency rooms); those effective among general populations and therefore likely to work for college students (e.g., increased enforcement of minimum drinking age laws); and those deemed promising but not yet fully evaluated (e.g., adopting campus policies to reduce high-risk use like eliminating keg parties).[27] The fourth tier, labeled "ineffective," included "informational, knowledge-based values clarification interventions when used alone." (This last category includes many of the practices that colleges had been using in the previous decade, presumably with little or no effect.)

The following discussion presents in outline form the main findings from the Task Force report (see the summary in table 7-1).[28]

Table 7-1.

NIAAA College Drinking Report: Three-in-One Framework

		Level of Operation		
Tier	Strategy	Individuals, including At-Risk and Dependent Drinkers	Student Population as Whole	Community
1: Effective among college students	1a) Combining cognitive-behavioral skills with norms clarification and motivational enhancement intervention	Yes	No	No
	1b) Offering brief motivational enhancement interventions in student health centers and emergency rooms	Yes	No	No
	1c) Challenging alcohol expectancies	Yes	No	No
2: Effective with general populations	2a) Increased enforcement of minimum drinking age laws	No	Yes	Yes
	2b) Implementation, increased publicity, and enforcement of other laws to reduce alcohol-impaired driving	No	Yes	Yes
	2c) Restrictions on alcohol retail density	No	No	Yes
	2d) Increased price and excise taxes on alcoholic beverages	No	No	Yes
	2e) Responsible beverage service policies in social and commercial settings	No	Yes	Yes

(*Continued*)

Table 7-1. (*Continued*)

Tier	Strategy	Individuals, including At-Risk and Dependent Drinkers	Student Population as Whole	Community
		Level of Operation		
	2f) The formation of a campus-community coalition	No	Yes	Yes
3: Promising	3a) Adopting campus-based policies to reduce high-risk use (e.g., reinstating Friday classes, eliminating keg parties, establishing alcohol-free activities and dorms	No	Yes	No
	3b) Increasing law enforcement at campus-based events that promote excessive drinking	No	Yes	No
	3c) Increasing public-ity about enforcement of underage drinking laws/eliminating "mixed" messages	No	Yes	Yes
	3d) Consistently enforcing campus disciplinary actions associated with policy violations	No	Yes	No
	3e) Conducting marketing campaigns to correct student mis-perceptions about alcohol use on campus	No	Yes	No

(*Continued*)

Table 7-1. (*Continued*)

Tier	Strategy	Individuals, including At-Risk and Dependent Drinkers	Student Population as Whole	Community
		Level of Operation		
	3f) Provision of "safe rides" programs	No	Yes	Yes
	3g) Regulation of happy hours and sales	No	Yes	Yes
	3h) Enhancing awareness of personal liability	Yes	Yes	Yes
	3i) Informing new students and parents about alcohol policies and penalties	Yes	Yes	No
4: Ineffective	4a) Informational, knowledge-based, or values clarification interventions when used alone	N/A	N/A	N/A

Source: NIAAA (2002: 25).

Tier 1 is made up of those strategies with evidence of effectiveness among college students who are problem, at-risk or alcohol-dependent drinkers. This tier includes several strategies:

- Combining cognitive-behavioral skills training with norms clarification and motivational enhancement interventions
- Offering brief motivational enhancement interventions
- Challenging alcohol expectancies

BASICS is one of the best-known programs:

BASICS is administered in the form of two individual sessions in which students are provided feedback about their drinking behavior and given the opportunity to negotiate a plan for change based on the principles of motivational interviewing. High-risk drinkers who participated in the BASICS program significantly reduced both drinking problems and alcohol consumption rates, compared to control group participants, at both the 2-year follow-up ... and 4-year outcome assessment periods. BASICS has also been found to be clinically significant in an analysis of individual student drinking changes over time.[29]

Tier 2 consists of those strategies for which there is evidence of success with general populations that could be applied to college environments. This tier includes strategies such as

- Increased enforcement of minimum legal drinking age laws
- Implementation, increased publicity, and enforcement of other laws to reduce alcohol-impaired driving
- Restrictions on alcohol retail outlet density
- Increased price and excise taxes on alcoholic beverages
- Responsible beverage service policies in social and commercial settings
- Formation of a campus and community coalition involving all major stakeholders

These strategies seek to change the broader environment, with many affecting not only college students but also those underage persons who are not in college.

A primary example of a Tier 2 strategy is the increased enforcement of the minimum legal drinking age (MLDA) laws. An examination of 241 empirical analyses of the MLDA published between 1960 and 2000 shows powerful evidence of an inverse relationship between the MLDA and both alcohol consumption and traffic crashes.[30] The MLDA is effective in spite of minimal enforcement. Public policies of this type have an impact on problematic drinking and alcohol-related problems among college students.[31]

Tier 3 includes strategies that show evidence of logical and theoretical promise, but they require more comprehensive evaluation to check on their results. Among the strategies are the following:

- Campus-based policies and practices that appear to be capable of reducing high-risk alcohol use, including eliminating keg parties, banning alcohol on campus, and expanding alcohol-free events
- Increased enforcement at campus-based events that promote excessive drinking

- Increased publicity about and enforcement of underage drinking laws on campus and eliminating "mixed messages"
- Conducting marketing campaigns to correct student misperception about alcohol use

Among the strategies listed in this tier are attempts to change the social norms that students perceive to be prevalent on a campus, usually by a marketing campaign that contrasts actual drinking behavior with perceived drinking behavior. Proponents of this approach claim to have had success in lowering drinking, but evidence published so far remains below the level necessary to label the approach a proven, as opposed to a promising, strategy.

Tier 4 lists strategies with evidence of ineffectiveness, or ineffectiveness when used alone:

- Informational, knowledge-based, or values clarification interventions about alcohol and the problems related to its excessive use, when used alone
- Providing blood alcohol content feedback to students

Purely informational programs assume that students lack the knowledge of the effects of alcohol, and that providing them with more information will change their behavior. By contrast, moving toward broader changes in the environment does change behavior.[32] Yet purely informational programs remain perhaps the most popular response to college drinking problems.

The NIAAA Task Force report provides support for moving from purely educational interventions (with limited or no evidence of effectiveness when used alone) to environmental strategies that have been proved effective.[33] Since the time the NIAAA report was published, new research has demonstrated that comprehensive environmental interventions (like the American Medical Association's "A Matter of Degree" or AMOD Program) can be effective in lowering the health and behavioral consequences of excessive college drinking.[34] Comparison of those campuses that implemented the AMOD environmental interventions most fully showed small but statistically significant improvements in alcohol consumption and in alcohol-related harms, including criminal ones, when compared with those institutions that had implemented the AMOD program poorly. Other recent research shows that "the state sets the rate"—that is, that public policies and effective enforcement play an important role in lowering the rate of binge drinking—but whether such policies change alcohol-related crime remains to be tested.[35]

This section has summarized the NIAAA Task Force report's findings about the effectiveness of different college prevention strategies. A critical issue concerns the general argument that broad environmental management strategies (that might include combinations of Tiers 1 through 3) will probably have the best effects on college populations.[36]

Five years later, NIAAA released an update to its Task Force report, *What Colleges Need to Know Now*.[37] The NIAAA argued:

> The news is mixed. Among college students and other 18- to 24-year-olds, binge drinking ... and, in particular, driving while intoxicated (DWI), have increased since 1998. The number of students who reported DWI increased from 2.3 million students to 2.8 million. The number of alcohol-related deaths also have increased. In 2001, there were an estimated 1,700 alcohol-related unintentional injury deaths among students 18–24, an increase of 6 percent among college students (that is, per college population) since 1998. In addition, it is estimated that each year, more than 696,000 students between the ages of 18 and 24 are assaulted by another student who has been drinking, and more than 97,000 students between the ages of 18 and 24 are victims of alcohol-related sexual assault or date rape. Clearly, alcohol-related problems on campus still exist.[38]

The NIAAA also reported that it had moved forward in redefining binge drinking, a term that had attracted considerable discussion since its use by Henry Wechsler and his colleagues in the Harvard School of Public Health College Alcohol Study: "A 'binge' is a pattern of drinking alcohol that brings blood alcohol concentration (BAC) to 0.08 gram-percent or above. For a typical adult, this pattern corresponds to consuming 5 or more drinks (male), or 4 or more drinks (female), in about 2 hours."[39]

Finally, the NIAAA update summarized the results of two special reports that assessed progress in both individual and environment prevention strategies for college students.[40] The NIAAA concluded,

> Research shows that several carefully conducted community initiatives aimed at reducing alcohol problems among college-age youth have been effective, leading to reductions in underage drinking, alcohol-related assaults, emergency department visits, and alcohol-related crashes. A close collaboration between colleges and their surrounding communities is key. This includes environmental approaches (such as more vigorous enforcement of zero tolerance laws, other drinking and driving laws, and strategies to reduce the availability of alcohol) as well as approaches that target the individual drinker (such as wider implementation of alcohol screening, counseling, and treatment programs).[41]

WHAT WORKS

What works? We can now answer this question by drawing on extensive evidence summarized in reviews, both in narratives and in numbers, of the many dozens of high-quality studies addressing this question. The findings vary, sometimes substantially, and sometimes contradict one another.

The evidence that has accumulated in the past few years helps us understand the apparent paradox of considerable progress in college-drinking prevention activity but yet no overall change in college drinking. Colleges have done a lot in the past 20 years, but most of what they've done employs approaches that at best have very small effects (and only in environments with little alcohol promotion). Other approaches, such as BASICS, although having demonstrated small effects, have been used on small fractions of college populations, producing little change at the population level. Still other approaches, like the AMOD and community-group approaches, also have small effects that don't necessarily extend beyond the intervention. The group interventions have not been done except when supported by outside funders, whose attention can shift away from college drinking as a priority.

At present, then, we have a better understanding of the seriousness of a public health problem and a growing understanding of how to carry out both individual and group interventions, but a firmer knowledge of the modest to small effect sizes, and wavering organizational and institutional commitment.

THE EFFECTS OF INDIVIDUAL INTERVENTIONS

Evidence about the effectiveness of interventions against college-drinking problems has begun to accumulate rapidly, particularly in the present decade. Carey and colleagues (2007) have conducted a meta-analysis that examines quantitatively the results of 62 studies conducted between 1985 and early 2007.[42] (Meta-analysis is used in fields such as medicine and psychology to assess how much of a difference—the "effect size"—a particular intervention makes, comparing a treatment group that receives the intervention to a control group that doesn't receive it.) Specifically excluded were interventions not given to individuals, such as social norms campaigns.

An elaborate and highly structured search found 62 studies that met the rigorous criteria for being included in the review, and effect size estimates (the mean difference between the treatment and control group, divided by a pooled standard deviation) were calculated by the authors for the major dependent variables measuring various aspects of drinking behavior. The studies usually included volunteers at larger public universities, with interventions mostly targeting heavy drinkers and freshmen; all studies used random assignment of subjects to treatment or control group.

The interventions included the types of approaches listed in Tier 1 and Tier 3 of the 2002 NIAAA Task Force report, with the most common being alcohol/BAC education (73 percent of the interventions), normative comparisons (56 percent), feedback on consumption (49 percent), motivational interviewing techniques (44 percent), moderation strategies (43 percent), feedback on problems (37 percent), goal setting (35 percent), and feedback on expectancies or motives (34 percent). Most of the studies reported on several intervention techniques.

The authors summarize their results in terms that add to the movement to reframe college-drinking interventions as successful: "Three major findings emerged: (a) individual-level alcohol interventions for college drinkers reduce alcohol use; (b) these interventions also reduce alcohol-related problems ...; and (c) the contrast between students who receive interventions and those in control conditions diminishes over time."[43] Whether measured immediately after the intervention or at short-term (4–13 weeks postintervention), intermediate (14–26 weeks postintervention), or long-term (27–195 weeks postintervention) intervals, various measures of drinking behavior were found to have decreased. For example, frequency of heavy drinking decreased at each follow-up except the long-term interval. But the effect sizes tended to be small. Interventions worked better on females than males. They worked less well on heavy drinkers or other high-risk groups.

These results add to the picture painted by the AMOD findings: college drinking behaviors can be changed, but the effects are usually small (so far), costly, and work least well among the heaviest drinkers.

THE EVALUATION OF SOCIAL NORMS CAMPAIGNS

One of the most popular approaches in college prevention efforts begins with the assumption that many college students misperceive how much alcohol abuse actually goes on. Survey evidence supports this assumption, with students believing that their peers drink significantly more than they actually do. Prevention takes the form of correcting these misperceived norms, and so this position is currently called the social norms approach.[44] Imaginative media campaigns help students adjust their impression of how much alcohol abuse actually occurs on campus. Its advocates point to success on a number of campuses, although press reports identify campuses where the approach has failed. The approach could be broadened to change norms about the propriety of those over 21 supplying minors with alcohol.

In its 2007 update, the NIAAA summarized available evidence about this approach in careful language under the rubric, "Still Promising, but Results Are Mixed and Questions Remain."

> As described in the original Task Force report, the social norms approach is based on the view that many college students think campus attitudes are much more permissive toward drinking than they really are and believe other students drink much more than they actually do.... The phenomenon of perceived social norms—or the belief that "everyone" is drinking and drinking is acceptable—is one of the strongest correlates of drinking among young adults and the subject of considerable research.... By and large, the approach most often used on campuses to change students' perception of drinking focuses on the use of social norms campaigns. These campaigns attempt to communicate the true rate of student alcohol use on campus, with the assumption that as students' misperceptions about other students' alcohol use are corrected, their own levels of alcohol use will decrease.
>
> The social norms approach is popular. Nearly half of the 747 4-year residential colleges and universities surveyed in a 2002 study reported having implemented a social norms campaign.... But are these campaigns successful? Research is mixed. The biggest obstacle in evaluating the effectiveness of social norms campaigns is the inconsistency that exists in the research methodology. For example, what constitutes a social norms program or campaign is not always clearly defined, and the components of the campaign often are not thoroughly evaluated....
>
> According to the most rigorous analysis conducted to date ... social norms approaches work best when combined with other interventions. They may be least effective in schools where very high levels of drinking are found and those that are located in communities with high alcohol outlet density. The more intense the social norms campaign in terms of the percentage of students exposed to its messages, the greater the effect on students' alcohol consumption. In this study, the largest reductions were found in the number of drinks consumed per week and the number of drinks consumed when students "party"—two messages that featured prominently in the study's social norms campaign. The study also showed that students' perceptions of what is normal drinking behavior influence the success of the campaign, confirming that social norms campaigns work by changing the way students view alcohol use.
>
> Just as environmental approaches work best when multiple interventions are used, social norms campaigns have demonstrated the most success when they are teamed with other prevention efforts.[45]

Some in the college prevention field had seen social norms marketing as a panacea, but current evidence supports a much more limited view of its role. A multisite randomized trial of the approach initially presented evidence that "students attending institutions that implemented an SNM [social norms marketing] campaign had a lower relative risk of alcohol consumption than students attending control group institutions."[46] More complete data from the same large study presents a more complex view, however, suggesting that social norms marketing campaigns are less effective when conducted on campuses ringed by many alcohol outlets.[47]

INTERNET-BASED PREVENTION

In just the past few years, prevention products that present students with information over the Internet have become popular in trying to reach college populations. One product, Alcohol.Edu, is claimed to now reach one out of four freshmen. But do these products work?

The NIAAA update reviews several studies that provide some support for these products. "Given these findings, it appears that increased alcohol screening and brief interventions are feasible and appropriate for identifying and addressing harmful drinking among college students."[48] A more recent evaluation concludes, "[f]indings hint toward evidence that interactive web-based tools can contribute to preventing high-risk student health behaviors in the campus environment, with self-reported evidence suggesting implementation among first-year students to be the most promising."[49] A number of papers that evaluate these programs are making their way toward publication; as of now, conclusions are premature.

The current state of college alcohol prevention efforts can be assessed by examining a recent publication from the Higher Education Center, *Experiences in Effective Prevention*.[50] Twenty-two model programs that were designated as such between 1999 and 2004 are described. The following five environmental management strategies are listed:

- Offer and promote social, recreational, extracurricular, and public service options that do not include alcohol and other drugs
- Create a social, academic, and residential environment that supports health-promoting norms
- Limit the availability of alcohol and other drugs both on and off campus
- Restrict marketing and promotion of alcohol and other drugs
- Develop and enforce campus policies and enforce local, state, and federal laws[51]

These programs are described in detail, including how they were implemented on the different campuses, but no details are presented about whether they were successful in actually reducing drinking or drinking-related problems.

WHAT PREVENTS SUCCESSFUL PREVENTION?

Why do universities adopt and then retain prevention practices that appear not to work as advertised? Like other parts of universities, most programs aren't evaluated rigorously. Each university probably has little or any evidence, even if the programs are evaluated, about efficacy, beyond the "clinical judgment" of staff. But each campus demonstrates its good faith effort to recognize and confront the problem of college drinking, perhaps with an eye toward a proper defense in case of litigation.

Besides, just like the DARE program persisted without evidence of efficacy, so do most college programs sail on without ever reaching port. They demonstrate one form of organizational rationality ("We know we've got a problem and we're working on it."). This shows good faith as well as "due diligence."

It is important to stress that any one university may not have systematic evidence of program efficacy, but it may have plenty of anecdotal evidence that the program works. If students attend alcohol prevention activities, this may be enough for many local observers to conclude that students are getting straight talk and good information. Under the prevailing and largely unexamined rules of American academic life, competent instruction in a planned curriculum with reasonable student completion rates often is all that need be offered to match institutional, parental, or donor expectations. If this is true for calculus or finance, why shouldn't it be true for less central endeavors like alcohol prevention? (To be fair, there has been a powerful movement toward assessment of instructional outcomes, but thus far the public rarely gets an opportunity to view its results.)

Efforts to curb college drinking become more or less permanent parts of college student affairs offices. We have discussed earlier a federal law that mandates biennial "reviews" of these efforts, and the Higher Education Center offers a checklist for complying with the law. But the federal law does not have any precise standards for complying or any serious consequences for not complying or complying just minimally. (Unlike the Clery Act, no watchdog group pushes for enforcement or helps whistleblowers file complaints.) As long as the boxes are checked off, the university "complies," and that part of its due diligence is completed.

Social norms campaigns and Alcohol.Edu are popular ways to demonstrate commitment required by federal law. These programs all can be used to generate "effort" statistics—number of campaigns, classes taught, orientation sessions presented, posters mounted, ads published, several hour training sessions, and nonduplicated head counts of attendees. They are matched by the often prodigious statistics about college judicial sanctions against alcohol policies.

Just like DARE, prevention programs have other functions that keep them going even if no rigorous evaluation shows successful outcomes. They provide a "home" for the problem of college drinking. They also provide an expert who can talk at new student orientation; visit classes; take phone calls; schedule task force meetings; talk to parents, alumni, and trustees; attend national meetings to share the latest news; and, in general, put a human face on the institution's well-meant efforts. Once that person or persons becomes a full-time staff member, then the institution's own personnel policies and other forms of bureaucratic inertia take over. While only faculty get tenure, other university employees who do their jobs diligently also have some expectations of long-term employment and soldier on in the local war on booze. Their supervisors may not know whether the programs have effects, but they do know when an employee works hard and loyally. Upper-level administrators seek stability, diligence, and performance in a role, not overnight breakthroughs in an intractable problem. The construction of college drinking as part of an entrenched culture can become justification enough to continue and perhaps expand efforts, regardless of evaluation results or their complete absence.

Why so little systematic evaluation? In a word: cost. Except for the relatively few campuses with significant outside funding, doing a competent job evaluating the outcomes of college Alcohol and Other Drug (AOD) programs costs too much money for many campuses.

But it isn't just cost. The prevailing culture of student affairs professionals downplays evaluation, and the larger academic culture does as well. It would be a rare psychology or sociology—or biology or chemistry—department that would do extensive evaluation of student outcomes. Much more than a decade of accrediting agency pressure to do outcomes evaluation of education programs has yielded a thin record. A new Web site (U-CAN) recently appeared with great fanfare to give parents or students outcome data, but in fact has only bare bones data about retention and graduation rates.[52] Data are important in their own right and give consumers something beyond the input data available from such sources as *U.S. News and World Report* and the College Board (an association of education organizations), or the Integrated Postsecondary Education Data System (IPEDS), but higher education as yet fails to provide much data on the impact or efficacy of its programs.

Another big barrier is that it is difficult to measure some of the key varia-bles that need to be part of any evaluation. Self-reported data on alcohol use is only the first major challenge. Getting good data on "dark side" issues, such as sexual assault, crime, drug use, violence, and so on is even harder, especially in a form that allows comparison across incidents or institutions.[53]

Evaluation also cuts against the deeply ingrained clinical mentality of many practitioners.[54] Trained in clinical fields, many of the leaders in cam-pus efforts count their victories by getting individual students to recognize they have a problem and perhaps even attempt to change. Working day after day with students in denial of growing addiction, these practitioners often have little patience, and less time, training, and professional inclina-tion, to put together the substantial work of an evaluation. And just like all of us, they often see little to gain from this form of evaluation, which might have the outcome of showing little or no major progress for their efforts.

The clinical mentality that dominates the college AOD field powerfully shapes its programs and evaluations. Implicit in the mentality is the assump-tion (shared with Alcoholics Anonymous [AA] and other movements) that the problem is "the man and not the bottle," that individual people have an underlying disorder (an alcohol use disorder) or disease (alcoholism).[55] The underlying disorder may be enhanced by the oversupply of alcohol, but fun-damentally, something deeper in the psyche is at fault. Progress begins with getting past denial and then going into a program or therapy.

THE TREATMENT GAP

Just as in the broader society, a substantial treatment gap exists for those students who meet the criteria of a substance use disorder. So the problem, as in the broader society, is that good treatment exists but isn't accessed by or accessible to those who need it. Sometimes individuals find their way out of alcohol use disorders on their own. Others turn to 12-step movements such as AA to help them abstain completely from alcohol.[56] But for some who have alcohol use disorders in college, only professional treatment helps. According to the NIAAA update of 2007, recent data show that

- 19 percent of college students ages 18–24 met the criteria for alcohol abuse or dependence
- 5 percent of these students sought treatment for alcohol problems in the year preceding the survey
- 3 percent of these students thought they should seek help but did not[57]

Again, as in the broader society, some of this treatment gap is due to the stigma attached to seeking mental health or substance abuse treatment. Some of it is the cost of treatment. A recent study by the General Accounting Office found that 80 percent of college students had health insurance.[58] However, just like in the broader society, health insurance often does not cover substance abuse treatment adequately. Even universities with extensive health care facilities report a problem in connecting their undergraduates in need of treatment with adequate providers. If Harvard and Duke have these problems, imagine how widespread they may be at institutions with more limited resources.

To respond to a common behavior such as college drinking, engaged in by millions of students at thousands of campuses, many colleges respond by trying to find an off-the-shelf solution that combines a low-cost (or even no-cost) solution with an approach that doesn't needlessly antagonize students who willingly pay thousands of dollars in tuition (and could easily transfer and pay that tuition to competitors). The NIAAA Task Force report and its 2007 update provide the gold standard, but of course many institutions may not be aware of that standard or they find ways to discount its advice.

Even for those who try to follow the best advice, it can be distorted. So while the Task Force report makes clear there is no simple or single solution, any individual campus can ignore Tier 1 as too expensive or complex, Tier 2 as perhaps too antagonistic to the local alcohol industry, and Tier 3 as an invitation to adopt strategies that are promising but not proven. Even Tier 4 has a qualification that would allow colleges to use its strategies if they were part of some comprehensive program.

Many interventions used by colleges rely on either voluntary student participation or "mandated" participation. The former has real limits on efficacy. Americans of any age deny they have problems with alcohol, but this is even more true for younger people. Prevention programs that rely on voluntary participation run into attendance problems, and several of the large surveys of college drinking have experienced trouble with response rates as well. But mandated participation has its own set of problems, including poor attendance and compliance.

The Institute of Medicine report about underage drinking lists a number of factors that impede college prevention programs:[59]

- Lack of data intended to identify specific campus problems for the "rational planning" of services
- Inconsistent enforcement of university policies and codes for student conduct

- Continued institutional reliance on informational approaches as a primary prevention strategy
- Limited student exposure to prevention activities
- Lack of use of counseling and treatment resources by students who may need those service the most
- Failure to screen and provide services for students through regular physician visits at college health clinics and emergency room visits, and for students who violate alcohol policies

Other obstacles to prevention include lack of clarity about its target, ambivalence about youth alcohol use, absence of evidence-based knowledge, the general problem of fidelity in fielding programs that match proven models, failure to anticipate conflict, hostile environments, poor evaluation capabilities, and the absence of cost estimates.

CONCLUSION

A *New Yorker* cartoon depicts a pack of wolves howling at the moon; one wolf turns to the other and says, "My question is, are we having an impact?"

Many practitioners who deal with college drinking have asked themselves and their colleagues that very question. Most attempts to answer it have been offered with evidence from individual colleges and universities–evidence usually covering a short time period of a year or two. As in many practical and clinical fields, daily work often goes forward without evaluation to guide practice.

The evidence about the successful institutionalization of college drinking as a social problem is substantial. National data exist in abundance about the scope and consequences of college drinking. Far better data now exist about what prevention programs work. A large, dedicated, and increasingly well-trained and professional cadre of specialists work in the field. Although no public evaluation is available, the Higher Education Center has helped build the infrastructure of college prevention. An NIAAA Task Force has reframed college drinking as a solvable social problem for higher education and has presented a comprehensive review of the field as well as an update on what works. Narrative evaluations of both individual and group interventions demonstrate progress. A quantitative evaluation of the field shows real effects of leading programs, although with small effect sizes. And a long-awaited evaluation of the social norms marketing approach presents some evidence of impact, although not in environments with heavy promotion of alcohol.

But with all of this forward motion, college drinking has not decreased in the past decade and may have even increased. To deal with the apparent contradiction between progress in the field of prevention and stasis in actual behavior, we turn to a concluding discussion of the status of college drinking as a social problem.

NOTES

1. Lucey in Chapman (2006).
2. NIAAA (1976: 2).
3. NIAAA (1976: 3).
4. Schneider & Porter-Shirley (1989: 10).
5. Schneider & Porter-Shirley (1989: 444).
6. Middlebrooks (2004). Available as a PowerPoint presentation at http://www.thenetwork.ws/resources.html, accessed April 5, 2008.
7. http://www.bacchusgamma.org/history.asp, accessed April 8, 2008.
8. Schneider & Porter-Shirley (1989: appendix 3).
9. For information about these groups, see the Web site of Inter-Association Task Force on Alcohol and Other Substance Abuse Issues (http://www.iatf.org).
10. http://www.centurycouncil.org/underage/underage.html, accessed April 5, 2008.
11. Shailagh & Gruley (2000: A-1).
12. http://www.socialnorms.org/, accessed April 5, 2008.
13. http://www.caph.gmu.edu/research.htm#CAS, accessed April 5, 2008.
14. Wechsler, Davenport, Dowdall, Moeykens, & Castillo (1994).
15. http://www.higheredcenter.org/pubs/enviro-mgnt.html, accessed June 19, 2008, originally published in 1998. This passage might alert the reader to one of the most significant challenges of the environmental approach in the new century. A number of pressures, including such diverse movements as the rise of distance education and the decline of *in loco parentis*, are changing the meaning of the traditional campus. Consequently, the assumption that all college students are powerfully tied to local campuses may be inaccurate.
16. http://www.higheredcenter.org/, accessed April 5, 2008.
17. Dowdall, DeJong, & Austin (2002) present a framework for evaluating programs. See http://www.higheredcenter.org/eval/manual/, accessed June 19, 2008.
18. http://www.rwjf.org/reports/grr/040869.htm, accessed April 8, 2008.
19. http://camy.org/, accessed April 5, 2008.
20. http://www.casacolumbia.org, accessed April 8, 2008.
21. CASA (1994).
22. CASA (2007).
23. Alcohol Alert: College Students and Drinking. http://pubs.niaaa.nih.gov/publications/aa29.htm, accessed April 5, 2008.
24. Dimeff (1999).

25. NIAAA (2002a: 8).

26. NIAAA (2002a: 2).

27. NIAAA (2002a: 25).

28. Detailed discussion of how the findings were generated and the content of each of the strategies can be found in the expert panel report.

29. NIAAA (2002a: 17).

30. Wagenaar & Toomey (2002).

31. Dowdall (2006).

32. DeJong & Langford (2002).

33. DeJong & Langford (2002).

34. Weitzman, Nelson, Lee, & Wechsler 2004).

35. Nelson, Naimi, Brewer, & Wechsler (2005); see also Dowdall (2006).

36. DeJong & Langford (2002).

37. NIAAA (2007a).

38. NIAAA (2007a: 1).

39. NIAAA (2007a: 2).

40. Larimer & Cronce (2007); Toomey, Lenk, & Wagenaar (2007).

41. NIAAA (2007a: 2).

42. Carey, Scott-Sheldon, Carey, & DeMartini (2007).

43. Carey et al. (2007: 2487).

44. Perkins (2003).

45. NIAAA (2007a: 7).

46. DeJong, Schneider, Towvim, Murphy, Doerr, Simonsen, Mason, & Scribner (2006).

47. Scribner, Mason, Theall, Simonsen, Schneider, Towvim, & DeJong (2008); DeJong (2007).

48. NIAAA (2007a).

49. Wall (2007).

50. DeJong, Anderson, Colthurst, Davidson, Langford, Mackay-Smith, Ryan, & Stubbs (2007).

51. DeJong et al. (2007: 8–9), emphasis in original.

52. http://www.ucan-network.org, accessed September 2, 2008.

53. For a discussion of these problems, see Dowdall & Wechsler (2002) and Dowdall, DeJong, & Austin (2002).

54. Freidson (1988).

55. Wiener (1981).

56. See Knapp (1996) and Zailckas (2005) for two moving narratives of young women, separated by a generation, who find their way out of college drinking.

57. NIAAA (2007a).

58. Government Accountability Office (2008).

59. Bonnie & O'Connell (2003: 203).

CHAPTER 8

What More Can Colleges Do?

During the past several decades college drinking was reframed. College drinking became a major social problem within higher education, with increased attention in the popular media, dramatically increased attention in the student press, but only modest increases within the higher education media. This attention gap reflects the crowded higher education agenda, especially the increased centrality of access, affordability, and accountability.

As the proportion of young people starting college approached half of the age-group, being a college student became almost a new stage of life.[1] Students' increased affluence made them into inviting targets of marketers, among the most successful of which was the local alcohol industry.[2] Other changes in consumption—more clubbing, off campus restaurants with full alcohol sales—changed the mix of daily life for college students.

The ecology of the college campus also changed. Centripetal forces, including pressure toward dry campuses, and enforcement of the 21-year-old minimum drinking age mandated by federal and state laws, probably pushed partying into the community and made pre-gaming even more popular. For a significant minority, often lifestyle leaders like the "Duke 500," heavy college drinking was viewed as an essential part of everyday life.

The broader culture reshaped campus attitudes as well. Americans increasingly adhere to a youth substance regime in which hard drugs were marginalized, while soft drugs like marijuana and familiar drugs like alcohol were seen as less harmful. Alcohol itself took on a Jekyll and Hyde personality.

Experts, including the Higher Education Center, the National Institute on Alcohol Abuse and Alcoholism (NIAAA), the Harvard School of Public Health College Alcohol Study, and National Center on Addiction and Substance Abuse at Columbia University (CASA), tried to frame it as more harmful than previously thought, while college students and younger teens increasingly viewed alcohol, or its abuse, as less harmful. Popular culture viewed college drinking as a harmless and fun-filled rite of passage, with classic films such as *Animal House* (1978) and more recent films such as *Old School* (2003) and *Superbad* (2007) linking college drinking to the very best parts of college life. For almost a third of American universities, where more than 50 percent of students binge drink, college drinking has become "normal deviance," that is, expected behavior on the part of most students.

Higher education responded to the changes. Attendance at the U.S. Department of Education's National Meeting, consultation with the Higher Education Center, participation in local and regional consortia and statewide and national networks, and subscription to listservs, along with the expanding body of research and other writing available through the Higher Education Center's Web site, all contributed to the establishment and then growing maturation of the college alcohol field.

While it has become fashionable in some quarters to talk about college heavy drinking as an epidemic, it is one that many students freely choose.[3] But what they want is shaped powerfully in popular culture, much of it skillfully manipulated by the advertising of the alcohol industry.[4] A significant core of college drinkers come to college not only expecting but also seeking a party-centered lifestyle, and colleges hardly stand in their way.

Data on comparable European countries show that the United States has a relatively low teen binge-drinking rate, probably in part because of its relatively high minimum drinking age law. Anecdotal evidence suggests that U.S. colleges began to adjust to binge drinking and extreme binge drinking during the past decade or so by a de facto form of harm reduction, using emergency room transports for high blood alcohol concentration (BAC) and passed-out students, while crafting good Samaritan policies to encourage quicker emergency calls. Campus public safety and law enforcement underwent significant professionalization, as did those parts of student affairs offices that deal with alcohol issues. The result may have saved lives at a time of extreme binge drinking, with the net result a small but significant rise in college-drinking fatalities. In the broader community, better and more effective emergency medical services may have slowed the rise in college-drinking deaths.

But several changes raise the possibility that it may be worse in the future. Efforts to lower the minimum drinking age appear to be gaining traction, with at least a half dozen states considering action on the drinking age. In the short run, at least, a lowering of the drinking age will probably result in increased college drinking and also increased fatalities. Leaders of the movement say it will induce students to choose responsibility (which of course most students currently do exercise), but they offer no evidence about how it would impact the binge drinking-centered college subculture of roughly one out of five college students. Lowering the minimum drinking age probably would transform college drinking once again, with pressure for more campus alcohol outlets, liberalization of student conduct codes (and consequently dramatically fewer alcohol violations), less mandated treatment, kegs in the dorms or in the quad, and fewer alcohol prevention and treatment experts. A facade of "responsible drinking" for those 18 to 21 would return, and incentives for the local alcohol industry to increase sales would be clear.

The primary impact of a decrease in the minimum drinking age would be felt in high schools. The decrease in the minimum drinking age would empower those high school students who are 18 and older to become suppliers for the whole school; siblings and friends who are 18–21 would add even more points of access. It is difficult not to conclude that all of this would result in increased drinking among high school students.

Those pushing for reduction in the minimum drinking age laws call for education and even licensing of those 18 to 21. Serious review of the available evidence by the NIAAA Task Force concluded that standalone education has not been proven effective.[5] Innovative entrepreneurial efforts like Alcohol.edu and My Student Body have yet to clearly establish their efficacy, whatever their promise. Full-blown attempts to change entire college environments produced actual change (though modest in scale), but these results can be undone with a change in local politics. Finally, social norms campaigns seem to work (again, modestly), under some circumstances, but not in environments with many alcohol outlets.

During the 1980s and 1990s, an interesting mix of new organizations arose in the evolving field of college alcohol work. These organizations reflected the prevailing ideas and values of the field at the time, especially the need to institutionalize college drinking as a social problem within higher education. Faced with an intractable problem, practitioners sought to establish programs that would endure beyond the years of their founding. Programs that emphasized education about the harmfulness of excessive drinking or reshaping of social norms helped institutionalize college drinking as a problem on higher education's agenda. The NIAAA Task Force called into question education as a standalone program and ended up concluding that insufficient evidence existed to support social norms campaigns as standalone programs as well.

Social norms became regarded as a promising practice, awaiting further research to confirm its value. A series of negative reports about its efficacy were called into question on methodological grounds, or on the grounds that its authors were biased against the approach. Fully two decades after its initial statement, social norms approaches were still being described as a promising practice. Publication of an elaborate test of social norms initially found support for the approach but then reported a "replication failure."

WASTING THE "BEST AND THE BRIGHTEST"

Reframing college drinking as a social problem doesn't rest solely on the growth of organizations or the accumulation of research about epidemiology or interventions. Some of the reframing rests on efforts to focus public consciousness on the problem.

The title of a recent report on college drinking and drugging gives its punch line: *Wasting the Best and the Brightest.* According to Joseph Califano, president of CASA, a think-tank pursuing a broad alcohol control agenda, the report "reveals a disturbing ambiance of hedonistic self-indulgence and alarming public health crisis on college campuses across this nation."[6] While much of the rest of his report focuses on health and behavioral consequences, the quoted phrase leaves the reader in no doubt that, for him at least, college drinking is both a moral and a health problem.

Califano's essay is one model of how college drinking came to be framed as a social problem. He reports as "shocking results" a finding that half of the 3.8 million full-time college students either "binge drink, abuse prescription drugs and/or abuse illegal drugs" and that almost one in four fit the medical criteria for substance abuse or dependence.

These "shocking results" are matched by Califano's estimate of how things have changed in just the short time. From 1993 to 2001,

[T]he proportion of students who:

- Binge drink frequently (three or more times in the past two weeks) is up 16 percent;
- Drink on 10 or more occasions in the past month is up 25 percent;
- Get drunk three or more times in the past month is up 26 percent;
- Drink to get drunk is up 21 percent.

Moreover, daily marijuana use has doubled; cocaine and heroin are up 52 percent. Abuse of prescription drugs has "exploded," with painkillers up

343 percent, stimulants up 93 percent, tranquillizers up 450 percent, and sedatives up 225 percent. This "explosion in the intensity of substance abuse among college students carries devastating consequences, with each year seeing 1,700 deaths, 700,000 student assaults, and almost 100,000 sexual assaults and rapes."[7]

Califano hits several key points in making college drinking a social problem: **seriousness** (1,700 deaths, other devastating consequences); **ubiquity** (half of college students binge); and finally, **rapidity** of change (an explosion of co-occurring prescription drug use). The CASA report also presents results of a survey of college administrators.[8] There are of course some real challenges in gathering these data. For one, on all but the smallest campus, any single administrator may have only limited knowledge of what goes on. The CASA report makes clear that few campuses rigorously evaluate these interventions, although many gather some kind of prevalence data. Moreover, while a survey of this type might identify whether a particular intervention is offered, whether the intervention is offered in a fashion faithful to its full planning and theory is hard to determine. Interventions might be offered to some students, but what proportion receives the full intervention is difficult to assess.

With all these qualifications in mind, the CASA report shows that the interventions effective with college students generally are offered by some campuses, whereas promising but unproven approaches are offered more frequently. Put more sharply, most colleges are still offering interventions toward the bottom end of the scale of effectiveness. One very helpful datum in the CASA report presents administrators' assessment of the barriers to progress against substance abuse. Very clearly, the widespread belief that heavy college drinking is viewed by students and others as a rite of passage leads the list.

THE U.S. SURGEON GENERAL'S *CALL TO ACTION*

One part of the reframing of college drinking as a social problem has been to situate it within what is perceived to be a larger problem, that of underage drinking. Acting U.S. Surgeon General Kenneth P. Moritsugu issued *The Surgeon General's Call to Action to Prevent and Reduce Underage Drinking* in 2007.[9] The 94-page report summarizes recent findings about the causes and consequences of underage drinking:

> Developed in collaboration with the National Institute on Alcohol Abuse and Alcoholism (NIAAA) and the Substance Abuse and Mental Health Services Administration (SAMHSA), *The Surgeon General's Call to Action to Prevent and Reduce Underage Drinking* identifies six goals for the nation to reduce the

number of underage drinkers and prevent children and adolescents from beginning to drink.

GOAL 1: Foster changes in American society that facilitate healthy adolescent development and that help prevent and reduce underage drinking.

GOAL 2: Engage parents, schools, communities, all levels of government, all social systems that interface with youth, and youth themselves, in a coordinated national effort to prevent and reduce drinking and its consequences.

GOAL 3: Promote an understanding of underage alcohol consumption in the context of human development and maturation that takes into account individual adolescent characteristics as well as environmental, ethnic, cultural, and gender differences.

GOAL 4: Conduct additional research on adolescent alcohol use and its relationship to development.

GOAL 5: Work to improve public health surveillance on underage drinking and on population-based risk factors for this behavior.

GOAL 6: Work to ensure that policies at all levels are consistent with the national goal of preventing and reducing underage alcohol consumption.[10]

From a public policy standpoint, what is particularly noteworthy about the *Call to Action* is the relative absence of discussion of any new public policy initiatives that might deal with underage drinking. Instead, the document stresses a developmental approach and (as indicated by Goal 6) an attempt to bring into sharper focus a national goal of reducing underage alcohol consumption, and of addressing the broader national goal of reducing binge drinking (see table 8-1).

The *Call* makes several references to college drinking. "The negative consequences of alcohol use on college campuses are widespread."[11] Strategies for colleges and universities "should examine their policies and practices on alcohol use by their students and the extent to which they may directly or indirectly encourage, support, or facilitate underage alcohol use. Colleges and universities can change a campus culture that contributes to underage alcohol use." Nine recommendations are offered, consistent with a developmental framework but curiously not citing the NIAAA four-tier framework or even federal laws or regulations.[12]

The *Call to Action* notes that

[C]olleges can be settings where underage alcohol use is facilitated—inadvertently or otherwise—and even openly accepted as a rite of passage and actively encouraged by some students and organizations. In fact, some parents and administrators appear to accept a culture of drinking as an integral part of the college experience. Such attitudes need to change and can change through ... a recognition of the university's responsibility to keep its campus safe for its students. Institutions of higher learning that accept this responsibility can build a developmentally appropriate protective scaffolding around their students by taking ... actions.[13]

The actions include fostering a culture in which alcohol isn't central, offering alcohol-free dorms and social choices, information about alcohol, and referral and counseling.[14] Colleges are also admonished to reduce risk factors and protect students from adverse consequences of alcohol use.[15] They also should "establish and enforce clear policies that prohibit alcohol use by underage students on their campuses" and "sponsor only interventions that research has confirmed are effective in preventing and reducing underage alcohol use."[16]

In essence, then, the Surgeon General places greatest emphasis on a culture of college drinking and on those forces that shape individual decisions to drink or drink excessively. Hardly anything is said about changing the environment of college drinking or about the availability of alcohol to minors.

What impact will the Surgeon General's *Call to Action* have on underage or college drinking? I asked that question of Ralph Hingson, director of NIAAA's Division of Epidemiology and Prevention Research and chair of the NIAAA Task Force Panel on Prevention and Treatment.[17]

> I think it will draw attention to the issue. The Surgeon General is a voice the American public listens to. It does not mean there will be an immediate change in behavior. When the Surgeon General's first report on smoking came about there were some very short term reductions in smoking, but the real impact of that report was not felt for twenty to thirty years. Ultimately, through a whole series of reports, they were able to get out the message that the smokers were not only harming themselves, but they were harming other people. When that information was made apparent to the public, then they started to demand clean, indoor air space and the airlines and restaurants and bars and hotels and so on are smoke free because people recognized the second hand effects.
>
> I think in the college area there are secondhand effects of drinking. There are just under 700,000 college students annually who are assaulted by another college drinking student, just under 100,000 date rapes that we know about, and about half of the traffic deaths in that age group involving drinking drivers are people other than the drinking drivers. There are a lot of people who are being negatively affected. I think it is important to continually keep the public aware that there are people other than the drinkers who are being affected. That will provide us with the same type of leverage [as] the second hand smoke provided by the anti-tobacco activists.[18]

SHOULD THE MINIMUM DRINKING AGE BE CHANGED?

Framing college drinking within the larger problem of underage drinking has led some to question the current minimum drinking age. In large part because of the rise of college drinking as a social problem, debate continues as to whether the minimum drinking age should be changed.

On the affirmative side, John McCardell, a former president of Middlebury College, has used print and other media to argue for scrapping the current minimum drinking age of 21. Through speeches to higher education groups, media appearances, essays and op-eds, and a Web site, McCardell has argued that "[t]he time has come to address the reality of alcohol in America."[19] McCardell and his group have achieved some success in opening up for debate what appeared to be a settled issue. In response, groups such as Mothers Against Drunk Driving (MADD) have released public statements and created a Web site that attempts to refute the other side's arguments, arguing for maintaining the current minimum age of 21.[20]

At the end of the summer of 2008, McCardell's group made national news about the drinking age:

> A year-old campaign by Middlebury College's former president to launch a discussion of lowering the legal drinking age from 21 to 18 has quietly gained the support of about 100 university presidents, the *Associated Press* reported Aug. 18.
>
> Duke University, Dartmouth College, Ohio State University, Syracuse University and Tufts University are among the institutions whose presidents have signed onto former Middlebury president John McCardell's Amethyst Initiative. McCardell has said his experience in a college environment has shown him that students will drink regardless of age-21 laws and that making most students' consumption illegal simply drives the activity underground and makes it more dangerous.
>
> But many researchers and groups such as Mothers Against Drunk Driving (MADD) consider the initiative's stance irresponsible, saying it ignores the progress age-21 laws have made in reducing drunk-driving deaths . . .
>
> The college presidents supporting the initiative have signed a statement that does not specifically call for the drinking age to be reduced from 21 to 18, but seeks a debate of the law that tied states' adoption of 21 as the legal drinking age to eligibility for federal highway funds. The statement does indicate that the presidents believe the laws are not working on college campuses, where they say a "culture of dangerous, clandestine binge drinking" has taken hold.
>
> Other college administrators were disinclined to sign off on the initiative. "I remember college campuses when we had 18-year-old drinking ages, and I honestly believe we've made some progress," University of Miami President Donna Shalala said. "To just shift it back down to the high schools makes no sense at all."[21]

Initial reaction to the Amethyst Initiative has been mixed. A few of the college presidents withdrew their support, while a few others joined the initiative. The NIAAA posted an information page on its Web site that provided readers with considerable research background on the issue.[22] Whatever the outcome of the Amethyst Initiative, it demonstrates that the issue of college drinking can still command attention across a broad national audience.

WHAT COLLEGES SHOULD DO

Ralph Hingson of the NIAAA sees cause for optimism in a mixture of public policy and college prevention activities.[23]

> The challenge for us in the field is to cast a wide net and look for all the types of interventions that make a difference in reducing the problem and recognize it is going to take more than just the colleges and more than action by a single segment from the college. Comprehensive college community interventions, which have been shown to be effective in reducing alcohol related problems involve multiple departments of city government to help—the school department, the health department, the police department, the city, social services, concerned private citizens, the city council, the mayor, and the college community need to be talking with the presidents, the alumni, the faculty, the staff, and the public safety and residence life people and the students. We need all of these people, in my view, working together to address the problem. Our institute [NIAAA] can help provide information about what kinds of programs and policies work, and we can encourage people to use these in collective actions. We have some evidence that some of these interventions will make a difference. I am optimistic we can make a difference in reducing excessive college drinking and related problems.

Each college has to deal with individual students on one campus *and* be supporters of effective public policy. They are required by federal regulation to explain laws. They should be especially careful to explain why the minimum legal drinking age is 21, and how lowering it won't happen anytime soon. (Perhaps colleges ought to explain why it shouldn't happen.)

Since the NIAAA Task Force Report on College Drinking (2002) was released, several studies have been published that add to the evidence about what works and why. The national evaluation of the American Medical Association's (AMA's) "A Matter of Degree" (AMOD) program has published data that support the broad environmental management framework.[24] The data from AMOD confirm that public policy has a role to play in lowering the negative outcomes of college drinking.

Colleges and universities should use evidence-based practices, and as we have seen, the NIAAA Task Force on College Drinking found that public policies such as enforcing the minimum drinking age laws are central. If social norms projects are used, they should embrace public policy issues, including components that talk about conformity with the minimum drinking age laws, discuss how underage students shouldn't break the law, and stress that overage students should not provide alcohol to minors. Finally, colleges and universities should play a greater role in shaping state policy about enforcing the minimum drinking age law and other public policies. Preventionists should take the lead on their campuses in discussions of public policy.

A major problem for the field is the tendency for individual colleges to adopt off-the-shelf "solutions" that may or may not fit the problems they face. Without attempting to engage in strategic planning that pinpoints population needs, adopting the "solution du jour" often fails to produce significant change. As promising as approaches like social norms or BASICS (Brief Alcohol Screening and Intervention for College Students) may seem, simply adopting one or the other (and applying them without much thought to diverse student populations) may prove futile. Similarly, having all freshmen do a few hours worth of online alcohol education may have some effect on knowledge but little on behavior. If colleges shape routine activities (through dorms or other forms of residences) and in turn these activities shape drinking behavior, then adding a few hours of activities to the thousands that make up a semester or a quarter is unlikely to result in significant change. Colleges have more power to shape student behavior than they think, even though systematic knowledge of how to use that behavior is slim.

Why wouldn't every college follow the prescriptions of the Higher Education Center or the NIAAA Task Force report, particularly in adopting Tier 1 and Tier 2 programs? Data show that college presidents are almost evenly split about taking more responsibility for this problem. Second, the Harvard College Alcohol Study data show how great variation is across colleges in binge drinking. No doubt some colleges see college drinking as at best a minor problem, correctly noting how low its prevalence is among their students. Others probably misperceive the scope of the problem. Still others see college drinking as a "bummer issue," attention to which can only bring trouble to the institution or, in extreme cases, professional death to the messenger bearing the bad news. At some colleges, other fires burn more brightly and scarce resources are moved toward grappling with any other of a number of notable academic or student affairs problems). Among the most pressing may be other behavioral health problems, ranging from student mental health needs (other than alcohol or other drugs), housing, other student conduct violations, and so on. In the past several years, school shootings at Virginia Tech and Northern Illinois have made campus safety and security rise on the agenda.

There are plenty of organizational reasons for shunning the most efficacious approaches. Even on large campuses, only a few people may be part of the decision to employ one approach or engage in planning, and individuals who have interests in or talents related to one approach may push for it over others. Put another way, those individuals may think their aptitudes and talents don't fit certain approaches. Organizationally, some of the approaches (like pushing for Friday classes or starting a task force) imply that alcohol prevention people will tread on other academic turf. Academic affairs departments and the faculty control class time, and vice presidents for community or external affairs may have considerable suspicion of efforts to round up the community in a crusade against drinking (antagonizing landlords, bar owners, politicians, and who knows who else).

Another factor is that colleges vary in how much attention they pay to student issues in general. For example, there are 28 Jesuit colleges (founded by the Roman Catholic religious order, the Society of Jesus, or the Jesuits). These colleges and universities all proclaim to have certain values, including *cura personalis* (Latin for care of the individual student). One would think that this value alone might make Jesuit college leaders attempt to respond to alcohol and drug issues, and at least some of these colleges could demonstrate that they have done just that. In 2007, 18 of the 28 Jesuit institutions formally agreed to join together in a consortium to address the problem.[25]

But there is another side to this story. Jesuit institutions have had a number of terrible student deaths caused by alcohol. Some have taken more than their share of criticism from their neighbors in the local media. Others report very high numbers of alcohol violations in their Clery Act data. (One Jesuit vice president pointed out to me that this may show a school leads the way in addressing the problem, however.)

This more critical side of the story was addressed in the pages of the prestigious Jesuit journal of opinion, *America*. Joseph Califano wrote a powerful attack on the Jesuit college presidents for acting like Pontius Pilate, washing their hands of any responsibility for the issue of college drinking. (One could hardly find a more odious comparison for the 28 leaders, 26 of whom are Catholic priests.) To date there has been no response in the pages of the journal from any of the presidents.

There are powerful institutional pressures that push attention away from student affairs issues in general and college drinking in particular. During the past decades many colleges and university professors have felt the push to do more research. Disposable time that faculty may have used to pursue conversations and other extracurricular activities with students (at least some of which might have had a social control function when directed at student conduct) has almost certainly been shifted into time spent in research. At the organizational level, countless colleges have been renamed universities, at least in part to signal a shift in focus toward research or toward professional master's degree programs. (Recall the sharp wit of the Columbia University poet John Ciardi who observed that "a university is a college that has forgotten its students.")

No doubt some of the name changes are purely cosmetic and respond more to marketing needs than anyone else. But many institutions that solely focused on undergraduate affairs now pursue advancement as universities that try to balance (or at least juggle) undergraduate teaching with graduate instruction and research.[26] Many institutions have made the shift from college to university in the past few decades, some with a nostalgic look over the shoulder at what's been left behind.

PRESIDENTIAL LEADERSHIP

How involved are college and university presidents in the issue of college drinking? The *Chronicle of Higher Education* commissioned several national surveys of college and university presidents that shed light on this issue. Presidents seem split down the middle on whether to take responsibility for college drinking. When asked to respond to the statement, "Colleges and universities should not be held responsible for the consequences of excessive student drinking," 45 percent of 764 presidents agreed, while 42 percent disagreed.[27]

College presidents are an obvious target for those who want change in college drinking as a social problem. Reports on the issue, including the 2002 NIAAA Task Force report, a summary of the College Alcohol Study results, and U.S. Senator Joseph R. Biden's report *Excessive Drinking on College Campuses*, were mailed to all presidents. Editorialists often focus their pens at presidents. And the Higher Education Center set up its own effort directed toward presidents, calling on them to be "vocal, visible, and visionary." But by 2007, membership in the Presidential Leadership Group set up by the Higher Education Center had only 44 members (out of more than 4,000 institutions of higher education).[28]

In 1997, the Higher Education Center's Presidential Leadership Group released the following recommendations for college presidents:

1. College presidents should work to ensure that school officials routinely collect data on the extent of the alcohol and other drug problem on campus and to make this information available.

2. College presidents should frame discussions about alcohol and other drug prevention in a context that other senior administrators, faculty, students, alumni, and trustees care about—excellence in education.

3. College presidents should define alcohol and other drug use not as a problem of the campus alone, but of the entire community, which will require community-level action to solve.

4. College presidents should use every opportunity to speak out and write about alcohol and other drug prevention to reinforce it as a priority concern and to push for change.

5. College presidents should work to ensure that all elements of the college community avoid providing "mixed messages" that might encourage alcohol and other drug abuse.

6. College presidents should demonstrate their commitment to alcohol and other drug prevention by budgeting sufficient resources to address the problem.

7. College presidents should appoint a campus-wide task force that (a) includes other senior administrators, faculty, and students, (b) has community representation, and (c) reports directly to the president.

8. College presidents should appoint other senior administrators, faculty, and students to participate in a campus-community coalition that is mandated to address alcohol and other drug issues in the community as a whole.

9. College presidents should lead a broad exploration of their institution's infrastructure and the basic premises of its educational program to see how they affect alcohol and other drug use.

10. College presidents should offer new initiatives to help students become better integrated into the intellectual life of the school, change student norms away from alcohol and other drug use, and make it easier to identify students in trouble with substance use.

11. College presidents should take the lead in identifying ways to effect alcohol and other drug prevention through economic development in the community.

12. As private citizens, college presidents should be involved in policy change at the state and local level, working for new laws and regulations that will affect the community as a whole.

13. Acknowledging that substance abuse is a problem that their schools have in common, college presidents should participate in state, regional, and national associations to build support for appropriate changes in public policy.[29]

With some notable exceptions, presidents have not become as extensively involved in this issue as hoped. For example, there have been only a few times during the past 15 years that the issue has been aired at the annual meeting of the American Council on Education (ACE), the largest umbrella organization in American higher education and in effect the largest membership organization for college presidents.[30]

A major exception was the speech by Donna Shalala to the ACE Annual Meeting in 1998, urging colleges and universities to engage with the issue of college drinking. Shalala was then secretary of health and human services in the Clinton administration, and that role alone would have guaranteed her a large and warm reception from the ACE. But she is also recognized as one of America's major leaders in higher education. In her distinguished career before joining Clinton's cabinet, she led the University of Wisconsin; she is presently president of the University of Miami.

Other leaders have attempted to influence higher education leadership as well. U.S. Senator Joseph R. Biden, Jr., addressed the Washington Higher Education Secretariat in 2000.[31] Biden urged the leaders of the nation's major higher education organizations to take action on college drinking, raising it higher on their agenda and following the U.S. Senate resolution he had sponsored about the issue. Neither the Biden or Shalala address appeared to have any noticeable impact, however. Few of the organizations place much emphasis on the issue, the major exceptions being NASPA (the student affairs leadership organization) and the NCAA (National Collegiate Athletic Association).[32]

Interviews with a number of the leaders of national higher education organizations make clear that college alcohol as a social problem is largely segregated into the area of student affairs.[33] In fact, the most important student affairs organization, NASPA, has begun to invest considerable resources in the issue, hosting its first standalone conference on the topic in 2007 and organizing a "knowledge community" on drug and alcohol questions. It also sponsors the peer-reviewed *NASPA Journal*, an outlet for research about the topic. The American College Health Association has also been active in pursuing interventions and research about the issue, and its peer-reviewed *Journal of American College Health* continues to publish on the topic.

A PROBLEM FOR HIGHER EDUCATION

Critics of American higher education have also addressed the problem of college drinking. For example, one of the most perceptive books about higher education, Anne Matthews' *Bright College Years* (1997), presented data from the initial Harvard study to note the widespread problem of student drinking.[34]

Derek Bok, with two terms as Harvard's president, has criticized higher education in his 2006 book *Our Underachieving Colleges*. He takes up the issue of college drinking in a discussion of why colleges need to both explain their rules and try to enforce them:

> This simple proposition is sometimes harder to live up to than one might think. Laws prohibiting under-age drinking and drug use, for example, present a peculiarly difficult problem because they are hard to enforce, widely disliked by students, and not rules the university itself has imposed. Even so, the way in which the institution responds can send a powerful message to students. The university cannot and should not establish a police state by subjecting undergraduates to constant surveillance in an effort to root out violations. Such policies would destroy the trust and confidence of students and drive a wedge between them and the administration. But if campus authorities are seen to avoid even efforts at enforcement and to wink at obvious violations, students are bound to gain the impression that it is legitimate to ignore laws they consider unnecessary or inconvenient.[35]

Bok comments that the professoriate is split on moral development as a goal, with only 55 percent in one survey saying it is "'very important' or 'essential' for a college to develop moral character." Bok poses the institutional choice this way:

> Should moral development be merely an option for students who are interested and for college authorities when it is not too costly or controversial? Or should it be an integral part of undergraduate education for all students and a goal demanding attention, effort, and, on occasion, even a bit of courage and sacrifice from every level of the college administration? After so many years of ambivalence and neglect, surely it is time to answer this question with the care and deliberation it deserves.[36]

One gets the feeling that administrators and researchers approach college drinking with a sense of embarrassment. Years ago college drinking could be described as higher education's dirty little secret, but years of media coverage have removed the secrecy, leaving only a sense of shame. Sometimes this takes the form of remorse that some great research university or prestigious college could turn out to have undergraduates who behave as poorly as anyone else's undergraduates. One exasperated college president complained at a higher education meeting that she couldn't believe she had spent so many years advancing through the faculty and the administration, only to end up dealing with such a mess.

Most of the national attention to higher education in the past few years has focused on the problems of accessibility, affordability, and accountability.

President Bush's secretary of education, Margaret Spellings, led a controversial movement culminating in her Commission on Higher Education. At an early stage in its deliberations, the Commission apparently included a discussion of college binge drinking, but the topic did not make it into the final report.[37]

CONCLUSION

From a handful of people addressing the problem of college drinking in the 1970s and earlier, college drinking has been reframed as a major social problem within higher education. College drinking appears to be higher education's most persistent social problem, and it will not change easily or quickly. As we have noted before, considerable research has revealed it is linked to a host of negative outcomes, including more than 1,700 deaths a year; 1 in 20 college women have nonconsensual sex in a period of time considerably less than a full academic year, and more than 70 percent do so because they are too intoxicated to give consent.

Especially since the early 1990s, the college-drinking field has expanded considerably, with national organizations joining the field. The Harvard School of Public Health College Alcohol Study played a central role in expanding knowledge about health and behavioral consequences not only to the drinker but also to those in the immediate environment. The Higher Education Center helped institutionalize the understanding of college drinking as a social problem. The social norms movement led to the establishment of programs at many colleges. The NIAAA Task Force established a framework for assessing the evidence supporting different types of interventions. For-profit organizations have begun to sell products such as Alcohol. Edu to large numbers of colleges.[38]

If the arguments of the preceding chapters are correct, changes in college drinking will come only partly from programs intended to lower risky drinking or to curb underage drinking, given their modest impact, small reach, or transitory effects. More important targets of attention are precollege behavior, college routine activities, broader patterns of alcohol use, the local and national alcohol industry, and government action. More recently, the problem of college drinking has been reframed as an entrenched culture. Recent statements about effective prevention by the Higher Education Center or about what colleges need to know now by the NIAAA, however, have yet to fully address how to change this culture.[39] In fact, almost all of the recent writing in the field tends to ignore the question of culture.[40]

But that doesn't mean that the college-drinking field should stop its often-fragmented efforts to take on the problem. The field has to acknowledge that working with individual high-risk students doesn't necessarily change the way college drinking is perceived as an issue. Moreover, once promising practices like social norms approaches taken alone seem to have modest (at best) or no (at worst) impact.[41] Programs like Alcohol.Edu have great advantages in reach and cost, but by themselves have only modest impact under the best circumstances. Among the most promising interventions are those that target indicated or high-risk students with personally engaging approaches based on motivational interviewing, combining Tier 1 effectiveness with economic personal outreach to large student populations.[42] The other side of the coin is that the college alcohol field has to come to terms with the success of the social norms movement and of the importance of paying attention to ways that students interpret their college reality.[43] If college drinking is indeed shaped by a culture, research and interventions have to begin to comprehend that culture and more explicitly address how to change it. The fragments of the field need to learn from each other and patch together some form of unified approach.

Reframing college drinking as a social problem within higher education has made substantial progress in taking what had been perceived solely as a personal problem and making it a public problem.[44] The challenge for the next period is to address simultaneously a health problem for an entire population within a highly individualistic culture of college drinking that still sees it as a harmless rite of passage. Even more challenging is the realization that a new generation of young Americans apparently views heavy episodic or binge drinking as less harmful than did an earlier generation, despite mounting evidence to the contrary. Finally, the organizational and institutional structure of higher education presents its own challenges; it is difficult to overcome the institutional inertia that militates against changing the way things operate.[45] The field of college-drinking prevention and treatment has to recognize its success in institutionalizing a social problem while moving beyond prevention approaches that are popular but weak in impact.

NOTES

1. Nathan (2005).
2. Morrison (2004) presents a guide to capturing what he claims is a $200 billion market.
3. Nathan (2005: concluding chapter).
4. http://camy.org/, accessed April 12, 2008.
5. NIAAA (2002a and b).

6. Califano (2007: 16).

7. Califano (2007: 17).

8. CASA's appended data show a few major and glaring errors, such as reporting that 10 percent of the schools are public, but then in the next table showing their religious affiliations.

9. U.S. Department of Health and Human Services, Office of the Surgeon General (2007). Available at http://www.surgeongeneral.gov/topics/underagedrinking/, accessed November 7, 2007.

10. http://www.surgeongeneral.gov/topics/underagedrinking/goals.html, accessed November 7, 2007.

11. U.S. Department of Health and Human Services, Office of the Surgeon General (2007: 12).

12. *Ibid.* (2007: 40–42).

13. *Ibid.*

14. *Ibid.* (2007: 52–53).

15. *Ibid.* (2007: 55).

16. *Ibid.* (2007: 71).

17. Author's interview with Ralph Hingson.

18. Author's interview with Ralph Hingson.

19. http://www.chooseresponsibility.org/, accessed November 25, 2007.

20. http://www.why21.org/, accessed April 14, 2008.

21. http://www.jointogether.org/news/headlines/inthenews/2008/college-leaders-seek-debate.html, accessed September 3, 2008.

22. http://www.niaaa.nih.gov/AboutNIAAA/NIAAASponsoredPrograms/drinkingage, accessed September 3, 2008.

23. Author's interview with Ralph Hingson.

24. Weitzman, Nelson, Lee, & Wechsler (2004).

25. The consortium is in the early stages of development, initially led by Loyola Marymount's Joseph LaBrie, SJ, one of the rising leaders in research about college drinking (see LaBrie, Lamb, Pedersen, & Quinlan 2006; and LaBrie, Pedersen, Lamb, and Bove 2006), and myself.

26. One of my colleagues who devoted his considerable energy and passion to undergraduate teaching was turned down for tenure because his publications didn't match the university's drive to advance in the *U.S. News and World Report* ratings. A jaundiced view from a senior professor was that he had "been sacrificed on the altar of preeminence."

27. *Chronicle of Higher Education* (2006: 29).

28. http://www2.edc.org/cchs/plg/members/, accessed May 8, 2007.

29. http://www2.edc.org/cchs/plg/recommendations.html, accessed May 8, 2007.

30. Just after the first publications of the Harvard School of Public Health College Alcohol Study in 1994, I chaired a session at the American Council on Education Annual Meeting that attracted a few dozen attendees. The Higher Education Center has had exhibits at the meeting as well.

31. For the current membership of the Washington Higher Education Secretariat, see http://www.whes.org/, accessed April 12, 2008.

32. As an indicator of where higher education as an institution places alcohol on its agenda, I investigated the Web sites of the major higher education organizations, those that are members of the Washington Higher Education Secretariat. I examined the number of hits for the term "alcohol" on the Web site (using Google's "Search only on the site" tool). It is readily apparent that only a few higher education organizations play much of a role on this issue.

33. I interviewed several leaders of these organizations, including the ACE's general counsel Sheldon Steinbach, NASPA's executive director Gwen Dungy and its 2007–08 president Jan Walbert, and the president of the Association of Jesuit Colleges and Universities, Charles Currie, SJ. I also approached another former president of the ACE and a former chancellor of one of the largest universities in the United States. Both said they knew little about the issue and would have deferred to others with expertise in student affairs.

34. Matthews (1997: 84).

35. Bok (2006: 163).

36. Bok (2006: 171).

37. Zemsky (2007).

38. Wall (2007) presents some evidence supporting the efficacy of this approach, but many in the college-drinking field will remain unconvinced until more comprehensive evaluation appears.

39. DeJong, Schneider, Towvim, Murphy, Doerr, Simonsen, Mason, & Scribner (2006); NIAAA (2007a).

40. In fact, of the 381 items reviewed in the current literature section of the Higher Education Center Web site between September 2006 and May 2008, only five mention culture in any way.

41. DeJong et al. (2006) and Scribner, Mason, Theall, Simonsen, Schneider, Towvim, & DeJong (2008) present data on a comprehensive evaluation of the social norms approach, finding support in the former publication but a "replication failure" in the second.

42. Interview with Joseph LaBrie.

43. See Chapman (2008) for an examination of how students and practitioners interpret the question of collegiate drinking.

44. Mills (1959).

45. Zegart (2007) presents a powerful case study of how slowly government and other nonprofit organizations change in response to even the most dramatic challenges. Dowdall (1996) reviews organizational theory about institutional inertia. Gumport (2007) discusses the organizational and institutional character of American higher education. The U.S. Department of Education (2007) examines how prevention programs survive within higher education.

Table 8-1.
The Surgeon General's "Healthy People 2010"

Goal 26-11. Reduce the proportion of persons engaging in binge drinking of alcoholic beverages.

Binge drinking is a national problem, especially among males and young adults. Nearly 15 percent of persons 12 or older reported binge drinking in the past 30 days, with young adults aged 18 to 25 years more likely (27 percent) than all other age groups to have engaged in binge drinking. In all age groups, more males than females engaged in binge drinking: among adults, the ratio was two or three to one. Rates of binge drinking varied little by educational attainment. People with some college, however, were more likely than those with less than a high school education to binge drink.

The perceived acceptance of problematic drug-using behavior among family, peers, and society influences an adolescent's decision to use or avoid alcohol, tobacco, and drugs. The perception that alcohol use is socially acceptable correlates with the fact that more than 80 percent of American youth consume alcohol before their 21st birthday, whereas the lack of social acceptance of other drugs correlates with comparatively lower rates of use. Similarly, widespread societal expectations that young persons will engage in binge drinking may encourage this highly dangerous form of alcohol consumption.

Passage of higher minimum purchase ages for alcoholic beverages during the mid-1980s reduced but did not eliminate under aged drinking. Many States are examining the use of additional restrictions and penalties for alcoholic beverage retailers to ensure compliance with the minimum purchase age.

To address the problem of binge drinking and reduce access to alcohol by underaged persons, several additional policies and strategies may be effective, including:

• Tougher State restrictions and penalties for alcoholic beverage retailers to ensure compliance with the minimum purchase age.

• Restrictions on the sale of alcoholic beverages at recreational facilities and entertainment events where minors are present.

• Improved enforcement of State laws prohibiting distribution of alcoholic beverages to anyone under age 21 years and more severe penalties to discourage distribution to underaged persons.

• Implementation of server training and standards for responsible hospitality. (Management and server training educate waitresses, waiters, bartenders, and supervisory staff on ways to avoid serving alcohol to minors and intoxicated persons).

• States could require periodic server training or use the regulatory authority of alcohol distribution licensing to mandate a minimal level of training for individual servers.

(Continued)

Table 8-1. (*Continued*)

• Institution of a requirement that college students reporting to student health services following a binge drinking incident receive an alcohol screening that would identify the likelihood of a health risk. An alcohol screening would provide student health services with the information needed to assess the student's drinking and refer the student to an appropriate intervention.

• Restrictions on marketing to underaged populations, including limiting advertisements and promotions. Although alcohol advertising has been found to have little or no effect on overall consumption, this strategy may reduce the demand that results in illicit purchase or binge consumption.

• Higher prices for alcoholic beverages. Higher prices are associated with reductions in the probability of frequent beer consumption by young persons and in the probability of adults drinking five or more drinks on a single occasion.

• Binge drinking among women of childbearing age (defined as 18 to 44 years) also is a problem because of the risk for prenatal alcohol exposures. Approximately half of the pregnancies in the United States are unintended, and most women do not know they are pregnant until after the sixth week of gestation. Such prenatal alcohol exposures can result in fetal alcohol syndrome and other alcohol-related neurodevelopmental disorders.

Source: http://www.healthypeople.gov/document/html/objectives/26-16.htm, accessed September 2, 2008.

CHAPTER **9**

How to Cope
with College Drinking:
What Students and
Parents Can Do

⁓

The approach to college drinking taken so far in this book raises some interesting difficulties—but also opportunities—regarding the more practical side of coping with this social problem. College drinking and the institutional response to it will not be easily or quickly changed, even if a broad and growing coalition of forces joins the efforts made so far. Up against this persistent and powerful social problem, what can individual students or parents do?

College drinking has been around a long time, and the level and type of abusive drinking may have even increased somewhat recently. The personal characteristics associated with excessive drinking are often unchangeable —factors like gender, age, race, religion, or economic status are more or less fixed for any one college student. Institutional factors associated with excessive college drinking do not change much either, such as the type of institution, its mission and location, the state's enforcement of the underage drinking laws, or alcohol's price or availability. Although some interventions work with individual college students and some with general populations, most of the major interventions now being used have little impact on the overall level of college drinking. Some of the interventions that work best are costly or unpopular. And it is not just a matter of individual choice: an important minority of college students already meet the criteria for a psychiatric diagnosis of alcohol dependence or abuse, and hardly could be said to be drinking completely voluntarily.

Most discussions of college drinking (especially the professional literatures of epidemiology and intervention) downplay the question of what students and parents can do. Instead, students are perceived as the targets of intervention, and efforts are made to change their perceptions of norms, or to reduce access to alcohol, or to change their college environments. Parents for the most part are just out of the picture entirely. In this chapter, I want to put greater emphasis on what students and parents can do.

Individuals can take steps to reduce the harm college drinking has on oneself or one's son or daughter.[1] We can specify some of the things that make high-risk drinking more likely to happen, and in turn, that knowledge can lead individual college students to make better choices. Even those students who are already dependent on alcohol can find ways to identify their problems and seek appropriate treatment and/or abstinence. Based on research from the emerging environmental perspective on college drinking, these steps involve avoiding high-risk environments, especially for those at highest risk. Addressing alcohol concerns during the high school years is absolutely essential, since many college-bound students begin alcohol use during high school.

Choosing a college or university is the next consideration. To help readers pick appropriate colleges, appendix D presents data on many leading colleges and universities. Once a student has enrolled in college, learning how to respond to alcohol problems may be critical to student success. For students, this may mean seeking sobriety by joining a 12-step program or seeking treatment for alcohol abuse or dependence. For parents, staying in touch with a newly independent student and offering assistance if trouble occurs may be critical.

BEFORE COLLEGE

The age of first alcohol use has been found to raise the risk of later alcohol dependence or abuse. Patterns of drinking in high school or earlier are often a precursor to serious problems in college. Bingeing in high school is a powerful predictor of college bingeing. College spokespeople have been quick to note that colleges inherit this problem in the form of students who are already experienced binge drinkers before they set foot on campus. It is doubtful whether large changes in college drinking on the population level (as opposed to particular individuals) can be accomplished without addressing precollege drinking.

Parents at Georgetown Prep, an exclusive and expensive private school in Washington, D.C., have gone well beyond the norm in taking on underage drinking, providing a national model for how to cope with this problem. Led by Mimi Fleury and her husband, parents invited experts in for a series of seminars and then wrote a detailed and helpful handbook for prep school parents. They banded together with other parents in the Washington area and then across the country to form "The Community of Concern" (see appendix A on resources for contact information). Now operating in 22 states, the Community of Concern provides detailed advice for parents who want to take action.

Robert Anastas, a student at Wayland High School in Massachusetts, founded SADD (Students Against Destructive Decisions, see appendix A for contact information) in 1981, to organize against underage drinking and drunk driving. There are now 350,000 students in chapters active in high schools that together enroll more than 7 million students.[2] On a much larger scale, Mothers Against Drunk Driving (MADD) chapters are found in every state, working on underage drinking and drunk driving issues.

With the support of Coors Brewing Company and the National Football League Players, mvparents.com provides a Web site with suggestions about how parents can strengthen developmental assets thought to be protective of teen drinking. While sponsorship by an alcohol industry powerhouse by itself does not delegitimize its efforts, the site seems to pay little attention to restricting sales to minors.

Even though brief—or perhaps because it is so brief—a two-page handout, "Parents, You're Not Done Yet. Have You Talked with Them about College Drinking?" deserves mention here. Sponsored by the Century Council, funded by big distillers, the advice is helpful and informative.[3]

AVOID COLLEGE ENTIRELY?

If being in college raises the risk of drinking and negative outcomes, the question of whether to go to college in the first place deserves discussion. Whatever may have been true a while ago, deciding not to go to college is not a realistic option for many people these days. The case for going to college is strong, with significant lifetime benefits, both nonmonetary and monetary. A recent comprehensive review for the College Board found that a typical college graduate in 2005 earned 62 percent more than a person who had graduated only from high school.[4] Other economic benefits to the college graduate included better health insurance and pensions, and lower unemployment rates. Many of the benefits of college education are non-monetary: better health, lower rates of smoking, healthier lifestyles, and perceptions of better personal health. The community benefits from college attendance as well, with higher levels of volunteer work, voting, and blood donations, and even greater openness to other opinions. College graduates have lower rates of substance use and abuse, including of alcohol, than those with just high school educations. This last point deserves emphasis, since in the long run, college graduates are less likely to abuse substances than are nongraduates.

CHOOSING A COLLEGE OR UNIVERSITY

As going to college shifted from an option available largely to the affluent minority to a requirement for entrance into the middle class for the majority of Americans, choosing a college became a much more urgent task. For many college-going Americans, this task involves searching online for information about requirements and financial aid, talking to high school guidance counselors and even costly private consultants, reading glossy view books and other written material, going to college fairs, and arranging campus visits. A vast amount of material in print and on the Internet claims to describe what colleges have to offer and how students live their lives at each institution. For relatively little cost, a prospective student or parent can access hundreds of pieces of information about each of the thousands of institutions across the country. A new Web site (knowhow2go.org) offers help for those unfamiliar with the college admission process.[5]

For many Americans thinking of college, choice is constrained by economic resources, limited ability to travel, and entrance requirements. Immediate family financial pressures push many to defer or even decline admission to college. But for a privileged minority, choice among selective colleges dominates the last few years of high school. "Selection" of a college is a complex bargaining process. Stevens describes the college admissions process at one selective Eastern college, but his analysis goes well beyond a single case to generate insights useful for a broad class of institutions.[6]

The National Institute on Alcohol Abuse and Alcoholism (NIAAA) Task Force on College Drinking presents the following ideas about picking a college.[7]

Like many parents, students, and administrators, you may be doing some research on colleges and universities. You've probably looked into:

- Academics
- Course offerings
- Athletic facilities
- Housing conditions
- School reputation

During your research, it's essential to remember a key issue, one that influences college students' quality of life every day: the culture of drinking at colleges in the United States.

An "Animal House" environment may seem exciting to students at first, but nothing affects health, safety, and academic performance more than a culture of excessive drinking. Many of the negative consequences associated with college alcohol abuse affect students who themselves are not drinking—and these are serious consequences: sexual assault, violence, vandalism, loss of sleep, and caring for friends and roommates in life-threatening states of alcohol poisoning.

There are a number of ways to investigate whether the schools you're considering are taking this problem seriously. Be sure that each school has created solid alcohol policies and is enforcing underage drinking laws. Collegedrinkingprevention.gov has made it easy for you to get this information for hundreds of colleges and universities in the United States.

The Task Force also had some specific suggestions; I have numbered them here, and highlighted the most important terms:

1. As you examine potential colleges, include in your assessment inquiries about **campus alcohol policies**.

2. During campus visits, ask college administrators to outline in clear terms how they go about **enforcing underage drinking prevention**, whether the school sponsors alcohol-free social events.

3. Ask what other socializing alternatives are available to students, what procedures are in place to notify parents about alcohol and substance abuse problems, what **counseling services** are available to students, and how energetic and consistent the follow-up is on students who exhibit alcohol abuse and other problem behaviors.

4. Inquire about housing arrangements and whether **alcohol-free dorms** are available.

5. Ask whether the college/university employs **student resident advisors** (RAs) or adults to manage/monitor dormitories.

6. If there are **fraternities and/or sororities** on campus, inquire about their influence on the overall social atmosphere at the college.

7. Ask if the school offers **Friday classes**. Administrators are increasingly concerned that no classes on Friday may lead to an early start in partying on the weekends and increased alcohol abuse problems.

8. Find out the average number of **years it takes to graduate** from that college.

9. Determine **the emphasis placed on athletics** on campus and whether tailgating at games involves alcohol.

10. Find out the number of **liquor law violations and alcohol-related injuries and deaths** the campus has had in previous years.

11. Finally, consider the **location** of the college and how it may affect the social atmosphere.

These are all reasonable things to ask, but it would take a great deal of effort to gather this information for even one school, let alone several under discussion, without some help. In the following sections, I comment on how a student or a parent might learn about each of the items numbered above, explaining how to use appendix D to find out much of the information for almost 400 leading institutions.

CAMPUS ALCOHOL POLICIES

The NIAAA's college Web site offers a way to access college alcohol policies at individual campuses. Point your browser to http://www.collegedrinking prevention.gov/policies/default.aspx and select the state and then the individual campus of interest.

Faden and Baskin selected 52 leading universities to find out how easy it was to find their alcohol policies at their Web sites.[8] They concluded, "In general, ... the information was difficult to find, was located in many areas of the Web site, and did not provide complete information about the school's alcohol policy."

Part of the problem in using this approach is the great variation in college alcohol policies. Appendix D presents a single item about policy, whether the college allows alcohol to those over 21, collected uniformly by a survey from *U.S. News and World Report*.

ENFORCING UNDERAGE DRINKING PREVENTION

This is one of the toughest items about which to get good, comparable information. Research on what colleges do usually just ask whether particular programs are being used, but does not establish whether the effort is extensive or sketchy, how faithful it is to the original design, or what kind of scope or reach it has.

Visitors to any one campus might learn a lot about prevention activities at each campus, but would probably find it hard to compare several campuses without some kind of checklist, perhaps based on what researchers have used. College guides like the *Fiske Guide* and *Princeton Review* contain occasional references to enforcement, but not systematic information on every one of the colleges.

By contrast, somewhat better data exist on how well the individual states do on this issue. MADD rates the states on how well they do in enforcing underage drinking by examining state laws and policing expenditures.[9]

COUNSELING SERVICES

Colleges vary greatly in what kinds of counseling services they provide and at what cost to individual students. Asking about the availability of counseling services could be revealing, but again making comparisons will be difficult. Many college Web sites will have separate pages describing the counseling center and its staff. Admissions staff members can probably answer questions.

ALCOHOL-FREE DORMS

The availability of alcohol-free dorms should be noted on the college's Web site or can be obtained from college admissions personnel. Questioners might probe how many students are housed in these dorms and whether there is a waiting list to get into the dorms. Questioners should clarify whether the dorms offer any special programming around wellness or health promotion, or whether the dorm is merely one in which alcohol isn't permitted, fairly common for those housing only freshmen and therefore many students under 21.

STUDENT RESIDENT ADVISORS

Admissions counselors should be able to clarify whether resident advisors (RAs) are upper-class undergraduates, graduate students, or other persons over 21.

FRATERNITIES OR SORORITIES

College guides like *Fiske* and *Princeton Review* offer frequent comments about the strength of the Greek system on campus, although the comments are not systematically made and it is hard to assess the quality of the information. The online edition of *U.S. News and World Report's America's Best Colleges* provides data under "Extracurriculars" on the number of fraternities and sororities, the number with chapter houses, and the percent who are members.

FRIDAY CLASSES

Admissions counselors will be able to answer questions about Friday classes in general, but only the registrar or perhaps an academic dean can answer whether students select or attend these classes in large numbers.

YEARS TO GRADUATION

Both the print and online versions of the *U.S. News and World Report's America's Best Colleges* report data about the average graduation rate, and readers interested in these data should consult these guides. Bear in mind that graduation rate reflects a number of issues, including the relative affluence of the student population, and may have little to do as such with alcohol use or abuse.

EMPHASIS PLACED ON ATHLETICS

Both the *Fiske Guide* and *Princeton Review* contain frequent comments about how important athletics are, though systematic or quantitative data are not given. The online version of *U.S. News and World Report* has a special section on athletics, but data may not be complete.

LIQUOR LAW VIOLATIONS

Chapter 4 on alcohol and crime should help decipher what information is available. A section of this chapter also explains how to access Clery Act data on campus crime and related issues. Appendix D presents detailed data on leading colleges.

LOCATION

The state in which a college is located has been demonstrated to be correlated with the college binge-drinking rate. Appendix D presents college location, and table 6-1 presents state binge drinking rates.

The specific location of a college is of course of great interest. Some colleges are ringed by alcohol outlets, whereas others are located in dry towns or counties. Both the *Fiske Guide* and *Princeton Review* make frequent reference to college location and to the availability of bars and clubs.

Visiting a campus and asking students and staff for information sound like good ideas. But bear in mind that researchers of social norms have found that students often misperceive alcohol use on their own campus. Even when asking a knowledgeable student about drinking on her campus, the answer likely may be far from accurate. Many admissions staffers are only a few years away from their own student days and also may have skewed perceptions.

USING COLLEGE GUIDES AND RANKINGS

Aside from actually visiting a specific college, prospective students and their families probably learn the most about colleges by consulting guides and rankings.

College rankings have gone from a parlor game for upper-middle-class parents to a thriving industry with major players. The shelves of the nearest chain bookstore are filled with guidebooks, rankings, and tracts promising inside information. On the Internet, rankings of colleges range from the best on sexual health, sponsored by the company that makes Trojan condoms, to the most public spirited, ranked by the *Washington Monthly*.[10]

The *Princeton Review* (a for-profit company with no ties to the university of the same name) claims to help more than half of all college bound students to "research, apply to, prepare for, and learn how to pay for their college education."[11] *The Best 361 Colleges: The Smart Student's Guide to Colleges* is based on surveys of 115,000 students, though the details about how the surveys are conducted do not permit a reader to assess the quality of the surveys. It is unlikely that anything approaching a scientific survey is done. For starters, the *Review* claims no attempt at a random sample of colleges, instead arguing that these are the best of the thousands of colleges in the country. But to my knowledge, the *Princeton Review* is currently the only publisher of data on drinking about a large number of individual colleges.

So with a very large grain of salt at hand, its data might shed some light on drinking at these 361 colleges. "Lots of beer drinking" happens at

53 percent of those campuses, while "hard liquor is popular" at 26 percent. The top 20 colleges with "Lots of Beer" include University of Wisconsin-Madison, Washington and Lee University, The University of Texas at Austin, Ohio University-Athens, and West Virginia University. At the other end of the scale, with almost no drinking: Brigham Young University, Wheaton College–Illinois, City University of New York–Queens College, College of the Ozarks, and Grove City College. Wheaton led those schools with little hard liquor consumption, while Louisiana State University hit the top of that category.

U.S. News and World Report collects data on whether a college permits alcohol at all for anyone on its campuses; these data are available from its premium content Web site, but they are not published in the popular print editions of its rankings. *Princeton Review* publishes data on whether beer, hard liquor, and other drugs are popular on campuses. Its Web site also makes available short videos on a few dozen campuses that mention drug and alcohol use.

The Fiske Guide to Colleges frequently mentions drug and alcohol issues.[12] Fiske notes, "We paid particular attention to the effect of the 21-year-old drinking age on campus life. Also, we noted efforts some schools' administrations have been making to change or improve the social residential life on campuses through such measures as banning fraternities and constructing new athletic facilities."[13] Also, it provides a ranking of social life (up to five "telephones").[14] Three telephones indicate a typical college social life; four, better-than-average; and five, "something of a party school, which may or may not detract from academic quality."[15]

And just once, in 1989, *Peterson's Guides* published an entire volume on drug and alcohol programs and policies.[16]

In this chapter, I offer some practical advice for those students and parents who want to choose a college taking into account its amount of drinking and drinking-related problems. This turns out to be harder to do than might first be imagined. Only one national survey has been done that looks at a scientifically adequate random sample of colleges. The Harvard School of Public Health College Alcohol Study surveyed 140 colleges beginning in 1993 and ending in 2001. But the College Alcohol Study promised its participating institutions confidentiality. Some voluntarily released their own College Alcohol Study data and posted the data on their Web sites, but this seems to be the exception. Other potential sources of data, such as the Core Institute or the American College Health Association (ACHA), or entering freshmen data from Alcohol.Edu, are generally kept confidential, though rigorous trolling through an institution's Web site might yield some data.

What publicly available data can help in choosing a college? A few of the college guides publish data about alcohol or drug use. *Princeton Review*'s popular guide, *The Best 361 Colleges*, claims to collect survey data about student perceptions of alcohol use. On the downside, *Princeton Review* doesn't really explain its methodology or sampling, so it is likely that neither meet current social science standards. Nor does it explain why one campus gets the "lots of beer" label and another does not—is it 50 percent or more? Nor does it justify why these student perception data should be taken as evidence about the actual amount of drinking, despite a wealth of evidence gathered by social norms researchers that students misperceive actual behavior, saying that their peers drink much more than they actually do.

Still, the *Princeton Review*'s *The Best 361 Colleges*, the *Fiske Guide*, and the *U.S. News and World Report* data, when taken together, are a rich body of evidence that students and parents should consult. Appendix D presents the data from all these sources for almost 400 leading schools. These are not a cross section of higher education today, but they do contain some of the most desired choices, including all those listed by the *Princeton Review* and *Fiske Guide*.[17] No attempt is made to present any other data, such as rankings on academics. The interested reader should consult the original sources for those data.

Appendix D presents the name of the institution, followed by its total student body size. Four columns follow reporting arrests and referrals data, which are explained in the next section. Then follows the "*Fiske Guide* Social" ratings (with 5 being the highest) of the social activity at the institution. The next piece of data is whether alcohol is allowed on campus; a "1" indicates yes, a "0" no. Two columns present the *Princeton Review* survey findings about whether beer or liquor is plentiful on campus, again with "1" indicating yes and "0" indicating no. The final column gives the state in which the college is located.

I have not attempted to rank the data in any way, and I would invite the reader to examine those schools of interest to see how each appears in terms of alcohol use, alcohol policy, or Clery Act data about alcohol. These data suggest questions that college admissions staff should answer ("*Fiske Guide* gives your campus a 5 on social life. Doesn't this mean it's a party school?" "*Princeton Review* reports that students say there's lots of beer and liquor at your school. What do you do about that to protect students?")

In addition to college guide data, a unique set of data exist about liquor law violations and campus crime, and these data are also presented in appendix D. In the next section, we discuss the Clery Act data.

USING THE U.S. DEPARTMENT OF EDUCATION CLERY ACT DATA

Yet another source of insight into alcohol use comes from the data published on a Web site of the U.S. Department of Education. To comply with the Clery Act (Campus Security Act), the Department gathers and makes public crime and other data gathered on a yearly basis. Reporting requirements are laid out in detail in a 200-page manual published by the Department.[18] Security on Campus, Inc. has begun offering two-day seminars funded by the U.S. Department of Justice to help college personnel comply more full with the Act. I attended one in Philadelphia in 2007, and much of what follows is based on that seminar.

The intent of the Clery Act was to publicize crimes on campus, with an eye toward helping students choose safer schools. An anomaly in the original law meant that data were collected about a narrow category of alcohol-related crimes (arrests for public drunkenness, for example, were excluded). College are required to report "liquor law violations," including violations of local law as well as violations of college policies about alcohol.

Information about "liquor law violations" are of some potential value to those seeking safer colleges. First, the data are published on all U.S. institutions, using what is by far the most sophisticated methodology available. Second, the data are about actual behavior, not just self-reported behavior or attitudes. Third, the U.S. Department of Education makes the data available on an easy-to-use Web site. As has been the case of education outcomes, graduation rates, and so on, colleges did not make any efforts to release data such as this until they were compelled to do so by a federal law. Rather than complaining about the alleged failings of the data, U.S. colleges ought to put some time, money, and energy into better ways of measuring it. And the price of accessing this data is right: free.

Appendix D presents alcohol and crime data for almost 400 leading institutions, including counts of how many liquor or drug law violations were given to students on a given campus. Several items are presented: "Arrests on Campus" for drug and for liquor law violations; followed by "Actions or Referrals on Campus," again for drug and for liquor violations separately. These items give the reader the best indication of how frequently drug and alcohol arrests and violations occur on each campus.

U.S. colleges vary enormously in size, and so one might want to compare how many students there are on a campus with the number of alcohol violations. Still, its main value to students and parents to suggest questions that could be posed to campus admissions staff ("Your campus had more than 400 liquor law violations, according to its own published Clery Act data. What can you tell us about the campus climate of alcohol use?"). Alternatively, one can compare groups of schools and then decide whether a choice might be made among them. For example, the eight Ivy League universities all have extremely selective admissions, but Columbia and Brown have fewer alcohol violations relative to their student populations than do Penn or Cornell. For another example, the 28 Jesuit colleges and universities share some great academic strengths, but why would one prefer those institutions with the highest number of violations to the many more moderate institutions?

In addition to the Clery Act data on leading institutions presented in appendix D, the data are publicly available on thousands of American colleges. Point your Web browser to http://www.ope.ed.gov/security/main.asp. The site provides you with a number of choices. If you are trying to find out information about one specific campus, choose "get data for one campus." Next, enter the name of the college. (In most cases, this is straightforward, but for some, like my own institution, Saint Joseph's University, it can get a bit tricky.) You usually can find the name by specifying the town, city, or even the state in which the college is located, and then selecting from the list presented.

Potential students and their parents have more informal ways of checking out the alcohol and drug scene on campuses of interest. Graduates of the same high school or prep school can be consulted; campus visits (and the informal comments of student guides or dorm residents) can yield impressions, though, again, social norms researchers have reported on how erroneous these impressions sometimes are. The presence of either membership or residential fraternities and sororities is an important indicator. A drive around the immediate vicinity of the campus will suggest how many bars and other alcohol outlets are nearby.

Some universities are engaging in current and public discussion. For example, driven by the extraordinary national attention devoted to the Duke lacrosse team rape allegations (which ended in the state attorney general dismissing all charges against the students in April 2007), Duke University placed on its Web site a candid discussion of its alcohol-related troubles.[19] Other universities publish their data on Web sites. For example, the University of Pennsylvania has published a great deal of its survey data for public inspection. But Penn is atypical: the more typical college administration is unfortunately less forthcoming.

A particularly well-motivated observer might try other methods of learning about alcohol and drug problems. Increasing numbers of daily newspapers are now available online, many with searchable archives, so one could search for a school name and then look for stories about drinking and its aftermath. A variation on this would be to use national newspaper archives to perform searches. What one finds hardly would be considered systematic knowledge and probably would reflect as much on the different editorial practices of individual newspapers than on any more general reality at each campus. Another source of information for the highly motivated is the college's student newspaper, many of which are available online in searchable forms.

What data do exist demonstrate that college drinking varies enormously across different schools. The Harvard College Alcohol Study found virtually no binge drinking at a few schools to more than 70 percent at the top school. Reading three college guidebooks makes one reach the same conclusion, but with far less firm evidence about the level or type of drinking than does the research literature. As we've seen, this research rarely identifies the institution or institutions on which it is based, whereas the college guides describe individual colleges by name.

CHOOSING A COLLEGE FOR STUDENTS IN RECOVERY

Students who have or are being treated for alcohol dependence or abuse, or who are currently sober and participating in Alcoholics Anonymous or other self-help programs have to be particularly careful in choosing a college. Making sure that treatment can be continued is critical for the first group, and college counseling or health services should be consulted early in the application process. For those in recovery, choosing a college means making sure that an appropriate 12-step program is available.[20] In some communities, like the Philadelphia area, Alcoholics Anonymous and other recovery groups maintain Web sites or telephone call-in centers to locate meetings.[21]

Fourteen colleges and universities are members of the Association for Recovery Schools (ARS), which

> [A]dvocates for the promotion, strengthening, and expansion of secondary and post-secondary programs designed for students and families committed to achieving success in both education and recovery. ARS exists to support such schools which, as components of the recovery continuum of care, enroll students committed to being abstinent from alcohol and other drugs and working a program of recovery.[22]

Brown University has pioneered services for students who seek sobriety through the fellowship of Alcoholics Anonymous. Beginning in the 1960s with the appointment of Bruce Donovan as its dean for Issues of Chemical Dependency, Brown has had a full-time administrator openly in recovery and available for advising students. The current dean, Kathleen McSharry, is one of several associate deans. "McSharry provides comprehensive academic support to students recovering from chemical dependency, collaborates with other offices on campus to establish policies and procedures regarding alcohol and other drugs on campus, and educates faculty, staff, and student leaders at high school and college campuses about drugs and their effects."[23]

At a few colleges, residences are available for students in sobriety. University House offers a residence for college men near the University of Minnesota. Students must be drug and alcohol free. University House is run by an active member of Alcoholics Anonymous.[24] At least one for-profit company operates a residence for recovering students near several colleges in Arizona.[25]

THE TRANSITION TO COLLEGE: STUDENTS ENTERING THE RED ZONE

Recent attention in college drinking has focused on the transition to college. Concerns about alcohol are represented among the many recommendations to colleges of a recent volume on "challenging and supporting the first-year student."[26]

Advice for the newly minted college student comes from all over. Readers of *U.S. News and World Report*'s 2007 edition of *America's Best Colleges* received personal advice from Koren Zailckas in her essay, "Booze News You Can Use." And she should know: the author of *Smashed: Story of a Drunken Childhood*, Zailckas (2005) survived high-bingeing in high school on Long Island and then at Syracuse University. Her book, according to my student reviewers, is a letter-perfect account of high-volume college drinking at a selective and expensive Eastern private university. Her *U.S. News* essay defines binge drinking and notes that most kids don't drink, providing the rest with scripts for turning down drinking: "While I clearly never said 'No,' you can. If you don't feel comfortable, say, 'I'm taking medication and can't drink' or 'I have an early exam' or 'I was up late last night and I'm still recovering.'"

Zailckas observes that figuring out what an enjoyable buzz is (with a blood alcohol concentration [BAC] of 0.15) is more difficult than one might think, since it depends on what you've eaten that day, what prescription drugs you're taking, and, if you're female, your menstrual cycles. Such topics as alcohol poisoning, secondhand effects, and "drunken sex is bad sex" all come in for comment, with a special warning for those 1 in 10 college students with a family history of alcoholism.

Many colleges provide advice to entering students about how to reduce the harm associated with freshman-year drinking. My freshman seminar students received this advice from our "crazy alcohol lady" in their first weeks on campus. As part of a broader program to curb high-risk drinking, Ellen Trappey visits freshman classes with a message tailored to students plunged into a very heavy drinking scene. She opens by saying clearly that state law forbids those under 21 from drinking, and more than a few of the entirely 18-year-old class smile somewhat wisely. Trappey, who is 27 but could easily pass for a college junior, gets the group to specify what it takes to get "buzzed" as opposed to "wasted." She then gives students handouts that show how many drinks it takes over different periods of time for a male or a female of a certain weight to get buzzed or wasted. She takes questions from the floor: "What BAC gets you a driving under the influence [DUI] in Pennsylvania? Can you mix Red Bull and vodka safely? Do you get in trouble for telling your resident assistant about a passed-out roommate?" Trappey presents other classes with specific information about the alcohol content of popular drinks so that students can gauge how much they actually consume.

The context is crucial: like many other campuses, my college went through a spell in which dozens of students, almost all of them freshman, had to be taken to local emergency rooms with very high BACs, some certainly life-threatening. One persistent campus rumor was that two dorms loaded with freshmen had gotten into a contest about who could get the most emergency room calls in a semester. Faced with an alcohol crisis, the university responded by hiring Trappey.

An unanswered question is whether these particular forms of harm reduction unwittingly communicate the message that there is "safe" binge drinking, that is, drinking below the level of life-threatening BACs but above both the state's BAC driving limits and the cutoffs for the elevated primary and secondary binge effects discussed earlier. The NIAAA Task Force report called into question the forms of purely educational efforts or education about BAC levels *when used alone*. But communicating about how to avoid alcohol poisoning inevitably raises the question of unwittingly encouraging nonlethal forms of heavy drinking.

A recent "back to college fact sheet" from the NIAAA warns parents: "As college students arrive on campus this fall, it's a time of new experiences, new friendships, and making memories that will last a lifetime. Unfortunately for many, it is also a time of excessive drinking and dealing with its aftermath—vandalism, violence, sexual aggression, and even death."[27] Summarizing evidence from its own Task Force report, the warning continues,

"the consequences of excessive drinking by college students are more significant, more destructive, and more costly than many parents realize. And
these consequences affect students whether or not they drink."

Claiming that "early weeks are critical," the NIAAA fact sheet proposes,
"[a]s the fall semester begins, parents can use this important time to help
prepare their college-age sons and daughters by talking with them about the
consequences of excessive drinking." The NIAAA zeroes in on the first few
weeks of college, called the Red Zone:

> Anecdotal evidence suggests that the first 6 weeks of the first semester are criti-
> cal to a first-year student's academic success. Because many students initiate
> heavy drinking during these early days of college, the potential exists for exces-
> sive alcohol consumption to interfere with successful adaptation to campus life.
> The transition to college is often difficult and about one-third of first-year stu-
> dents fail to enroll for their second year.

Up against the challenge of the Red Zone, what can parents do? The
NIAAA suggests, "They can inquire about campus alcohol policies, call
their sons and daughters frequently, and ask about roommates and living
arrangements. They should also discuss the penalties for underage drinking
as well as how alcohol use can lead to date rape, violence, and academic
failure."[28]

The NIAAA advises parents to use the Task Force's "award-winning Web
site (collegedrinkingprevention.gov) for more information and resources.

HOW STUDENTS CAN LEARN MORE

Students who want to learn more about alcohol or get help with its use
should make use of their college's counseling service or alcohol and drug
counselor. Many colleges have specialized services available for free, at least
for the initial consultation. One Web site allows an individual anonymous
screening for alcohol problems.[29] Some colleges provide screening information on the Internet: The University of California–Los Angeles, for example, has a series of aids available to students.[30]

As discussed in an earlier chapter, many colleges make efforts to educate
their own students about alcohol and other drug problems. Such products as
Alcohol.Edu contain considerable information about college drinking. Students interested in learning more about college drinking should consult appendix A, which lists many resources, including those with a Web presence.
Among the most helpful on a personal level are Columbia University's "Go

Ask Alice," a college student health advice site with down-to-earth information expressed in language light on unnecessary moralizing. "Go Ask Alice" features a section on alcohol and other drugs, with plenty of other typical college health questions answered as well. Both men and women will find the self-help classic *Our Bodies, Ourselves* an excellent source of nonjudgmental advice as well.[31] Finally, the NIAAA Task Force on College Drinking Web site (collegedrinkingprevention.gov) is a superb source of scientifically sound advice and information, as is the U.S. Department of Education's Higher Education Center for the Prevention of Alcohol and Other Drug Abuse and Violence Prevention (higheredcenter.org).

DEALING WITH ALCOHOL EMERGENCIES

Students who are experiencing a health emergency or witnessing one should always call 911 immediately. Many colleges now have "Good Samaritan" policies that promise no one gets into trouble for helping others in emergency situations, and it is just plain common sense for students to call emergency services immediately. Students with treatment needs should consult their college's counseling services or their own personal physician. Treatment services in a particular community might be listed in the "blue pages" of the phone book. A federal agency, the Substance Abuse and Mental Health Services Administration, maintains a service locator feature on its Web site.[32] Some local governments like New York City also have 311 numbers to locate services or information.

COLLEGES AND PARENTS: A CHANGING RELATIONSHIP

For many years, colleges and universities had a ritualized relationship with parents. After looking over the shoulder of a college-bound child as she or he completed admissions applications and opened the fat acceptance letter, parents became the functional equivalent of a higher education teller machine, dispensing funds to cover tuition, room and board, and other sundries. Except for the occasional invitation to a Parents' Weekend, mom and dad were expected to shell out and shut up until graduation rolled around. Colleges and universities kept parents at a distance. If anything happened on campus, it was as if Las Vegas rules applied: what happens here stays here. Parents were rarely informed about their children's academic and non-academic happenings. The taken-for-granted assumption was that colleges expected little or nothing from parents (aside from the tens of thousands of dollars, that is to say). Aside from greetings from the dean of students and perhaps a preview of this year's sports prospects, parents dropped off students at student orientation and were expected to leave as soon as the last minifridge or stereo had been dropped off at the dorm.

These rules were well entrenched by the time Congress passed the Buckley Amendment also known as the Family Educational Rights and Privacy Act (FERPA). This literally wrote into federal law the wall that separated parents from their college-going students, requiring colleges not to reveal student academic grades or nonacademic gaffes. (That colleges could do so for nonemancipated students often was ignored in favor of strengthening the wall.) The result has been a practice within many college student affairs administrations of not involving parents in student conduct issues (except for the most serious).

One of the consequences of the rising concern about college drinking in the 1990s was to cause a significant number of colleges to rethink these institutional arrangements. In several well-publicized experiments, especially those supported by the Robert Wood Johnson Foundation in its "A Matter of Degree" Program, colleges began to explore parental notification of parents when their children broke college rules.

The NIAAA Task Force offers the following advice for parents of college students:

- Pay special attention to your son's or daughter's experiences and activities during the crucial first six weeks on campus. With a great deal of free time, many students initiate heavy drinking during these early days of college, and the potential exists for excessive alcohol consumption to interfere with successful adaptation to campus life. You should know that about one-third of first-year students fail to enroll for their second year.

- Find out whether a program during orientation educates students about campus policies related to alcohol use. If there is one, attend with your son or daughter, or at least be familiar with the name of the person who is responsible for campus counseling programs.

- Inquire about and make certain you understand the college's "parental notification" policy.

- Call your son or daughter frequently during the first six weeks of college.

- Inquire about their roommates, the roommates' behavior, and how disagreements are settled or disruptive behavior dealt with.

- Make sure that your son or daughter understands the penalties for underage drinking, public drunkenness, using a fake identification, driving under the influence, assault, and other alcohol-related offenses. Indicate to them that you have asked the college/university to keep you informed of infractions to school alcohol policies. (For alcohol policies on college campuses see www.collegedrinkingprevention.gov/policies)

- Make certain that they understand how alcohol use can lead to date rape, violence, and academic failure.

The NIAAA's college-drinking prevention site includes the following sound advice for parents of a college student facing an alcohol-related crisis:

- Be aware of the signs of possible alcohol abuse by your son or daughter (e.g., lower grades, never available or reluctant to talk with you, unwilling to talk about activities with friends, trouble with campus authorities, serious mood changes).

- If you believe your son or daughter is having a problem with alcohol, do not blame them, but find appropriate treatment.

- Call and/or visit campus health services and ask to speak with a counselor.

- Indicate to the Dean of Students, either in person or by email, your interest in the welfare of your son or daughter and that you want to be actively involved in his or her recovery despite the geographic separation.

- If your son or daughter is concerned about his or her alcohol consumption, or that of a friend, have them check out www.alcoholscreening.org for information about ongoing screening for problems with alcohol.

- Pay your son or daughter an unexpected visit. Ask to meet their friends. Attend Parents' Weekend and other campus events open to parents.

- Continue to stay actively involved in the life of your son or daughter. Even though they may be away at college, they continue to be an extension of your family and its values.[33]

COLLEGE SAFETY AND SECURITY

Thanks to the courage and persistence of one family, we now know a lot more about crime on campus. After their daughter Jeanne was raped and murdered at Lehigh University, Connie and Howard Clery set out to find out how safe campuses were. Sadly, their effort to get colleges to release crime data was a struggle over two decades, and even today colleges often don't comply with the federal law about campus safety and security named after their daughter.

The horrific 2007 massacre at Virginia Tech has probably changed a lot of conversations about campus safety. Students and parents are probably much more likely to ask colleges for assurances that safety is at the top of the list of administrative concerns. Even taking into account Virginia Tech's 33 deaths, American college campuses rarely have murders.

By contrast, as the noted behavioral scientist and epidemiologist Ralph Hingson has shown, more than 1,700 college students die each year as the result of alcohol. Some, perhaps many, of the murder and manslaughter deaths involve alcohol. Other deaths, like Rider University student Gary DeVercelly, are the result of alcohol poisonings. Other deaths, from accidental injury including car crashes, are far more numerous.

Of the other college student deaths, most if not almost all could have been prevented. Many college student deaths are caused by car crashes involving alcohol. Activist groups such as MADD argue that vigorous enforcement of existing law could make such crashes far less frequent. Mandatory "passive" seat belt laws, regular use of roadblocks and random traffic stops, mandatory use of BAC monitoring, and stricter monitoring of convicted DUI offenders could combine to prevent many of these crashes. (In the not-so-distant future, auto manufacturers could make cars inoperable by anyone with alcohol in their bloodstream, perhaps coming close to eliminating car crashes of this type.) Some of these changes can be part of policing and prevention activities directed at college students and staff.

With quick action in taking a high-BAC person to an emergency room, most alcohol poisoning deaths probably could be prevented. In addition to adequate campus security and student life protocols for students, prevention activities can include a "Good Samaritan" exception so that students who may have been drinking illegally or immoderately are not punished for calling 911 or local authorities to bring a drunk student to the emergency room. Better training of RAs and RDs (resident directors) as well as broader education of students through Alcohol.Edu or other programs can raise the awareness level.

These activities take the form of "harm reduction."[34] Harm reduction begins with the recognition that even with minimum drinking laws in place and vigorous enforcement (hardly the reality at present), many people in our society, including college students, will use alcohol unwisely. To save lives and promote public health, harm reduction has to be part of any community's response to substance use, regardless of what else is done to minimize abuse. These efforts don't have to be mutually exclusive alternatives, though sometimes they are treated that way. Some argue that harm reduction is just a fancy word for enabling; is it not just teaching students how to drink heavily without paying the price? But others point out that saving lives will always trump preventing heavy drinking.

The best estimate of student deaths resulting from alcohol puts the figure at 1,700 across the nation. Any one college may have a single student death or more every year, but for the most part these deaths are not reported accurately in the media or other public places. The result is that students underestimate the harm alcohol abuse holds. One way to improve this situation is to report student deaths accurately in campus newspapers. There are many obstacles to doing this, including a well-founded concern about prolonging the mourning of friends and family. But the present situation, in which alcohol-related car crashes are reported as unfortunate and unavoidable accidents, has a heavy costs in the long run.

Aside from choosing a college, important choices include living arrangements that powerfully shape routine activities and social networks. The NIAAA puts it succinctly: "The proportion of college students who drink varies with where they live. Drinking rates are highest in fraternities and sororities followed by on-campus housing (e.g., dormitories, residence halls). Students who live independently off-site (e.g., in apartments) drink less, while commuting students who live with their families drink the least."[35] Much of what's going on here probably is self-selection. But even though this correlational data cannot tell us about causes, they do suggest rethinking where a student should live. At a minimum, considering living in a fraternity or sorority should trigger a vigorous discussion of the wisdom of that choice.

CONCLUSION

A persistent and long-term social problem like college drinking will not be changed overnight. In the meantime, students and parents can cope with this problem by addressing factors that raise the risk of excessive drinking and that can be modified. Particularly critical are high school drinking, choosing a college, and navigating through the Red Zone. Self-help advice and anonymous screening can help students identify problems. Using college and off-campus treatment services and maintaining sobriety through a 12-step program will help those who begin to abuse, continue to abuse, or are dependent on alcohol.

NOTES

1. Haines, Barker, & Rice (2006) present findings about the kinds of self-protective behaviors that college students use, though without evaluating how effective these behaviors actually are. Neighbors, Larimer, Lostutter, & Woods (2006) discuss the "harm reduction" approach, more popular in other countries than at present in the United States.

2. http://www.sadd.org/numbers.htm, accessed September 24, 2007.

3. http://www.centurycouncil.org/lib/downloads/parents.pdf, accessed September 19, 2007.

4. Baum & Ma (2007: 9).

5. http://www.knowhow2go.org/, accessed September 26, 2007.

6. Stevens (2007).

7. http://www.collegedrinkingprevention.gov/collegeparents/choosingRightCollege. aspx, accessed September 25, 2007.

8. Their report is available at http://www.collegedrinkingprevention.gov/ CollegePresidents/evalCollegeAlcoholPolicies.aspx, accessed September 23, 2007.

9. MADD (2002).

10. The data on sexual health are available at http://www.prnewswire.com/ cgi-bin/stories.pl?ACCT=104&STORY=/www/story/09-10-2007/0004659655&EDAT, accessed September 14, 2007. The *Washington Monthly*'s rankings are at http://www2. washingtonmonthly.com/features/2007/0709.collegeguide.html, accessed September 23, 2007.

11. *Princeton Review* (2007: back cover).

12. Fiske (2007: xvi).

13. *Ibid.*

14. Fiske (2007: xix).

15. *Ibid.*

16. Schneider & Porter-Shirley (1989).

17. I included the 28 Jesuit colleges and universities and several other institutions I had personal knowledge of to come up with 400 in total.

18. U.S. Department of Education, Office of Safe and Drug Free Schools (2005).

19. http://www.dukenews.duke.edu/reports/ccireport.pdf, accessed April 12, 2007.

20. http://www.alcoholics-anonymous.org, accessed September 26, 2007.

21. http://www.sepennaa.org/, accessed September 26, 2007.

22. http://www.recoveryschools.org/about_mission.html, accessed September 26, 2007.

23. http://brown.edu/Administration/Dean_of_the_College/people/Kathleen_Mc Sharry.php, accessed September 26, 2007.

24. http://www.aa-uk.org.uk/alcoholics-anonymous-reviews/2005/05/university-house-offers-sober.html, accessed June 8, 2007.

25. http://www.gatehousecollegecampus.com/locations/index.php, accessed September 26, 2007.

26. Upcraft, Gardner, & Barefoot (2005: 520).

27. http://www.collegedrinkingprevention.gov/NIAAACollegeMaterials/college FactSheetForParents.aspx, accessed September 24, 2007.

28. *Ibid.*

29. http://www.alcoholscreening.org/, accessed September 24, 2007.

30. http://www.sps.ucla.edu/assist.html, accessed September 24, 2007.

31. Boston Women's Health Book Collective (2005).

32. http://findtreatment.samhsa.gov/, accessed September 24, 2007.

33. http://www.collegedrinkingprevention.gov/NIAAACollegeMaterials/parentBro chure.aspx, accessed April 12, 1007.

34. Marlatt (1998); Neighbors, Larimer, Lostutter, & Woods (2006).

35. http://pubs.niaaa.nih.gov/publications/StrategicPlan/NIAAASTRATEGICPLAN. htm, accessed April 12, 2007.

Afterword: 2013—Changing the Culture of College Drinking

Has anything changed since 2009, when the first edition of this book was published? This afterword, written especially for the new, reprinted edition, addresses that question by updating some of the major themes in this book, introducing some fresh evidence, and raising questions about the objective reality of college drinking, its construction as a social problem, and the prospects of changing the culture of college drinking.

COLLEGE DRINKING AS A SOCIAL PROBLEM

It has now been a decade since the National Institute on Alcohol Abuse and Alcoholism (NIAAA) Task Force on College Drinking published its landmark 2002 report, which was mailed to every college president in the United States. In it, college drinking, no longer a harmless rite of passage (think of the image of John Belushi from *Animal House*), was reframed as a major public health problem. NIAAA's college website (http://www.collegedrinkingprevention.gov) has had millions of hits since the report was published. Scientific papers commissioned by the Task Force appeared in the major journal in the field, now called the *Journal of Studies on Alcohol and Drugs,* and several publications went on to become citation classics.[1] Since the 2002 Task Force report, NIAAA has released several updates about college drinking, including most recently an April 2012 publication, *College Drinking.*

Abusive and underage college drinking are significant public health problems, and they exact an enormous toll on the intellectual and social lives of students on campuses across the United States.

Drinking in college has become a ritual that students often see as an integral part of their higher-education experience. Many students come to college with established drinking habits, and then the college environment can exacerbate the problem. Research shows that more than 80 percent of college students drink alcohol, and almost half report binge drinking in the 2 weeks prior to being interviewed.

Virtually all college students experience the effects of college drinking—whether they drink or not.[2]

Possibly because of its construction as a health issue, college drinking continues to be viewed largely as a "student affairs" problem, attended to by the vice president in charge of that activity and the board of trustees' student affairs committee. To gauge its standing, consider its placement on the trustees' agenda. The Association of Governing Boards of Universities and Colleges (AGB) represents college and university trustees, who carry the enormous responsibility of choosing the campus president in addition to other leaders. The president and trustees set the agenda for each institution. The AGB staff publishes a biennial list of the top public policy issues facing higher education, which is in effect its estimate of the current agenda at the national level for higher education.[3] For 2010–2011, the list included the following:

- Continued fiscal pressure
- Advancing student success
- Increased interest in the regulation of higher education
- Greater expectations for P–20 alignment
- Productivity, efficiency, affordability
- Student-aid policy
- Increasingly negative perceptions about higher education
- The evolving relationship between higher education and the government
- Tax policies

College drinking as an issue simply doesn't appear on this list, but two of the items might include some backwash from the issue. The impact of college drinking on completing a college degree usually has been assumed to be negative, so at least some of the problems in "advancing student success" might be deepened by college drinking. Many of the news stories tied to college drinking, including deaths, injuries, and rapes and other crimes, as well as activities like hazing, also play a role in the "increasingly negative perceptions about higher education."

Individual college agendas simply do not mirror AGB's estimates of national higher education issues, although it would be surprising if most of these issues were not among the concerns of governing boards at many institutions. Like most student affairs issues, as noted previously, college drinking is not an explicit item on individual college and university agendas.[4]

At some colleges and universities, college drinking has been raised to the top of the institutional agenda by a single tragic event or scandal. Several high-profile institutions have been the focus of media stories about college campus scandals (such as the Duke lacrosse rape case), and recently these scandals have involved alcohol-related issues, such as sexual harassment, sexual assault, and hazing. In 2010, pledges at Yale's Delta Kappa Epsilon fraternity were forced to chant sexist phrases (including the notorious "No means yes, yes means anal") at women undergraduates, several of whom filed a complaint with the U.S. Department of Education, stating that their civil rights had been infringed.[5] Another sensational story about hazing, this time at Dartmouth College, appeared in *Rolling Stone* magazine.[6] The story alleged many negative things about one of the most prestigious American universities, ranked 90th in the world by the *Times Higher Education World University Rankings* in 2011. The Dartmouth student newspaper interpreted the article as an attack on the school's culture.[7] Binge drinking and sexual assault both figured in the piece.

REFRAMING COLLEGE DRINKING

By the mid-1990s, Harvard School of Public Health College Alcohol Study researchers, led by Henry Wechsler, had begun to concentrate on binge drinking as one of the central problems college drinkers faced. By the next decade, other researchers had used the concept to define a harmful drinking pattern in the general population.[8] Binge drinking has become established as a central focus of federal alcohol health discourse.[9]

The concept has continued to be controversial, with some critics claiming that it distorts an older conception of problematic drinking or that it is better labeled as extreme or excessive drinking.[10] The concept of binge drinking has now been used by governments and private researchers across North America and Europe and is cited in the World Health Organization's most recent global status report on alcohol and health.[11]

This book has argued that there is a major difference between actual college drinking behavior and its construction as a social problem. Long-term trends in college drinking show little change over a period of decades, although occasionally there are fluctuations. Binge drinking increased slightly (from 41.7 to 44.7 percent) during the period from 1999 to 2005.[12] But the uptick of the early 2000s was followed by a slight decline in the last half of the decade. Data from the National Survey on Drug Use and Health for 2002–2010 confirm that among young adults, college binge drinking has hardly changed, while noncollege binge drinking may have declined slightly.[13] Binge drinking has increased slightly among women college students but not among men.[14] Attention to college drinking as an issue has increased considerably over the long haul among the general public (as indexed by stories in the *New York Times*) but has received less attention from university leaders (as indexed by stories in the *Chronicle of Higher Education* and *Inside Higher Education*).

THE IMPACT OF COLLEGE DRINKING

NIAAA has published a new snapshot of the impact of college drinking in a single year.[15] The consequences of excessive and underage drinking affect virtually all college campuses, college communities, and college students, whether they choose to drink or not.

- **Death**: 1,825 college students between the ages of 18 and 24 die from alcohol-related unintentional injuries, including motor vehicle crashes.
- **Injury**: 599,000 students between the ages of 18 and 24 are unintentionally injured under the influence of alcohol.
- **Assault**: 696,000 students between the ages of 18 and 24 are victims of alcohol-related assault, including sexual assault or date rape.
- **Sexual Abuse**: 97,000 students between the ages of 18 and 24 are victims of alcohol-related sexual assault or date rape.
- **Unsafe Sex**: 400,000 students between the ages of 18 and 24 had unprotected sex, and more than 100,000 students between the ages of 18 and 24 report having been too intoxicated to know if they consented to having sex.
- **Academic Problems**: About 25 percent of college students report academic consequences of their drinking including missing class, falling behind, doing poorly on exams or papers, and receiving lower grades overall.
- **Health Problems/Suicide Attempts**: More than 150,000 students develop an alcohol-related health problem, and between 1.2 and 1.5 percent

of students indicate that they tried to commit suicide within the past year due to drinking or drug use.

- **Drunk Driving**: 3,360,000 students between the ages of 18 and 24 drive under the influence of alcohol.

- **Vandalism:** About 11 percent of college student drinkers report that they have damaged property while under the influence of alcohol.

- **Property Damage:** More than 25 percent of administrators from schools with relatively low drinking levels and over 50 percent from schools with high drinking levels say their campuses have a "moderate" or "major" problem with alcohol-related property damage.

- **Police Involvement:** About 5 percent of 4-year college students are involved with the police or campus security as a result of their drinking, and 110,000 students between the ages of 18 and 24 are arrested for an alcohol-related violation such as public drunkenness or driving under the influence.

- **Alcohol Abuse and Dependence:** 31 percent of college students met criteria for a diagnosis of alcohol abuse and 6 percent for a diagnosis of alcohol dependence in the past 12 months, according to questionnaire-based self-reports about their drinking.

A key question that deserves thorough reexamination is whether a culture of college drinking lies at the heart of the issue. Rich ethnographies of that culture have been published in the past few years, the most recent at several high-binge universities in the Midwest.[16] A recent evaluation of college academic achievement has focused national attention on how the lifestyles and choices of students may undercut their academic progress, leaving them "academically adrift."[17] The public image of the contemporary American university has become tarnished, at least in part because of binge drinking and other alcohol-related problems, such as hazing and campus crime.[18] The impact of the recent economic recession, followed by deep cuts in public education dollars, has led to a period of increasingly negative discussions of American higher education.

Sociologist Thomas Vander Ven used student accounts of recent drinking at two midwestern universities in his *Getting Wasted: Why College Students Drink Too Much and Party So Hard*, as the following Amazon.com summary makes clear:[19]

> College students rely on "drunk support": contrary to most accounts of alcohol abuse as being a solitary problem of one person drinking to excess, the college

drinking scene is very much a social one where students support one another through nights of drinking games, rituals and rites of passage. Drawing on over 400 student accounts, 25 intensive interviews, and one hundred hours of field research, Vander Ven sheds light on the extremely social nature of college drinking. Giving voice to college drinkers as they speak in graphic and revealing terms about the complexity of the drinking scene, Vander Ven argues that college students continue to drink heavily, even after experiencing repeated bad experiences, because of the social support that they give to one another and due to the creative ways in which they reframe and recast violent, embarrassing, and regretful drunken behaviors. Provocatively, *Getting Wasted* shows that college itself, closed and seemingly secure, encourages these drinking patterns and is one more example of the dark side of campus life.[20]

Vander Ven's account helps to understand the culture of heavy drinking at colleges where a large majority of students indulge in binge drinking. What is less clear is how many campuses more or less have this type of culture, given that only about a third of four-year colleges have a majority of students who binge drink. *Getting Wasted* does a commendable job of exploring part of the cultural reality of heavy alcohol use at colleges at the high end of the distribution, but it also tends to downplay harmful parts of the experience. For example, the most reputable epidemiological evidence about alcohol-related deaths among college students is presented in a footnote (p. 192, note 42), and then the author notes that this is an estimate, not "documented alcohol fatalities."

In 2002, the NIAAA Task Force report placed a culture of college drinking at the center of the discussion, but the short 2012 report from the same agency, *College Drinking*, did not even use the word "culture."[21] Instead, NIAAA argued,

> Although the majority of students come to college already having some experience with alcohol, certain aspects of college life, such as unstructured time, the widespread availability of alcohol, inconsistent enforcement of underage drinking laws, and limited interactions with parents and other adults, can intensify the problem. In fact, college students have higher binge-drinking rates and a higher incidence of drunk driving than their non-college peers.
>
> The first 6 weeks of freshman year is an especially vulnerable time for heavy drinking and alcohol-related consequences because of student expectations and social pressures at the start of the academic year.

ALCOHOL AND CRIME

The evidence continues to support the argument that alcohol and college crime are powerfully connected. There is little doubt that alcohol plays a role in much of the crime and even violence on college campuses and that alcohol use is a major risk factor for college student victimization.

On-campus disciplinary actions at all American institutions of higher education rose to 185,005 in 2008, 185,590 in 2009, and 186,487 in 2010.[22] These figures may reflect both rising amounts of alcohol-related crime and increased attention to alcohol issues by college security officials. In any case, alcohol arrests are far more numerous than other kinds of reported crime. For 2008 to 2010, the U.S. Department of Education's data on campus crimes show 53 murders or manslaughters, 8,217 forcible/nonforcible sex offenses, and 557,082 liquor law violations.[23] These data certainly raise the question, how well have colleges and universities been dealing with campus crime, including alcohol-related crime?[24]

COLLEGE DRINKING, SOCIAL LIFE, AND SEX

The reporting of campus crime remains a major challenge, even after the many years since passage of the Clery Act in 1990. This is particularly problematic in the case of rape and sexual assault. A telephone survey of 2,000 women at four-year colleges found that 230 had experienced rape, but only 16 percent of forcible rape victims had filed a formal report with law enforcement.[25] Less than 3 percent of women who had experienced incapacitated rape, or drug- or alcohol-facilitated rape, had made formal reports. So the most common form of nonconsensual sex among college students is also virtually never reported to the authorities, and college women are less likely to report rape than noncollege women.[26]

Security efforts have increased, but there has been little change in heavy drinking and its consequences (including getting into trouble with the police or a woman reporting being a victim of sexual assault or rape) in the period from 1993 to 2005 at heavy drinking colleges.[27]

A recent "Dear Colleague" letter from the Department of Education to all higher education institutions underscores how much work needs to be done to guarantee student safety and security.[28] The letter notes that Title IX of the Education Acts of 1972 prohibits discrimination on the basis of sex in educational programs receiving federal funds, and then argues that sexual harassment and sexual violence (including sex against a person's will or when one is incapacitated by drugs or alcohol) fall under this prohibition. The letter suggests that each institution's Title IX coordinator be trained on the "link between alcohol and drug abuse and sexual harassment and violence and best practices to address that link." As they work to implement this new mandate, colleges can draw on a growing body of evidence about how to prevent campus crime and lower substance abuse.[29]

PUBLIC ALCOHOL POLICY

Evidence that public alcohol policy can play an important role in shaping alcohol consumption among the general population and among youth continues to build.[30] In the cross-national perspective, the United States falls somewhere toward the middle of the developed world in the strength of its alcohol control policies. It is distinctive in having a minimum drinking age of 21, higher than in almost any other developed country. Some have argued that this higher drinking age causes higher rates of binging in the United States.

Friese and Grube examined 2007 data on 16 European countries (for youths 15–16 years of age) and on the United States (for students in the 10th grade, roughly the same age).[31] They concluded that there was "no evidence that young Europeans drink more responsibly than their counterparts in the US." A greater proportion of young Western Europeans (except for Icelanders) currently binge drink than do young Americans. A majority of Western European nations report higher rates of intoxication, and more intoxication, before age 13 than does the United States.

An international team of leading experts on alcohol policy used the growing research literature to assess policy options.[32] The result was a list of 42 strategies or interventions, of which 19 were rated as "particularly good choices," presented here under bolded terms that indicate the general policy areas of each intervention:

- **Pricing and taxation**
  - Alcohol taxes
- **Regulating physical availability**
  - Ban on sales
  - Minimum legal purchase age
  - Rationing
  - Government monopoly of retail sales
  - Restrictions on density of outlets
  - Different availability by alcohol strength
- **Modifying the drinking environment**
  - Enhanced enforcement of on-premises laws and legal requirements

- **Drunk-driving countermeasures**
  - Sobriety check points
  - Random breath testing
  - Lowered blood alcohol content (BAC) limits
  - Administrative license suspension
  - Low BAC for young drivers ("zero tolerance")
  - Graduated licensing for novice drivers
- **Restrictions on marketing**
  - Legal restrictions on exposure
- **Treatment and early intervention**
  - Brief interventions with at-risk drivers
  - Mutual help/self-help attendance
  - Medical and social detoxification
  - Talk therapies

It is worth emphasizing that an additional category (like those listed in bold), "Education and persuasion," had six interventions listed, but none were judged "particularly good choices." Included among them were classroom education, college student normative education, brief interventions with high-risk students, mass media campaigns, warning labels and signs, and social marketing. So those interventions, often popular on American campuses, turn out to be of little help, according to this panel of international experts.

REFRAMING PREVENTION

The most recent NIAAA bulletin on college drinking notes, "Ongoing research continues to improve our understanding of how to address this persistent and costly problem. Successful efforts typically involve a mix of prevention, intervention, and treatment strategies that target individual students, the student body as a whole, and the broader college community."

Among those that target individual students, screening and brief intervention programs are highlighted. "A focus on individual intervention and treatment is significant, as research shows that 19 percent of college students between the ages of 18 and 24 meet the criteria for alcohol abuse and dependence, but only 5 percent seek treatment assistance."[33]

The NIAAA also suggests strategies that target the campus and surrounding community, including strategies that

- provide alcohol education,
- limit alcohol availability and enforce underage-drinking laws,
- provide alcohol-free campus activities,
- notify parents of alcohol-related infractions, and
- adjust academic schedules to include more Friday classes and reduce the number of long weekends during the semester.

NIAAA observes how widely social norm approaches (correcting student misperceptions about peer drinking) have been implemented, often in individual or online applications, but notes they are less effective as part of campus-wide campaigns. By contrast, evidence has accumulated about the efficacy of campus-community partnerships, which could include the following:

- Publicizing and enforcing underage-drinking and zero-tolerance laws for drivers under age 21
- Establishing partnerships between the college and the local residential and business communities to reduce access to alcohol and to address violations
- Increasing the price of alcohol

NIAAA concludes, "Strong leadership from a concerned college president in conjunction with an involved campus community and a comprehensive program of evidence-based strategies can help address harmful student drinking." This is important, for it raises the crucial question of how the accumulating knowledge about what works and why has been implemented on real college campuses.

The variation in how colleges attempt to address drinking problems is remarkable. Data collected in 2008 at 351 four-year colleges were used to identify four classes of institutions. The largest class (with 38 percent of colleges in the sample) had many alcohol policies and practices, while the smallest class (13 percent of colleges) had few or no policies or practices; the remaining institutions had some but lacked others. Six years after the landmark NIAAA Task Force report of 2002, there was hardly any uniform pattern.[34] Why so much variation? Again, thinking about higher education as a social institution and how individual colleges and universities operate helps to understand the disparity.

The American system of higher education . . . combines very large size, extreme decentralized control, great institutional diversity, sharp institutional competition and substantial status hierarchy. Its most important feature is the radical disbursement of authority. It is a system comprised both of major private sectors, in which over 2,000 private universities and colleges of all sizes operate under individual boards of control, devising their own viable niches, and of numerous public sectors in which another 1,600 institutions fall primarily under the 50 states rather than under the national government.[35]

In part, the NIAAA report of 2002 wanted these thousands of institutions to begin to move in more or less a single direction, but that has hardly happened. A few institutions chose to emphasize change in college drinking; many more probably adapted policies and practices that appeared to comply with federal regulations and that were compatible with existing institutional priorities and budgets. The result was that at the national level there has been little change in college drinking, even though at the local level most colleges can say they have taken some kind of action on the issue.

Six years after the NIAAA report of 2002, a team of researchers at the University of Minnesota assessed its implementation.[36] They found that most administrators were familiar with the report, although more than 1 in 5 were not. Almost all colleges reported using educational programs (which the report had noted were ineffective when used alone); half of the institutions used intervention programs with high-risk students. Few used the kind of community-based alcohol control strategies that both American and international researchers claim are most efficacious.

One particularly rich new source of ideas about prevention comes from NIAAA's "rapid response" program of pairing 15 colleges that have experienced alcohol crises with five teams of prevention and intervention experts from several fields. A special supplement of the *Journal of Studies on Alcohol and Drugs* published papers that summarized the results.[37] Among the studies were the following:

- James F. Schaus, MD, and colleagues at the University of Central Florida found that brief motivational interviews proved effective for high-risk drinkers seen in a busy college health clinic. Compared with a control group, students who participated in two sessions reported consuming less alcohol six months later and had fewer drinking-related problems nine months later.
- Hortensia Amaro, PhD, and colleagues at Northeastern University in Boston developed a one-on-one counseling program for students with alcohol and drug policy violations. Six months later, students who received the intervention were drinking less than counterparts who had not been through the program.

- Joseph A. LaBrie and colleagues at Loyola Marymount University in Los Angeles evaluated the long-term effectiveness of a motivational-enhancement group intervention for first-year college women. Participants consumed significantly less alcohol across ten weeks of follow-up, but not at six-month follow-up, suggesting the need for booster sessions during the first year of college.

- Two separate studies developed programs in which colleges worked closely with their surrounding communities, using measures such as increased police patrols in problem neighborhoods and raising student awareness of their responsibilities as community residents. The studies found reductions in heavy drinking and a decrease in the number of off-campus incidents involving students. One study was led by Mark D. Wood, PhD, of the University of Rhode Island, and the other by Robert F. Saltz, PhD, of the Pacific Institute for Research and Evaluation, working with two universities in Washington State.

- Another study found that colleges have made online alcohol-policy information more available and accessible to students, parents, and other interested parties. This shift may reflect a greater engagement of colleges and universities in the issue of drinking on campus in general, according to lead author Vivian B. Faden, PhD, acting director of NIAAA's Office of Science Policy and Communications.

A randomized clinical trial found that a popular online alcohol education product, AlcoholEdu for College, had beneficial short-term effects (during the first semester of college), lowering victimization and several of the most common alcohol-related problems.[38] This type of program had been thought of as promising, but this study presents actual persuasive evidence.

One of the first tangible products of U.S. health care reform, the Affordable Care Act of 2010, was the new National Prevention Strategy, which identifies drug abuse and excessive alcohol use as two of the top targets for prevention.[39] Particularly noteworthy are the clear emphasis on college drinking as an issue and the shift toward a broad environmental approach (including public policy changes).

WHAT MORE CAN COLLEGES DO?

In the past few years, the Obama administration has shifted emphasis away from a primarily criminal justice "war on crime" and taken a broader perspective on alcohol and drug use that includes greater use of the nation's health care assets. The 2011 National Drug Control Policy makes the following comments about college students:

> Underage drinking and substance use among college students threaten not only the present well-being of millions of students, but also our Nation's future capacity to maintain its leadership in the fiercely competitive global economy. Studies have shown that drinking and substance use are a significant problem on our Nation's college and university campuses. Nearly 4 million college students age 18 to 22 reported binge drinking in the past 30 days, and 20 percent reported past-month use of marijuana or other illegal drugs.
>
> While the problem is significant, use of SBIRT [screening, brief intervention, and referral to treatment] in campus health centers has shown promising results. Notably, a study funded by SAMHSA [Substance Abuse and Mental Health Services Administration] and conducted by the University at Albany–State University of New York found that SBIRT programs in campus health centers can help address college drinking. At a 6-week follow-up, students reported decreased alcohol use, more accurate perceptions of other students' drinking, and increased use of strategies to enhance self-esteem and self-worth. Results of the study also indicate that changes in alcohol use were positively correlated with changes in perceptions of drinking among peers. This year, the ONDCP [Office of National Drug Control Policy] in partnership with [the U.S. Department of] Education, will disseminate information on SBIRT to campus health centers and school administrators and provide university officials with screening tools and information on substance use that can be accessed on the schools' websites and in orientation materials by both parents and students.[40]

Dartmouth College's President Jim Kim, a noted expert in the use of public health to deal with third-world health problems such as tuberculosis and human immunodeficiency virus (HIV), founded the Learning Collaborative on High-Risk Drinking, a coalition of more than 30 colleges, many of them among the most elite in the country, to deal with alcohol problems.[41] But little has been heard in the past several years from the Amethyst Initiative, in which more than 130 colleges and universities called for a national discussion of whether the minimum drinking age should be changed. A *Yale Daily News* columnist urged Yale's president to take up the issue, noting that the Amethyst Initiative's statement had "all but died from public view."[42]

What more can colleges and universities do? Brandon Busteed, a social entrepreneur who created the largest online alcohol prevention program (AlcoholEdu for College), points out, "The three biggest problems in making environmental management work are a lack of leadership, financial support, and campus-level data to measure and chart progress. Leadership must come from the top: trustees, presidents, and vice presidents for student affairs."[43] With some notable exceptions, many college presidents and trustees simply haven't displayed the kind of leadership needed. Colleges are insured well enough to see the occasional lawsuit as a smaller cost than paying for adequate prevention services. For the most part, data collection about college drinking follows the familiar higher education reluctance to create solid measurement of outputs and outcomes.

Busteed points out that high-risk drinking rates have hardly changed overall but then notes success at a few schools of the thousand or so he visited. Frostburg State University reported a drop of 27 percent over ten years, and even notorious party schools such as Indiana, Pitt, and Arizona State reported one-year drops. Why?

> Although the tactics and strategies vary, common elements include strong campus-communication strategies, increased and consistent enforcement of campus alcohol policies and the legal drinking age, and mandatory education for all incoming students. More important, all of the universities made alcohol-abuse prevention an institution-wide priority, combining the influence of the president's office and all relevant campus groups through task forces. . . . The successful institutions have held themselves accountable . . . tracked their progress . . . and shaped strategic plans for reducing high-risk drinking by establishing definable goals, both annual and long-term, and examining systematic changes to residence life configurations and social spaces on their campus.[44]

STUDENTS AND PARENTS

The most recent NIAAA bulletin on college drinking makes an intriguing point: "An often overlooked preventive factor involves the continuing influence of parents. Research shows that students who choose not to drink often do so because their parents discussed alcohol use and its adverse consequences with them."[45] Evidence suggests that parents could play a significant though indirect role in college drinking prevention.[46]

Appendix D of this revised edition of *College Drinking* presents updated data on crime and alcohol violations at hundreds of selected institutions of higher education in this country. A U.S. Department of Education website called College Navigator (http://nces.ed.gov/collegenavigator/) provides these data for thousands of institutions. Prospective students and their parents can use this information to ask pointed questions of a college or university before admission. Learning about the presence of major risk factors—big-time athletic programs, residential fraternities, large numbers of alcohol outlets surrounding the campus—may also help.

CHANGING THE CULTURE

The major argument of this book is that college drinking has been reframed from a harmless rite of passage to arguably the major public health problem facing college students. The most recent data show that there has been little or no decline in college drinking rates for decades. Concern (as indexed by newspaper stories) has risen. Most colleges do something, but clearly it is not enough. Yet we know more about what is effective and why. A series of interventions (in some combination yet to be fully mapped) will help to change the culture.

Changing the culture of student drinking requires changing the organizational culture of the American college or university. What has been locked in a silo, as one of many student affairs issues, has to be reexamined as a problem for the university and its community. Universities have to be partners with their communities, and both would benefit greatly from more vigorous leadership by their states. Many college and university campuses have almost become gated communities, isolated from the concerns of surrounding neighborhoods. Effective public health practice may require thinking that goes beyond the campus.[47]

College and university problems are interconnected. Binge drinking, sexual assault, and campus crime all arise as individual problems, and many of the practitioners, administrators, researchers, and student activists attempt to deal with them individually, without always seeing the connections. But the limits of this one-by-one approach are apparent. Douglas Fierberg, an attorney experienced in litigation about one campus life problem, recently wrote an essay whose title makes this clear: "To End Fraternity Hazing, End Boozing First."[48] One could make the same argument about rape, since among the one in 20 women who have been raped, more than 70 percent report that they were not able to give consent because they were intoxicated. Prevention programs proliferate, but they often ignore or downplay the role of alcohol.[49]

Changing the culture also means changing the material culture, that is, the availability and price of alcohol in the campus community. States could do much more to bring into balance the modest taxes placed on alcohol products with the costs of the extensive set of state programs, from health to criminal justice, that address alcohol-related problems. Environmental change should include much more attention to the social availability of alcohol in college communities.

A recent national summit meeting, "Proceeding in Partnership: The Future of Campus Safety," presented ideas that can help change the culture. The

conference was held at Lehigh University, the site of the tragic rape and murder of Jeanne Clery, which led to important reforms in higher education. The
co-sponsor with Lehigh was the Clery Center for Security on Campus, Inc.,
a nonprofit foundation that promotes campus safety. (Disclosure: I am on the
Clery Center's board of directors, was a panelist, and am the co-editor of the
conference proceedings, which are available online.)[50]

Many ideas emerged at the conference. That Lehigh and the Clery Center
could collaborate confirmed that universities and their sometime critics can work
together for better campus safety. Several panels brought together campus presidents, activists, practitioners, administrators, and researchers, all attempting to
get past the silo mentality that has been a barrier to collaboration in the past.

The keynote speaker, Robert Carothers, told a story of how he became president of the University of Rhode Island (URI) and then changed its culture.
He believes that the documented change in a flagship state university such as
URI is a powerful argument for that type of change being possible almost
anywhere. But it took determined and persistent presidential leadership at a
truly impressive and, one must say, relatively rare level to effect that change.
Many colleges and universities give much less attention to the issue than is
necessary to change both student and organizational cultures. The pressures
toward the corporate university may even lead away from concern about the
individual student.[51] At least one person in the audience at Lehigh was re-
minded of the words of an American poet who claimed that a university was a
college that has forgotten its students.

Carothers became president of the University of Rhode Island in 1991. URI
was a classic party school back then and won "best party school" honors from
the *Princeton Review* in both 1993 and 1994. More importantly, it was perceived as such by New England teens, who often pronounced its initials as
"You Are High." A flagship state university in a heavy-drinking state, URI was
ringed by fraternities, sororities, liquor outlets, and nearby summer beach
houses rented to undergraduates. Carothers told a tale of a new president,
alarmed at the level of partying and binge drinking, who then took steps to
address the issue. What he did, how long and persistently, and with what resistance, is noteworthy.

Many opposed Carothers's efforts, beginning with the students who felt
threatened by his attempts at enforcing norms fairly across the campus. Not
only the Greeks but also other elements of the student body had a stake in
the old ways of heavy drinking. Landlords stood to lose if heavy alcohol use
was changed in the nearby beach houses they rented. Young alumni couldn't
bear to lose a storied world at football tailgates. Attendance dropped at Home-
coming. But Carothers persisted.

Some of the resistance was predictable. But some was surprising. Why, for example, would the campus police be anything but supportive of efforts to enforce laws and norms about excessive drinking? It turned out that many police were collecting significant overtime from policing potentially disruptive campus events and simply didn't want their pay diminished by better student behavior. Neighbors were fearful that a URI crackdown would push the problem out into their communities. But the URI-sponsored Narragansett Coalition found that didn't happen. Carothers observed, "There was a lot of abuse out there, but it didn't get any greater and didn't get any less."

A key obstacle to progress is often working with the community. Colleges have plenty of experience working with students, and that in part explains why efforts such as social norming are so popular (even if often ineffective). It's quite another matter to engage with a broader community, when years if not decades of mutual suspicion and distrust may make interactions go less smoothly. Yet another problem is how long it may take to change the culture. Discussions of college drinking usually assume a series of short-term programs will somehow change patterns of behavior that have been established for years.

Carothers also pointed out some organizational challenges. The lines of authority within the university may complicate a response. Public safety personnel often take different tacks than do student health and wellness staff. Student preferences for off-campus and largely unmonitored residences may be at odds with university efforts to provide on-campus and supervised living quarters. Sometimes only the president can knit these concerns together and lead a unified response.

In sum, a vigorous effort to change the culture may step on many toes and generate much resistance within colleges and the surrounding community. The effort may also chafe against staff who would be quite happy to continue their daily work in familiar and unchallenging ways. Cultural change might disrupt the kind of conflict-free life many seek.

College drinking persists unchanged on many campuses not just because personal behavior is hard to change. On some campuses, party-centered heavy drinking reflects and sustains a special kind of culture.[52] College drinking is also supported and shaped by a specialized community experience that contemporary universities foster, even if not fully intentionally. Changing that culture is probably not possible without a vigorous change in the organizational culture of the university, supported and led by its president.

In retrospect, it is hard to avoid the conclusion that the discourse about the culture of college drinking underestimated how hard it would be for presidents to get engaged on this issue and then make headway in the face of resistance. The economic challenges of the past few years make the university even more difficult to manage. State-funded flagships have had severe funding challenges; at the other end of the scale, even elite liberal arts colleges face an uncertain future. Few presidents take up the challenge, but Carothers's efforts at URI shows that it is possible.[53]

Finally, changing the culture of college drinking requires a shift in the awareness of the role alcohol plays in college life.[54] Many of the student life and academic problems of college students are shaped by alcohol, so we need a better sense of how many of these are "alcohol-attributable." Campus newspapers, for example, often fail to contextualize reports of campus crime or victimization, scrubbing any mention of alcohol use in a way that may lessen understanding of its role. College officials prefer to "dodge a bullet" by keeping the details of problems from public scrutiny, but they are passing up a chance to teach valuable lessons. Almost two decades ago, it was accurate to say that many colleges were in denial about alcohol. Today, the trivialization or "casualization" (to use Peggy Reeves Sanday's term) of college troubles often disguises the important and often decisive role alcohol plays in the underside of college life.[55]

CONCLUSION

Remember that image of John Belushi as Bluto in *Animal House*? He personified the binge drinker as carefree and happy, destined ultimately to become the 43rd president of the United States.[56] In 2013, as the evidence about the harm of binge drinking continues to accumulate, the cultural image persists. A new Broadway musical called *Animal House* is in preparation.

Has anything changed?

Higher education has begun to transform rapidly, and some observers think even more dramatic modifications are on the horizon. One estimate is that 10 percent of college students today have already taken a course online. Even elite institutions such as Stanford have begun to invest in large-scale online education, and what was once a well-bounded campus now spans "two counties, three Zip Codes, and six government jurisdictions." Stanford's president is now on sabbatical, looking for an opportunity to think, with distance learning topping his list of topics. "Stanford, like newspapers and music companies and much of traditional media a little more than a decade ago, is sailing in seemingly placid waters. But Hennessy's digital experience alerts him to danger. He says, 'There's a tsunami coming.'"[57] Some institutions, such as New York University (NYU), have deemed themselves global campuses. On a recent visit to Abu Dhabi in the United Arab Emirates, I saw a large building sporting the familiar NYU violet, with student and faculty housing nearby in a high-rise. What constitutes a campus, a college community, or a university town is being transformed, and so are the ways of life of undergraduates. These changes will reshape college drinking.

When choosing the title of this book, I weighed whether I should follow the 1953 classic study *Drinking in College*, emphasizing that young American college students are more like their noncollege peers than not. I chose *College Drinking* instead to emphasize how college students had somewhat distinctive drinking patterns and that these had been reframed, not as harmless rites of passage, but as major public health problems.

This afterword has taken note of several developments in that reframing. Institutions such as URI and the vigorous efforts of practitioners and researchers have produced a fascinating body of evidence that suggests the culture of college drinking can be changed, at least under some circumstances and with considerable effort and effective leadership. Whether the culture is changed at a single campus or across the country is, to some degree, a decision. Like states and communities, colleges to some extent choose their own rates of drinking, but they don't choose them just as they please; organizational and student cultures shape those rates, and in turn, they shape the contemporary university.

NOTES

1. Goldman, Boyd, & Faden (2002); Hingson, Heeren, Zakocs, Kopstein, & Wechsler (2002).

2. NIAAA (2012).

3. Association of Governing Boards (2011).

4. Another way of assessing how college drinking fared as an issue on the higher education agenda is to note its absence from any of the following recent writings about higher education problems: *Measuring Up: The National Report Card on Higher Education* (2008); *A Test of Leadership: Charting the Future of U.S. Higher Education* (Spellings Report) (2006); William Bowen, *Crossing the Finish Line: Completing College at America's Public Universities* (2009); *Chronicle of Higher Education Almanac* (2012); Derek Bok, *Our Underachieving Colleges* (2006); Robert Zemsky, *Making Reform Work: The Case for Transforming American Higher Education* (2009).

5. http://www.yaledailynews.com/news/2010/oct/15/dke-apologizes-for-pledge-chants, accessed April 30, 2012.

6. Reitman (2012).

7. http://thedartmouth.com/2012/03/29/news/rollingstone, accessed April 3, 2012.

8. Naimi, Brewer, Mokdad, Denny, Serdula, & Marks (2003).

9. http://www.cdc.gov/alcohol/fact-sheets/binge-drinking.htm, accessed April 9, 2012; http://www.cdc.gov/vitalsigns/BingeDrinking/index.html, accessed April 9, 2012.

10. E.g., Martinic & Measham (2008).

11. Anderson & Baumberg (2006); Smith & Foxcroft (2009); Secretary of State for the Home Department (2012); World Health Organization (2011).

12. Hingson, Zha, & Weitzman (2009).

13. Substance Abuse and Mental Health Services Administration (2011). For data on trends in college versus noncollege binge drinking, see the following table: http://www.samhsa.gov/data/NSDUH/2k10NSDUH/2k10Results.htm #3.1.6, accessed June 8, 2012.

14. Grucza, Norberg, & Bierut (2009).

15. http://www.collegedrinkingprevention.gov/Stats/Summaries/snapshot .aspx, accessed January 25, 2012; see also NIAAA (2012).

16. Vander Ven (2011).

17. Arum & Roska (2011).

18. Sloan & Fisher (2011); Reitman (2012).

19. Vander Ven (2011).

20. http://www.amazon.com/Getting-Wasted-College-Students-Drink/dp/0814788327, accessed April 30, 2012.

21. NIAAA (2012).

22. http://ope.ed.gov/security/index.aspx, accessed January 31, 2012.

23. Dowdall (in press, The role of alcohol abuse).

24. Katel (2011).

25. Wolitzky-Taylor, Resnick, Armstadter, McCauley, Ruggiero, & Kilpatrick (2011).

26. For a more extensive discussion of these issues, see Dowdall (in press, Campus crime).

27. Nelson, Xuan, Lee, Weitzman, & Wechsler (2009).

28. Ali (2011).

29. Dowdall (in press, Campus crime); Dowdall (in press, The role of alcohol abuse).

30. Brand, Saisana, Rynn, Pennoni, & Lowenfels (2007); Paschall, Grube, & Kypri (2009).

31. Friese & Grube (n.d.).

32. Babor (2010: 242).

33. NIAAA (2012).

34. Lenk, Erickson, Nelson, Winters, & Toomey (2012).

35. Quoted in Tuchman (2009: 5).

36. Nelson, Toomey, Lenk, Erickson, & Winters (2010).

37. For a summary, see http://www.nih.gov/news/health/jun2009/niaaa-15 .htm, accessed April 10, 2012.

38. Paschall, Antin, Ringwalt, & Saltz (2011).

39. Executive Office of the President (2011).

40. Executive Office of the President (2011: 28).

41. See http://now.dartmouth.edu/2011/06/high-risk-drinking-collabo rative-begins-work-with-32-member-schools/, accessed April 30, 2012; for the collaborative's website, see http://www.nchip.org/, accessed April 30, 2012.

42. http://www.yaledailynews.com/news/2012/feb/27/zelinsky-levin -should-influence-the-drinking-age/, accessed April 30, 2012.

43. Busteed (2008).

44. Busteed (2010).

45. NIAAA (2012).

46. Abar & Turrisi (2008).

47. For an extensive discussion of this point, see http://www.countyhealth rankings.org, accessed March 14, 2012.

48. Fierberg (2012).

49. Fogg (2009).

50. Kiss & Dowdall (2012).

51. Tuchman (2009).

52. Vander Ven (2011).

53. It is instructive to compare URI with another New England flagship ("Wannabe U.," probably University of Connecticut) that underwent extensive institutional change with hardly a mention of the issue of college drinking; see Tuchman (2009).

54. Wechsler & Nelson (2008)

55. Sanday (2007).

56. Miller (2007).

57. Auletta (2012).

REFERENCES FOR AFTERWORD: 2013

Abar, C., & Turrisi, R. (2008). How important are parents during the college years? A longitudinal perspective of indirect influences parents yield on the college teens' alcohol use. *Addictive behaviors*, 33(10), 1360–1368.

Ali, R. (2011). *"Dear Colleague" letter on Title IX compliance*. Washington, DC: U.S. Department of Education.

Anderson, P., & Baumberg, B. (2006). *Alcohol in Europe: a public health perspective. A report for the European Commission*. London: Institute for Alcohol Studies.

Arum, R., & Roska, J. (2011). *Academically adrift: limited learning on college campuses.* Chicago: University of Chicago Press.

Association of Governing Boards of Universities and Colleges. (2011). *Top public policy issues for higher education in 2011 and 2012.* Washington, DC: Association of Governing Boards of Universities and Colleges.

Auletta, K. (2012). Get Rich U.: there are no walls between Stanford and Silicon Valley. Should there be? *New Yorker*, April 30, 2012, 38–47.

Babor, T. (2010). *Alcohol: no ordinary commodity: research and public policy* (2nd ed.). New York: Oxford University Press.

Brand, D. A., Saisana, M., Rynn, L. A., Pennoni, F., & Lowenfels, A. B. (2007). Comparative analysis of alcohol control policies in 30 countries. *PLoS medicine*, 4(4), e151.

Busteed, B. (2008). The mistake colleges make about student drinking. *The Chronicle of Higher Education*, May 2.

Busteed, B. (2010). Is high-risk drinking at college on the way out? *The Chronicle of Higher Education*, March 10.

Dowdall, G. W. (in press). Campus crime. In Miller, S., Gover, A., & Renzetti R., eds., *Routledge handbook of gender and crime studies.* New York: Routledge.

Dowdall, G. W. (in press). The role of alcohol abuse in campus crime victimization. In Sloan, J., & Fisher, B., eds., *Campus crime* (3rd ed.). Springfield, IL: Charles C. Thomas.

Executive Office of the President. (2011). *National Drug Control Strategy.* Washington, DC: Executive Office of the President.

Fierberg, D. (2012). To end fraternity hazing, end boozing first. *The Chronicle of Higher Education*, April 29.

Fogg, P. (2009). Rape-prevention programs proliferate, but "It's hard to know" whether they work. *The Chronicle of Higher Education*, November 15.

Friese, B., & Grube, J. W. (n.d.) *Youth drinking rates and problems: a comparison of European countries and the United States.* Berkeley, CA: Prevention Research Center.

Goldman, M. S., Boyd, G. M., & Faden, V. (2002). College drinking, what it is, and what to do about it: a review of the state of the science. *Journal of Studies on Alcohol*, (14).

Grucza, R. A., Norberg, K. E., & Bierut, L. J. (2009). Binge drinking among youths and young adults in the United States: 1979–2006. *Journal of the American Academy of Child and Adolescent Psychiatry*, 48(7), 692–702.

Hingson, R. W., Heeren, T., Zakocs, R. C., Kopstein, A., & Wechsler, H. (2002). Magnitude of alcohol-related mortality and morbidity among US college students ages 18–24. *Journal of Studies on Alcohol*, 63(2), 136–144.

Hingson, R. W., Zha, W., & Weitzman, E. R. (2009). Magnitude of and trends in alcohol-related mortality and morbidity among U.S. college students ages 18–24, 1998–2005. *Journal of studies on alcohol and drugs. Supplement*, (16), 12–20.

Katel, P. (2011). Crime on campus: Are colleges doing enough to keep students safe? *CQ Researcher*, 21(5), 97–120.

Kiss, A., & Dowdall, G., eds. (2012). *Proceeding in partnership: the future of campus safety.* Wayne, PA: Security on Campus, Inc.

Lenk, L. M., Erickson, D. J., Nelson, T. F., Winters, K. C., & Toomey, T. (2012). Alcohol policies and practices among four-year colleges in the United States: prevalence and patterns. *Journal of Studies on Alcohol and Drugs,* 73(3), 361–367.

Miller, C. (2007). *The National Lampoon's* Animal House *book.* Los Angeles: National Lampoon Press.

Naimi, T. S., Brewer, R. D., Mokdad, A., Denny, C., Serdula, M. K., & Marks, J. S. (2003). Binge drinking among US adults. *Journal of the American Medical Association,* 289(1), 70.

National Institute on Alcohol Abuse and Alcoholism. (2012). *College drinking.* Bethesda, MD: NIAAA.

Nelson, T. F., Toomey, T. L., Lenk, K. M., Erickson, D. J., & Winters, K. C. (2010). Implementation of NIAAA College Drinking Task Force recommendations: how are colleges doing 6 years later? *Alcoholism: Clinical and Experimental Research,* 34(10), 1687–1693.

Nelson, T. F., Xuan, Z., Lee, H., Weitzman, E. R., & Wechsler, H. (2009). Persistence of heavy drinking and ensuing consequences at heavy drinking colleges. *Journal of Studies on Alcohol and Drugs,* 70(5), 726–734.

Paschall, M. J., Antin, T., Ringwalt, C., & Saltz, R. F. (2011). Effects of AlcoholEdu for College on alcohol-related problems among freshmen: a randomized multicampus trial. *Journal of Studies on Alcohol and Drugs,* 72, 642–650.

Paschall, M. J., Grube, J. W., & Kypri, K. (2009). Alcohol control policies and alcohol consumption by youth: a multi-national study. *Addiction,* 104, 1849–1855.

Reitman, J. (2012). Confessions of an ivy league frat boy: inside Dartmouth's hazing abuses. *Rolling Stone,* March 28.

Sanday, P. (2007). *Fraternity gang rape: sex, brotherhood, and privilege on campus* (2nd ed.). New York: New York University Press.

Secretary of State for the Home Government. (2012). *The government's alcohol strategy.* London: Her Majesty's Government.

Smith, L., & Foxcroft, D. (2009). *Drinking in the UK: an exploration of trends.* London: Joseph Rowntree Foundation.

Substance Abuse and Mental Health Services Administration. (2011). *Results from the 2010 National Survey on Drug Use and Health: summary of national findings,* NSDUH Series H-41, HHS Publication No. (SMA) 11-4658. Rockville, MD: Substance Abuse and Mental Health Services Administration.

Tuchman, G. (2009). *Wannabe U: inside the corporate university.* Chicago: University of Chicago Press.

Vander Ven, T. (2011). *Getting wasted: why college students drink too much and party so hard.* New York: New York University Press.

Wechsler, H., & Nelson, T. F. (2008). What we have learned from the Harvard School of Public Health College Alcohol Study: focusing attention on college student alcohol consumption and the environmental conditions that promote it. *Journal of Studies on Alcohol and Drugs,* 69(4), 481–490.

Wolitzky-Taylor, K. B., Resnick, H. S., Armstadter, A. B., McCauley, J. L., Ruggiero, K. J., & Kilpatrick, D. G. (2011). Reporting rape in a national sample of college women. *Journal of American College Health*, 59(7), 582–587.

World Health Organization. (2011). *Global status report on alcohol and health*. Geneva: World Health Organization.

APPENDIX A

Sources for Further Information

A Matter of Degree
(http://www.ama-assn.org/special/aos/alcohol1/aboutus.htm)
The American Medical Association's innovative program is designed to reduce binge drinking on college campuses. The evaluation of AMOD is discussed on a separate Web site (http://www.hsph.harvard.edu/amod/).

Alcohol and Drug Abuse Institute, University of Washington
(http://depts.washington.edu/adai/)
This comprehensive site about research on alcohol and drugs features a library with links to more than 600 research organizations.

Alcohol Epidemiology Program, University of Minnesota
(http://epihub.epi.unm.edu/alcohol/default.htp)
This site provides research about the causes and correlates of alcohol.

Alcohol Policies Project, Center for Science in the Public Interest
(http://www.cspinet.org/booze/index.html)
This site offers information about public policy issues involving alcohol.

Alcohol Policy Information System, National Institute on Alcohol Abuse and Alcoholism
(http://www.alcoholpolicy.niaaa.nih.gov/)

This site provides data and analyses about both federal and state alcohol policies and their effects.

Alcohol Research Center
(http://www.arg.org/)
This independent center is dedicated to research about alcohol.

Alcohol Screening
(http://www.alcoholscreening.org/)
This site provides anonymous screening for alcohol problems.

Alcoholics Anonymous (AA)
(http://www.alcoholics-anonymous.org)
The most important self-help group established this Web site, which includes information about how to find an AA meeting for a particular town or city. The Web site includes the full text of the "Big Book" about AA.

American College Health Association
(http://www.acha.org/)
This higher education professional organization is devoted to health issues.

American College Personnel Association
(http://www.myacpa.org/)
This higher education professional association is dedicated to student affairs professionals.

Association of Recovery Schools
(http://www.recoveryschools.org/)
This site provides information about colleges and universities with special programs for students in recovery.

The BACCHUS Network
(http://www.bacchusgamma.org/)
This network of students and higher education staff is dedicated to comprehensive prevention and safety through peer education.

Center for Substance Abuse Prevention (CSAP) (http://prevention.samhsa.gov/)
"CSAP works with states and communities to develop comprehensive prevention systems that create healthy communities in which people enjoy a

quality life. This includes supportive work and school environments, drug- and crime-free neighborhoods, and positive connections with friends and family."

Center for Substance Abuse Treatment
(http://csat.samhsa.gov/)
This government-sponsored site "promotes the quality and availability of community-based substance abuse treatment services for individuals and families."

Center on Alcohol Marketing and Youth (CAMY)
(http://camy.org/)
Located at Georgetown University, CAMY studies the marketing of alcohol to young people.

Century Council
(http://www.centurycouncil.org)
A nonprofit organization funded by leading distillers, the Century Council is dedicated to fighting drunk driving and underage drinking.

Choose Responsibility
(http://www.chooseresponsibility.org)
"CHOOSE RESPONSIBILITY is a nonprofit organization founded to stimulate informed and dispassionate public discussion about the presence of alcohol in American culture and to consider policies that will effectively empower young adults age 18 to 20 to make mature decisions about the place of alcohol in their own lives."

College Drinking Prevention
(http://www.collegedrinkingprevention.gov/)
Original documents and publications of the landmark 2002 Task Force on College Drinking are found on this Web site. The original Task Force Report ("A Call to Action: Changing the Culture of Drinking on College Campuses") and the special supplement to the *Journal of Studies on Alcohol* with important reviews of the literature are included. The site has special sections for students, college presidents, parents, and other groups.

College Parents of America
(http://www.collegeparents.org)
"College Parents of America is the only national membership association dedicated to advocating and to serving on behalf of current and future college parents."

Community Anti Drug Coalitions of America (CADCA)

(http://cadca.org/)

CADCA's mission is "to strengthen the capacity of community coalitions to create and maintain safe, healthy and drug-free communities. CADCA supports its members with training and technical assistance, public policy advocacy, media strategies and marketing programs, conferences and special events."

The Community of Concern

(http://www.thecommunityofconcern.org/)

"Through our booklet, *A Parent's Guide for the Prevention of Alcohol, Tobacco and Other Drug Use*, parents, students, schools and other organizations have joined together to form the Community of Concern. Our mission is to educate parents and build partnerships so that we may coordinate our efforts to keep our children alcohol, tobacco and other drug free."

Core Institute

(http://www.siu.edu/~coreinst/)

"Core Institute is the leading research, assessment and development organization serving alcohol and drug prevention programs across the nation."

DrugStrategies

(http://www.drugstrategies.org)

"A nonprofit research institute that promotes more effective approaches to the nation's drug problems."

Go Ask Alice!

(http://www.goaskalice.columbia.edu/)

This site is offered by Columbia University's Health Services and deserves to be visited by any college student who wants factual and down-to-earth answers to personal health questions. The site features 40 questions and answers about alcohol alone, plus many other health topics of interest to college students.

Harvard School of Public Health College Alcohol Study

(http://www.hsph.harvard.edu/cas/)

This Web site lists the more than 80 papers and other publications of the College Alcohol Study, as well as biographical information about its director Henry Wechsler.

Higher Education Center for Alcohol and Other Drug Abuse and Violence Prevention
(http: www.edc.org/hec)
"The Higher Education Center's purpose is to help college and community leaders develop, implement, and evaluate programs and policies to reduce student problems related to alcohol and other drug use and interpersonal violence." The center is funded by the U.S. Department of Education and is a component of the Educational Development Center, a nonprofit organization.

Inter-Association Task Force on Alcohol and Other Substance Abuse Issues
(http://www.iatf.org)
This coalition of higher education and other groups seeks to advance substance abuse prevention and sponsors the National Collegiate Alcohol Awareness Week.

Join Together
(http://www.jointogether.org)
Join Together is "the nation's leading provider of information, strategic planning assistance, and leadership development for community-based efforts to advance effective alcohol and drug policy, prevention, and treatment."

Marin Institute
(http://www.marininstitute.org/)
"The Marin Institute fights to protect the public from the impact of the alcohol industry's negative practices. We monitor and expose the alcohol industry's harmful actions related to products, promotions and social influence, and support communities in their efforts to reject these damaging activities."

Monitoring the Future Study
(http://www.monitoringthefuture.org)
"Monitoring the Future is an ongoing study of the behaviors, attitudes, and values of American secondary school students, college students, and young adults."

Mothers Against Drunk Driving (MADD)
(http://www.madd.org/)
"The mission of MADD is to stop drunk driving, support the victims of this violent crime and prevent underage drinking."

MVParents.com
(http://mvparents.com/)
This Web site provides ideas for parents to strengthen development through the teen years; it is partly sponsored by the Coors Brewing Company.

National Alcohol Screening Day
(http://www.mentalhealthscreening.org/events/nasd/)
"National Alcohol Screening Day (NASD) is an annual event that provides information about alcohol and health as well as free, anonymous screening for alcohol use problems."

National Association of Student Personnel Administrators (http://www.naspa.org)
This organization supports professionals in higher education student affairs, such as vice presidents for student life or deans of students.

National Center on Addiction and Substance Abuse at Columbia University
(http://www.casacolumbia.org/)
"The National Center on Addiction and Substance Abuse (CASA) at Columbia University is the only nation-wide organization that brings together under one roof all the professional disciplines needed to study and combat abuse of all substances—alcohol, nicotine as well as illegal, prescription and performance enhancing drugs—in all sectors of society."

National Clearinghouse for Alcohol and Drug Information
(http://ncadi.samhsa.gov/)
The Substance Abuse and Mental Health Administration's National Clearinghouse for Alcohol and Drug Information.

National Council on Alcoholism and Drug Dependence (NCADD)
(http://www.ncadd.org/)
"Founded in 1944 by Mrs. Marty Mann, a pioneer in the alcoholism field, the National Council on Alcoholism and Drug Dependence, Inc. (NCADD) provides education, information, help, and hope to the public."

National Institute on Alcohol Abuse and Alcoholism
(http://www.niaaa.nih.gov/)
The Web site of the premier federal research agency on alcohol, the site contains a rich collection of short bulletins (Alcohol Alerts) as well as lengthy documents.

National Institute on Drug Abuse (NIDA)
(http://www.nida.nih.gov/)
"NIDA's mission is to lead the Nation in bringing the power of science to bear on drug abuse and addiction. This charge has two critical components. The first is the strategic support and conduct of research across a broad range of disciplines. The second is ensuring the rapid and effective dissemination and use of the results of that research to significantly improve prevention, treatment and policy as it relates to drug abuse, and addiction."

National Social Norms Resource Center (NSNRC)
(http://www.socialnorm.org/)
"The NSNRC is an independent center that supports, promotes and provides technical assistance in the application of the social norms approach to a broad range of health, safety and social justice issues, including alcohol-related risk-reduction and the prevention of tobacco abuse."

The Network Addressing Collegiate Alcohol and Other Drug Issues
(http://www.thenetwork.ws/)
"Begun in 1987 by U.S. Department of Education, the Network is a voluntary membership organization whose member institutions agree to work toward a set of standards aimed at reducing alcohol and other drug problems at colleges and universities. It now has approximately 1,600 members nationwide."

Office of National Drug Control Policy (ONDCP)
(http://www.whitehousedrugpolicy.gov/)
"The principal purpose of ONDCP is to establish policies, priorities, and objectives for the Nation's drug control program. The goals of the program are to reduce illicit drug use, manufacturing and trafficking, drug-related crime and violence, and drug-related health consequences."

One in Four
(http://www.oneinfourusa.org/).
One in Four, Inc. is a "501 (c) 3 non-profit organization dedicated to prevent rape by the thoughtful application of theory and research to rape prevention programming. One in Four provides presentations, training, and technical assistance to men and women, with a focus on all-male programming targeted toward colleges, high schools, the military, and local community organizations."

Our Bodies, Ourselves

(http://ourbodiesourselves.org)

"Our Bodies Ourselves (OBOS), also known as the Boston Women's Health Book Collective (BWHBC), is a nonprofit, public interest women's health education, advocacy, and consulting organization." OBOS publishes the premier women's self-help book that includes a chapter on mind-altering substances such as alcohol.

Outside the Classroom, Inc.

(http://www.outsidetheclassroom.com/)

"Outside the Classroom is a Boston-based company that was founded to address epidemic-level public health issues affecting education, corporate, and government institutions. The company's mission is to deliver tangible results to its customers by providing measurable reductions in the negative consequences associated with these health issues. In an effort to deliver on this promise, Outside the Classroom has remained focused on one of the largest of these problems: high-risk drinking."

Pacific Institute for Research and Evaluation

(http://www.pire.org/)

"Pacific Institute for Research and Evaluation (PIRE) is one of the nation's preeminent independent, nonprofit organizations focusing on individual and social problems associated with the use of alcohol and other drugs."

Partnership for a Drug-Free America

(http://www.drugfree.org/)

"The Partnership for a Drug-Free America is a nonprofit organization uniting communications professionals, renowned scientists, and parents. Best known for its national drug-education campaign, the Partnership's mission is to reduce illicit drug use in America."

Project Cork

(http://www.projectcork.org/)

"Cork's mission is to assemble and disseminate current, authoritative information on substance abuse for clinicians, health care providers, human service personnel, and policy makers. Project Cork produces a bibliographic database, offers current awareness services, produces resource materials, responds to queries, and collaborates in professional education efforts."

Promising Practices: Campus Alcohol Strategies

(http://www.promprac.gmu.edu/)

"Promising Practices: *Campus Alcohol Strategies* strives to contribute to reducing alcohol-related problems among college and university students by motivating institutions of higher education to share their resources and strategies. Resulting from national solicitations, the project's *Sourcebook* incorporates a wide range of strategies designed to assist campuses in their efforts to prevent or reduce alcohol-related problems."

Rutgers University Center of Alcohol Studies

(http://alcoholstudies.rutgers.edu/)

"The Center of Alcohol Studies (CAS) is a multidisciplinary institute dedicated to acquisition and dissemination of knowledge on psychoactive substance use and related phenomena with primary emphasis on alcohol use and consequences."

Security on Campus, Inc.

(http://www.securityoncampus.org/)

"Security on Campus, Inc. is a unique 501(c)(3) non-profit grass roots organization dedicated to safe campuses for college and university students. It was co-founded in 1987 by Connie [and] Howard Clery, following the murder of their daughter at Lehigh University."

Students Against Destructive Decisions (SADD)

(http://www.sadd.org/)

"SADD's mission simply stated: To provide students with the best prevention and intervention tools possible to deal with the issues of underage drinking, other drug use, impaired driving, and other destructive decisions."

Substance Abuse and Mental Health Services Administration

(http://www.samhsa.gov/)

This federal agency Web site lists a wide variety of helpful material about the treatment of substance abuse. It includes a toll-free number that a person can call in a crisis, and a way to locate treatment facilities for substance abuse.

U.S. Department of Education Office of Postsecondary Education Campus Security Statistics Search Page

(http://www.ope.ed.gov/security/Search.asp)

This site provides data from the Clery Act about crime on thousands of individual college campuses.

U.S. Department of Education Office of Safe and Drug-Free Schools

(http://www.ed.gov/about/offices/list/osdfs/index.html)

This federal agency administers programs designed to keep colleges and schools drug free.

Underage Drinking Enforcement Training Center

(http://www.udetc.org/)

"The Underage Drinking Enforcement Training Center was established by the Office of Juvenile Justice and Delinquency Prevention (within the U.S. Department of Justice) to support its Enforcing Underage Drinking Laws Program."

Washington Higher Education Secretariat (WHES)

(http: //www.whes.org)

Most of the major higher education associations in the United States are members of WHES.

Why 21?

(http://why21.org/)

This coalition of organizations such as MADD supports the current minimum drinking age laws.

APPENDIX B

Methods and Data

This book is an assessment of how American higher education deals with its most persistent social problem.[1] The book's methodology comes close to what some call an "institutional ethnography."[2] Understanding higher education as an institution can be made a great deal easier by regularly reading two of its leading general newspapers, *The Chronicle of Higher Education* and *Inside Higher Education* (I also read each paper's headlines on a daily basis). I came to appreciate how extensive and probing the coverage of college drinking (let alone other issues in higher education) was in the pages of *The New York Times*.

In addition to the sources cited in the notes, this book was based on interviews with the following people (whom I cannot thank enough for their willingness to participate). In the end, I decided to forego extensive direct quotes that would have made the book richer but much longer, but the interviews were invaluable in shaping my understanding of college drinking.

- Catherine Bath, Security on Campus
- Kathleen Bogle, La Salle University
- Joan Bradley, Saint Joseph's University
- Brian Busteed, Outside the Classroom, Inc.
- S. Daniel Carter, Security on Campus, Inc.
- Ralph Castro, Stanford University
- Robert Chapman, Drexel University
- Tom Colthurst, Higher Education Center
- Charles Currie, SJ, Association of Jesuit Colleges and Universities
- Laurie Davidson, Higher Education Center

- William DeJong, Boston University
- Beth DiRicco, Higher Education Center
- Fred Donodeo, National Institute on Alcohol Abuse and Alcoholism
- Jean Dowdall, Witt Kieffer Inc.
- Gwen Dungy, National Association of Student Personnel Administrators
- Vivian Faden, National Institute on Alcohol Abuse and Alcoholism
- Debbie Fickler, Saint Joseph's University
- Kaye Fillmore, School of Nursing, University of California San Francisco
- George Hacker, Center for Science in the Public Interest
- Ralph Hingson, National Institute on Alcohol Abuse and Alcoholism
- Stephanie Ives, University of Pennsylvania
- Maria Kefalas, Saint Joseph's University
- Joseph LaBrie, SJ, Loyola Marymount University
- Ting-Kai Li, M.D., National Institute on Alcohol Abuse and Alcoholism
- Richard Lucey, U.S. Department of Education
- Richard Malloy, SJ, Saint Joseph's University
- Joseph McShane, SJ, Fordham University
- Kathleen McSharry, Brown University
- Patrick Meehan, United States Attorney for the Eastern District of Pennsylvania
- Andrea Mitchell, Alcohol Research Group
- Jeanne H. Neff, The Sage Colleges
- Joseph Powell, Commonwealth of Pennsylvania Bureau of Drug and Alcohol Programs
- Christopher Rodgers, Fordham University
- Maureen Rush, University of Pennsylvania
- Barbara Ryan, Higher Education Center
- Robert Saltz, Alcohol Research Group
- James Sandoval, University of California Riverside
- Ginger Mackay-Smith, Higher Education Center
- Sheldon Steinbach, American Council on Education
- Robert Straus, University of Kentucky
- Pat Swinton, University of Southern California
- Sue Thau, Community Anti-Drug Coalitions of America
- Jan Walbert, Arcadia University, and National Association of Student Personnel Administrators

- Henry Wechsler, Harvard School of Public Health
- Elissa Weitzman, Harvard Medical School

I've also learned a great deal from informal conversations with practitioners or administrators on different campuses that I visited, including the following:

- Boston College
- Brown University
- Buffalo State College
- Canisius College
- College of the Holy Cross
- Fordham University
- Harvard University
- La Salle University
- Lehigh University
- Loyola College in Maryland
- Loyola Marymount University
- Marymount College
- Moravian College
- Pacific Lutheran University
- Providence College
- Rutgers University
- Saint Joseph's University
- Santa Clara University
- Simmons College
- Stanford University
- Sweet Briar College
- Temple University
- University of California San Diego
- University of Delaware
- University of Iowa
- University of Miami
- University of Oregon
- University of the Pacific
- University of Pennsylvania
- University of Rhode Island
- University of San Francisco
- West Chester University

NOTES

1. Henry Wechsler and I (Dowdall & Wechsler 2002) prepared an examination of the methodological issues in studying college drinking for the National Institute on Alcohol Abuse and Alcoholism (NIAAA) Task Force on College Drinking.

2. DeVault (2006). For further discussion and examples of institutional ethnographies, see the August 2006 issue of the journal *Social Problems*.

APPENDIX C
Timeline of Important Events Shaping College Drinking

1919–1933	Prohibition
1930s	The Great Depression
1939	Alcoholics Anonymous is founded.
1953	Straus and Bacon publish *Drinking in College*.
1954	American Medical Association (AMA) declares alcoholism a disease.
1960	Jellinek publishes *The Disease Concept of Alcoholism*.
1961–1975	The Vietnam War
Early 1970s	Twenty-nine states lower the drinking age.
1971	National Institute of Alcohol Abuse and Alcoholism (NIAAA) is created.
	The voting age is lowered to 18.
1975	BACCHUS (Boost Alcohol Consciousness Concerning the Health of University Students) founded at University of Florida.
1976	NIAAA publishes *The Whole College Catalog about Drinking*.
1980	Mothers Against Drunk Driving (MADD) is founded.
1982	Students Against Drunk Driving (SADD) is founded.

1983	Inter-Association Task Force on Alcohol and Other Substance Issues is founded (IATF is the sponsor of National Collegiate Alcohol Awareness Week).
1984	National Minimum Drinking Age Act of 1984 is passed.
1985	GAMMA (Greeks Advocating Mature Management of Alcohol) is founded.
	University of Maryland basketball star, Len Bias, dies from a cocaine overdose.
1986	Perkins and Berkowitz first publish on social norms approach.
	Drug-Free Schools and Communities Act is passed.
1987	Special issue of *Journal of American College Health* on college drinking is published.
	First U.S. Department of Education National Meeting on Alcohol and Other Drug Prevention in Higher Education attracts 182 attendees.
	The first Fund for the Improvement of Post-Secondary Education (FIPSE) grants are provided to colleges for Alcohol and Other Drug (AOD) prevention.
	The Network Addressing Collegiate Alcohol and Other Drug Issues is founded.
	Minimum drinking age of 21 is in effect.
	Security on Campus, Inc. is founded by Connie and Howard Clery after their daughter Jeanne was murdered in her dorm room at Lehigh University in 1986.
1988	Federal law requires drug-free workplace policies.
	U.S. Surgeon General's Workshop on Drunk Driving is held.
1989	Exxon Valdez oil spill off Alaska involves alcohol.
	The Crime Awareness and Campus Security Act of 1990 (The Clery Act) is passed.
1991	The Century Council is founded by American distillers.
	Louis Eigen publishes the white paper "Alcohol Practices, Policies, and Potentials of American Colleges and Universities" on college drinking.
1993	Widespread rates of binge drinking are documented in the first College Alcohol Study by Harvard.
	Higher Education Center for the Prevention of Alcohol and Drug Problems is founded.

1994	Ryan, Colthurst, and Segars publish *College Alcohol Risk Assessment Guide*.
	The National Center on Addiction and Substance Abuse (CASA) at Columbia University publishes *Rethinking Rites of Passage: Substance Abuse on America's Campuses*.
	Wechsler, Davenport, Dowdall, Moeykens, and Castillo publish "Health and Behavioral Consequences of Binge Drinking in College" in the *Journal of the American Medical Association*.
1995	Wechsler and colleagues devise the "5/4" definition of binge drinking in *American Journal of Public Health* paper.
	Federal Zero Tolerance Law is passed.
	Student alcohol deaths at MIT and several other campuses raise visibility of college drinking.
1998	U.S. Secretary of Health and Human Services Donna E. Shalala presents "Preventing Substance Abuse on College Campuses" to the national meeting of the American Council on Education.
1999	U.S. Surgeon General launches National Alcohol Screening Day.
2000	Law mandates a 0.08 blood alcohol concentration (BAC) national standard for driving under the influence.
	U.S. Senator Joseph R. Biden, Jr. publishes *Excessive Drinking on America's College Campuses*.
	The first U.S. Department of Education model program awards are given.
	Outside the Classroom, Inc. is founded and proposes to publish "alcohol.edu."
2002	NIAAA Task Force Report, "A Call to Action: Changing the Culture of Drinking at U.S. Colleges," is released.
	Journal of Studies on Alcohol Supplement, "College Drinking: What It Is, and What to Do About It: A Review of the State of the Science" is published.
	U.S. Senate holds hearing, "Under the Influence: The Binge Drinking Epidemic on College Campuses."
2003	National Academy of Science/Institute of Medicine publishes *Reducing Underage Drinking*.
2004	The National Alliance to Prevent Underage Drinking is founded.
	NIAAA Council approves the definition of "binge drinking."

The law mandates that 0.08 BAC or above defines drunk driving.

2006   The Substance Abuse and Mental Health Administration (SAMHSA) publishes the *Comprehensive Plan for Preventing and Reducing Underage Drinking*.

Duke lacrosse team members indicted for alleged rape of stripper during night of heavy drinking.

S.T.O.P. (Sober Truth on Preventing) Underage Drinking Act is passed by Congress and signed by President George Bush.

2007   CASA releases *Wasting the Best and the Brightest: Substance Abuse at America's Colleges and Universities*.

NIAAA issues *What Colleges Need to Know Now: An Update on College Drinking Research*.

The first National Association of Student Personnel Administrators special symposium on college drinking is held.

U.S. Surgeon General's Report on Underage Drinking is released.

Special issues of both *Addictive Behaviors* and *Journal of American College Health* on college drinking are released.

The U.S. Department of Education releases *Experiences in Effective Prevention*.

2008   John McCardell launches "The Amethyst Initiative" to question the minimum drinking age.

Source: Robert Wood Johnson Foundation (2002); Mantel (2006); interviews with Barbara Ryan and Thomas Colthurst (2006 and 2007).

APPENDIX D

Alcohol and Crime Data for Colleges

In the first edition of this book, appendix D presented data about crime reports and disciplinary actions at almost 400 leading U.S. colleges and universities; this revised version of the appendix presents an update to those data.

I have designed the new appendix to more fully live up to the spirit of the Clery Act (see Chapter 3). The Clery Act was intended in part to help students and their families choose a "safe" college by forcing institutions that receive federal funding to reveal what kinds of crimes occurred on or near the campus, to issue campus alerts and publish an annual security report, and to improve campus safety and security reporting. (For more information about the act and its requirements, see http://www2.ed.gov/admins/lead/safety/campus.html.)

The Clery Act is not perfect and has attracted criticism from a number of quarters. But it is the only more or less reliable source of data about the type and amount of crime on college campuses across the country. Its critics could help to make it more useful by providing practical advice rather than global commentary.

One change to the act that would make campus crime data more useful is moving from a simple count of crimes to a measure of crime per capita. Such a measure would take into account how colleges differ greatly in size and thus in the number of students at risk. But this is not as simple as it sounds. Some colleges have almost completely residential populations; others have only commuting students who are present for a small number of hours per week; and an increasingly large number of institutions are online in whole or part, with some students who visit the campus only by clicks of a mouse. Even at residential colleges, many students spend summer and vacation breaks away from campus, and even when in residence, they spend parts of their lives at off-campus locations, such as bars and restaurants. Also, some crimes, such as sexual assault and rape, are underreported (see the afterword for recent evidence of this). Thus, simply presenting the number of full-time students in the denominator of a crime rate based on crimes known to the police doesn't work very well as a true measure of campus crime. We need more research to guide us in creating crime rates for colleges. (For an attempt to use Clery Act data to generate a ranking of "safe" campuses, see http://www.thedailybeast .com/articles/2010/09/14/most-dangerous-college-campuses-ranked.html.)

DATA ON COLLEGE ALCOHOL AND DRUG USE

Table D-1 presents the most recent data about student drinking and drug use available, as reported in the American College Health Association's National College Health Assessment (ACHA-NCHA). I present only the data for the spring semester of 2011; data are available on every semester back to 2001 online at the ACHA website (http://www.acha-ncha.org/reports_ACHA-NCHA original.html). These data have been collected from 105,781 students at two- and four-year institutions, a broader set than many other data sources, such as the College Alcohol Study cited so often in this book. The ACHA-NCHA data are limited, however, because they are not taken from a random sample of either students or institutions. But they help to paint a picture of alcohol and drug use, one that appears not to have changed much since the last CAS survey in 2001.

DATA ON CRIMINAL OFFENSES ON ALL CAMPUSES

Table D-2 displays the most recent data available on criminal offenses aggregated for every institution of higher education in the country. These data include all postsecondary institutions eligible to receive federal funds, which is a far broader collection than the group of four-year institutions sampled by the College Alcohol Study.

Table D-1.
**Alcohol Use Data from the National College Health Assessment Reference
Group Summary, 2011**

A. Alcohol use (percent)

	Male	Female	Total
Never used	22.6	20.6	21.3
Used, but not in last 30 days	11.7	13.4	12.8
Used 1–9 days	46.1	52.2	50
Used 10–29 days	17.9	13.2	14.9
Used all 30 days	1.7	0.6	1
Any use within the last 30 days	65.7	66	65.9

**B. Reported number of times students consumed five or more drinks in a sitting
within the last two weeks (percent)**

	Male	Female	Total
N/A, don't drink	23.7	22.1	22.6
None	34.1	48.4	43.3
1–2 times	25	21.4	22.7
3–5 times	13.5	7	9.3
6 or more times	3.7	1.1	2.1

C. Consequences of drinking occurring in the last 12 months (percent)*

	Male	Female	Total
Did something you later regretted	35.3	34.2	34.6
Forgot where you were or what you did	33.1	29	30.4
Got in trouble with the police	5.4	2.6	3.6
Had sex with someone without giving your consent	1.6	2.4	2.1
Had sex with someone without getting their consent	0.7	0.3	0.5
Had unprotected sex	18.7	15.2	16.5
Physically injured yourself	16.4	13.9	14.9
Physically injured another person	3.8	1.5	2.3
Seriously considered suicide	1.9	1.5	1.7
Reported one or more of the above	52.8	48.7	50.1

*Students responding "N/A, don't drink" were excluded from this analysis.
Source: http://www.acha-ncha.org/reports_ACHA-NCHAoriginal.html, accessed November 1, 2011.

Table D-2.
Criminal Offenses and Disciplinary Actions at Institutions of Higher Education, by Location and Sector, 2010

Location and sector	Murder	Negligent man-slaughter	Forcible sex offenses	Nonforcible sex offenses	Robbery	Aggravated assault	Burglary	Motor vehicle theft	Arson	Drug arrests	Liquor law violations
				Criminal offenses						Disciplinary actions	
On campus											
Public, 4-year or above	9	0	1,431	15	689	1,139	10,401	1,638	458	20,566	92,818
Private nonprofit, 4-year or above	5	0	1,240	8	445	673	8,356	660	228	18,062	86,517
Private for profit, 4-year or above	0	0	22	1	78	54	362	67	2	215	525
Public, 2-year	1	1	218	9	328	444	2,469	1,039	42	2,518	5,868
Private nonprofit, 2-year	0	0	8	0	20	54	132	10	4	120	299
Private for profit, 2-year	0	0	2	2	103	57	233	134	3	261	293
Public, less-than-2-year	0	0	6	0	21	67	65	11	2	230	98
Private nonprofit, less-than-2-year	0	0	0	0	44	7	50	12	0	3	2
Private for profit, less-than-2-year	0	0	5	0	79	37	156	49	1	29	12
Total	15	1	2,932	35	1,807	2,532	22,224	3,620	740	42,004	186,432
Residence halls*											
Public, 4-year or above	1	0	1,038	12	125	431	5,714	5	276	16,976	83,855
Private nonprofit, 4-year or above	1	0	945	5	55	258	5,232	2	149	15,329	77,171
Private for profit, 4-year or above	0	0	9	0	1	21	115	0	2	175	476
Public, 2-year	0	0	64	6	19	82	754	0	3	1,579	4,662
Private nonprofit, 2-year	0	0	6	0	2	9	66	0	3	98	284
Private for profit, 2-year	0	0	0	2	1	1	62	0	0	192	251
Public, less-than-2-year	0	0	1	0	0	3	1	0	0	11	5
Private nonprofit, less-than-2-year	0	0	0	0	0	0	0	0	0	0	0
Private for profit, less-than-2-year	0	0	0	0	0	0	4	0	0	0	0
Total	2	0	2,063	25	203	805	11,948	7	433	34,360	166,704

Noncampus

Public, 4-year or above	0	0	194	0	77	164	878	205	23	243	768
Private nonprofit, 4-year or above	1	0	68	0	60	112	475	96	9	608	2,923
Private for profit, 4-year or above	0	0	15	0	55	64	386	73	3	609	795
Public, 2-year	0	0	13	0	26	60	102	56	1	44	261
Private nonprofit, 2-year	0	0	1	0	2	1	3	1	0	2	1
Private for profit, 2-year	0	0	9	0	6	8	50	14	0	211	203
Public, less-than-2-year	0	0	0	0	0	0	1	4	0	24	5
Private nonprofit, less-than-2-year	0	0	0	0	2	0	10	0	0	0	0
Private for profit, less-than-2-year	0	0	0	0	1	0	5	2	0	0	0
Total	1	0	300	0	229	409	1,910	451	36	1741	4956

Public property

Public, 4-year or above	5	2	129	0	629	478	0	640	28	397	1,764
Private nonprofit, 4-year or above	7	0	83	5	971	501	0	613	10	163	979
Private for profit, 4-year or above	0	1	10	0	62	55	0	109	12	35	17
Public, 2-year	6	0	93	29	341	298	0	320	1	137	207
Private nonprofit, 2-year	0	0	2	0	18	45	0	14	1	1	0
Private for profit, 2-year	1	0	5	1	150	140	0	180	0	32	23
Public, less-than-2-year	0	0	3	0	44	30	0	25	0	49	4
Private nonprofit, less-than-2-year	0	0	2	0	58	29	0	16	0	6	0
Private for profit, less-than-2-year	0	1	25	0	379	227	0	293	7	51	59
Total	19	4	352	35	2,652	1,803	0	2,210	59	871	3053

Total

Public, 4-year or above	14	2	1,754	15	1,395	1,781	11,279	2,483	509	21,206	95,350
Private nonprofit, 4-year or above	13	0	1,391	13	1,476	1,286	8,831	1,369	247	18,833	90,419
Private for profit, 4-year or above	0	1	47	1	195	173	748	249	5	859	1,337
Public, 2-year	7	1	324	38	695	802	2,571	1,415	55	2,699	6,336
Private nonprofit, 2-year	0	0	11	0	40	100	135	25	5	123	300
Private for profit, 2-year	1	0	16	3	259	205	283	328	4	504	519
Public, less-than-2-year	0	0	9	0	65	97	66	40	2	303	107
Private nonprofit, less-than-2-year	0	0	2	0	104	36	60	12	0	9	2
Private for profit, less-than-2-year	0	1	30	0	459	264	161	344	8	80	71
Total	35	5	3,584	70	4,688	4,744	24,134	6,281	835	44,616	194,441

Source: http://ope.ed.gov/security/GetAggregatedData.aspx, accessed December 1, 2011.

*Included in on-campus

DATA ON ALCOHOL AND CRIME FOR SELECTED COLLEGES AND UNIVERSITIES

Table D-3 presents data for several hundred institutions, including those discussed in major guidebooks for choosing colleges, such as *Fiske Guide to Colleges* and the Princeton Review's *Complete Book of Colleges*. Readers interested in examining current data about many aspects of college life, including criminal offenses and drug and alcohol violations, should use the National Center for Education Statistics' College Navigator tool, available at http://nces.ed.gov/collegenavigator. The College Navigator is fairly easy to use, but instructions for finding data on any U.S. campus can also be found on this book's companion website, collegedrinkingbook.com.

TABLE D-3.

Alcohol and Crime Data for Selected Colleges and Universities, 2010

Name	Size	Murder	Negligent homicide	Forcible sex	Nonforcible sex	Robbery	Aggravated assault	Burglary	Vehicle theft	Arson	Drug	Liquor
				Criminal offenses							Violations	
Adelphi University	7,917	0	0	1	0	0	0	2	1	0	3	76
Agnes Scott College	917	0	0	0	0	0	0	5	1	0	1	4
Albion College	1,602	0	0	2	0	1	1	4	0	3	15	47
Alfred University	2,309	0	0	1	0	1	1	4	0	0	63	103
Allegheny College	2,153	0	0	3	0	0	1	9	0	0	12	90
Alma College	1,422	0	0	1	0	0	1	0	0	0	2	73
Alverno College	2,759	0	0	0	0	0	0	1	0	0	5	1
American University	12,795	0	0	1	0	0	2	17	3	0	77	386
Amherst College	1,794	0	0	14	0	1	0	6	1	2	55	180
Antioch University—Midwest	645	0	0	0	0	0	0	0	0	0	0	0
Arizona State University	70,440	0	0	6	0	3	12	95	18	6	0	989
Auburn University	25,078	0	0	1	0	0	1	15	5	0	6	228
Austin College	1,314	0	0	0	0	0	0	3	0	0	6	13
Babson College	3,300	0	0	3	0	0	2	3	0	0	59	51
Bard College	2,273	0	0	5	0	0	0	14	0	0	36	117
Bard College—Simon's Rock	380	0	0	1	0	0	0	5	0	0	22	54
Bates College	1,725	0	0	2	0	0	3	15	0	0	65	18
Baylor University	14,900	0	0	0	0	1	3	5	1	2	9	11
Bellarmine University	3,342	0	0	0	0	1	0	3	2	0	20	124
Beloit College	1,397	0	0	6	0	0	0	9	0	0	86	65
Bennington College	811	0	0	0	0	0	0	0	0	0	13	91
Bentley University	5,684	0	0	3	0	0	5	18	0	3	227	514
Berea College	1,613	0	0	0	0	0	0	17	6	1	10	18
Birmingham Southern College	1,542	0	0	1	0	0	0	0	0	0	23	42

(continued)

Name	Size	Criminal offenses									Violations	
		Murder	Negligent homicide	Forcible sex	Nonforcible sex	Robbery	Aggravated assault	Burglary	Vehicle theft	Arson	Drug	Liquor
Boston College	14,868	0	0	6	0	1	3	8	1	1	96	1,058
Boston University	32,727	0	0	8	0	1	2	59	0	1	55	569
Bowdoin College	1,762	0	0	7	0	0	0	6	0	0	19	146
Bradley University	5,813	0	0	4	0	3	1	23	0	0	29	32
Brandeis University	5,642	0	0	0	0	0	2	10	0	2	28	13
Brigham Young University—Provo	33,841	0	0	1	0	0	1	17	1	1	1	0
Brown University	8,705	0	0	9	0	0	1	39	0	0	20	15
Bryant University	3,606	0	0	6	0	0	0	2	0	0	58	515
Bryn Mawr College	1,751	0	0	2	0	0	0	4	0	0	7	15
Bucknell University	3,615	0	0	5	0	0	1	7	0	1	18	175
California Polytechnic State University—San Luis Obispo	18,360	0	0	1	0	1	1	29	3	1	0	0
Calvin College	3,991	0	0	0	0	0	0	16	0	0	9	29
Canisius College	5,111	0	0	1	0	0	0	12	0	0	29	216
Carleton College	2,020	0	0	3	0	0	0	13	0	0	63	40
Carnegie Mellon University	11,340	0	0	1	0	0	1	12	3	1	14	19
Case Western Reserve University	9,837	0	0	3	0	3	0	32	0	0	20	299
Catawba College	1,324	0	0	0	0	0	1	10	0	0	5	56
Catholic University of America	6,967	0	0	1	0	2	0	14	0	0	9	238
Centenary College of Louisiana	904	0	0	2	0	1	1	8	1	1	1	4
Centre College	1,242	0	0	1	0	0	0	4	0	0	0	60
Chapman University	6,881	0	0	3	0	0	0	9	0	1	21	149

Claremont McKenna College	1,278	0	1	0	1	23	3	0	2	20
Clark University	3,451	0	5	2	3	15	1	1	46	173
Clarkson University	3,330	0	0	0	0	3	1	0	17	234
Clemson University	19,453	0	2	0	3	45	19	1	74	446
Coe College	1,357	0	1	0	1	7	0	1	10	117
Colby College	1,825	0	0	0	0	6	0	0	22	123
Colgate University	2,903	0	2	0	0	13	1	0	167	281
College of Charleston	11,532	0	6	0	2	4	1	0	68	153
College of the Atlantic	370	0	1	0	0	0	0	0	1	1
College of the Holy Cross	2,899	0	2	0	1	12	0	0	17	408
College of William and Mary	8,000	0	3	0	1	23	1	1	3	198
Colorado College	2,091	0	6	0	1	11	0	5	192	232
Colorado School of Mines	5,287	0	0	0	0	8	0	0	0	36
Columbia University in the City of New York	25,208	0	4	1	1	26	0	1	113	189
Connecticut College	1,887	0	8	0	1	3	0	2	101	260
Cooper Union for the Advancement of Science and Art	1,004	0	0	0	0	0	0	0	0	0
Cornell College	1,191	0	3	0	0	0	0	0	16	46
Cornell University	20,939	0	3	0	1	13	2	4	57	259
Creighton University	7,662	0	1	0	0	8	2	2	42	170
CUNY Hunter College	22,407	0	0	0	0	5	0	0	5	0
CUNY Queens College	20,906	0	0	1	1	16	0	1	22	36
Dartmouth College	6,141	0	12	0	2	4	0	0	20	31
Davidson College	1,742	0	4	0	1	18	0	1	11	122
Denison University	2,275	0	11	0	4	7	0	3	84	185
DePaul University	25,145	0	2	0	6	17	0	3	61	639
DePauw University	2,390	0	8	0	3	11	0	0	21	168
Dickinson College	2,414	0	5	0	0	15	0	0	45	170
Drew University	2,697	0	3	0	0	0	0	0	90	287
Drexel University	23,637	0	1	0	2	20	2	0	75	407

(continued)

		Criminal offenses									Violations	
Name	Size	Murder	Negligent homicide	Forcible sex	Nonforcible sex	Robbery	Aggravated assault	Burglary	Vehicle theft	Arson	Drug	Liquor
Duke University	15,016	0	0	12	0	3	5	30	12	1	18	344
Duquesne University	10,161	0	0	2	0	0	0	8	1	0	42	323
Earlham College	1,326	0	0	1	0	0	0	5	0	0	4	0
Eckerd College	2,346	0	0	5	0	1	2	44	11	2	120	83
Elon University	5,709	0	0	2	0	0	1	5	0	0	35	595
Emerson College	4,566	0	0	0	0	0	3	5	0	1	54	392
Emory University	13,381	0	0	10	0	2	2	14	10	0	46	169
Fairfield University	5,181	0	0	5	0	0	3	13	0	0	92	1,291
Fisk University	580	0	0	0	0	1	1	1	0	0	1	3
Flagler College—St. Augustine	2,753	0	0	0	0	0	1	0	0	0	1	56
Florida Institute of Technology	8,985	0	0	0	0	1	2	6	0	0	20	140
Florida State University	40,416	0	0	4	0	11	10	90	10	9	2	214
Fordham University	15,158	0	0	6	0	0	5	24	0	0	105	890
Franklin and Marshall College	2,335	0	0	0	0	2	0	4	0	0	6	69
Franklin W. Olin College of Engineering	346	0	0	0	0	0	0	0	0	0	0	0
Furman University	2,996	0	0	1	0	0	4	6	5	1	15	190
George Mason University	32,562	0	0	5	0	1	2	22	5	0	65	259
George Washington University	25,135	0	0	10	0	2	0	71	0	2	162	264
Georgetown University	16,937	0	0	8	0	2	1	38	1	0	38	444
Georgia Institute of Technology–Main Campus	20,720	0	0	2	0	2	2	26	13	0	67	255
Gettysburg College	2,485	0	0	6	0	0	1	12	1	0	55	199
Gonzaga University	7,738	0	0	7	0	0	0	19	10	2	71	523

Institution										
Gordon College	1,599	0	1	0	0	0	1	0	0	1	10
Goucher College	2,299	0	2	0	1	0	4	0	0	43	252
Grinnell College	1,655	0	2	0	0	0	12	0	8	1	7
Guilford College	2,828	0	1	0	0	0	10	0	0	63	83
Gustavus Adolphus College	2,455	0	3	0	0	0	0	0	0	37	163
Hamilton College	1,861	0	7	0	0	0	18	1	0	46	122
Hampden-Sydney College	1,058	0	2	0	0	0	10	1	2	19	64
Hampshire College	1,529	0	11	0	0	0	16	1	0	5	40
Hampton University	5,254	0	0	0	2	11	36	0	0	4	6
Hanover College	1,006	0	0	0	0	0	9	0	0	3	100
Hartwick College	1,531	0	2	0	0	0	11	0	0	28	60
Harvard University	27,594	0	31	0	8	5	35	0	0	10	23
Harvey Mudd College	773	0	1	0	0	0	13	0	0	1	1
Haverford College	1,177	0	8	0	0	0	6	2	0	0	15
Hendrix College	1,467	0	0	0	1	2	3	0	0	18	45
Hiram College	1,389	0	1	0	0	5	24	0	0	18	112
Hobart and William Smith Colleges	2,173	0	2	0	0	0	11	1	0	93	218
Hofstra University	11,579	0	5	0	0	1	9	2	0	175	55
Hollins University	1,024	0	4	0	0	0	8	1	0	8	23
Hood College	2,447	0	0	0	0	1	10	1	0	20	52
Hope College	3,202	0	2	0	0	0	2	0	0	4	69
Houghton College	1,272	0	2	0	0	0	5	0	0	3	10
Howard University	10,379	0	7	0	20	6	15	5	0	17	8
Illinois Institute of Technology	7,774	0	0	0	1	1	10	0	0	7	47
Illinois Wesleyan University	2,094	0	0	0	0	0	5	0	0	6	323
Indiana University of Pennsylvania—Main Campus	15,126	0	6	0	1	2	10	2	0	65	252
Indiana University—Bloomington	42,464	0	15	0	4	7	52	7	2	176	1,042
Iowa State University	28,682	0	7	0	1	14	24	2	1	3	527

(continued)

		Criminal offenses									Violations	
Name	Size	Murder	Negligent homicide	Forcible sex	Nonforcible sex	Robbery	Aggravated assault	Burglary	Vehicle theft	Arson	Drug	Liquor
Ithaca College	6,949	0	0	1	0	0	1	10	0	2	289	870
James Madison University	19,434	0	0	5	0	0	3	21	1	1	21	573
John Carroll University	3,692	0	0	3	0	0	0	14	0	3	48	186
Johns Hopkins University	20,977	0	0	0	0	1	0	1	0	0	38	212
Juniata College	1,593	0	0	2	0	0	0	0	0	0	4	33
Kalamazoo College	1,369	0	0	1	0	0	0	9	0	0	10	80
Kansas State University	23,588	0	0	6	0	0	3	25	2	0	11	363
Kenyon College	1,632	0	0	1	0	0	1	12	2	0	57	210
Knox College	1,392	0	0	4	0	1	0	4	0	1	21	25
La Salle University	6,636	0	0	0	0	3	1	4	1	0	32	190
Lafayette College	2,414	0	0	3	0	1	1	22	0	2	30	80
Lake Forest College	1,443	0	0	4	0	0	3	10	0	0	40	259
Lawrence University	1,557	0	0	2	0	0	0	0	0	0	10	19
Le Moyne College	3,502	0	0	1	0	0	0	8	0	0	34	186
Lehigh University	7,051	0	0	1	0	1	0	18	0	0	10	170
Lewis and Clark College	3,584	0	0	3	0	0	1	6	1	2	106	227
Louisiana State University and Agricultural and Mechanical College	29,451	0	0	5	0	5	10	13	13	3	1	0
Loyola Marymount University	9,223	0	0	3	0	2	0	25	4	1	277	124
Loyola University—Baltimore	6,061	0	0	2	0	2	3	3	1	0	36	618
Loyola University—Chicago	15,951	0	0	1	0	0	0	3	1	0	168	615
Loyola University—New Orleans	4,772	0	0	0	0	0	0	2	2	0	18	34
Lynchburg College	2,643	0	0	3	0	1	4	13	0	0	14	143

Institution												
Macalester College	2,033	0	0	7	0	0	0	4	0	0	112	181
Manhattanville College	2,695	1	0	0	0	0	1	5	0	0	24	263
Marist College	6,140	0	0	2	0	0	0	22	0	0	31	198
Marlboro College	279	0	0	2	0	0	1	0	0	0	5	1
Marquette University	11,806	0	0	3	0	0	1	36	1	1	50	866
Massachusetts Institute of Technology	10,566	0	0	3	0	2	1	22	1	0	5	22
Mercer University	8,236	0	0	1	0	1	0	5	1	0	5	32
Mercyhurst College	4,388	0	0	1	0	0	3	7	0	0	21	385
Miami University–Oxford	17,472	0	0	12	0	0	5	14	3	2	20	543
Michigan State University	46,985	0	0	14	0	8	8	95	12	2	117	109
Michigan Technological University	6,971	0	0	2	0	0	0	4	1	1	4	63
Middlebury College	2,532	0	0	4	0	0	0	27	0	0	63	16
Mills College	1,589	0	0	0	0	0	0	2	2	0	18	12
Millsaps College	1,060	0	0	0	0	0	0	9	1	0	15	24
Monmouth University	6,506	0	0	8	0	0	0	14	1	1	7	125
Montana Tech of the University of Montana	2,304	0	0	0	0	0	0	0	1	0	4	89
Moravian College and Moravian Theological Seminary	2,032	0	0	0	0	1	1	5	0	0	5	64
Morehouse College	2,586	0	0	0	0	3	2	26	0	1	8	13
Mount Holyoke College	2,344	0	0	3	0	0	0	9	0	0	11	22
Muhlenberg College	2,515	0	0	4	0	1	0	7	0	0	32	173
New Jersey Institute of Technology	8,934	0	0	0	0	2	3	7	2	0	21	14
New Mexico Institute of Mining and Technology	1,775	0	0	1	0	0	3	1	0	0	0	0
New York University	43,797	0	0	1	0	0	0	53	0	0	48	341
North Carolina State University–Raleigh	34,376	0	0	5	0	1	12	34	13	0	80	165
Northeastern University	29,519	0	0	2	0	3	3	16	4	0	35	550
Northwestern University	20,481	0	0	3	0	0	0	33	0	0	47	309

(continued)

Name	Size	Criminal offenses									Violations	
		Murder	Negligent homicide	Forcible sex	Nonforcible sex	Robbery	Aggravated assault	Burglary	Vehicle theft	Arson	Drug	Liquor
Oberlin College	3,000	0	0	7	0	0	1	31	8	6	79	135
Occidental College	2,102	0	0	7	0	0	1	15	1	0	147	389
Oglethorpe University	1,155	0	0	0	0	0	0	0	0	0	5	3
Ohio Northern University	3,570	0	0	2	0	0	0	8	0	0	2	166
Ohio University—Main Campus	25,108	0	0	12	0	1	2	34	2	4	126	521
Ohio Wesleyan University	1,911	0	0	4	0	0	0	1	0	5	1	47
Oregon State University	23,753	0	0	9	0	0	1	36	11	1	0	299
Pennsylvania State University—Main Campus	45,233	0	0	5	0	2	3	63	2	14	199	475
Pepperdine University	7,604	0	0	2	0	0	0	30	1	0	9	21
Pitzer College	1,080	0	0	0	0	0	0	10	1	0	35	37
Pomona College	1,560	0	0	2	0	0	1	52	2	0	30	101
Presbyterian College	1,266	0	0	0	0	0	5	35	0	0	19	60
Prescott College	1,132	0	0	0	0	0	0	0	0	0	2	0
Princeton University	7,724	0	0	13	0	0	1	30	4	5	37	33
Providence College	5,034	0	0	2	0	1	0	8	2	0	72	504
Purdue University—Main Campus	41,063	0	0	5	0	1	4	41	2	0	8	368
Quinnipiac University	8,166	0	0	4	0	0	2	3	0	0	66	437
Randolph-Macon College	1,222	0	0	4	0	0	1	7	0	0	1	85
Reed College	1,477	0	0	7	0	0	1	7	2	5	90	93
Rensselaer Polytechnic Institute	6,704	0	0	1	0	0	0	1	0	0	8	9
Rhode Island School of Design	2,406	0	0	2	0	0	1	3	1	0	33	40
Rhodes College	1,721	0	0	3	0	0	0	2	0	0	10	63

Institution											
Rice University	5,879	0	1	0	0	0	31	4	0	8	35
Rider University	5,776	0	2	0	0	0	22	3	0	4	269
Ripon College	1,065	0	2	0	0	1	6	0	1	26	130
Rockhurst University	2,895	0	1	0	0	0	3	0	0	14	163
Rollins College	3,226	0	2	0	0	0	2	1	2	57	296
Rose-Hulman Institute of Technology	1,980	0	0	0	0	0	2	0	0	13	1
Rutgers University—New Brunswick	38,912	0	11	0	5	7	76	7	2	134	1,031
Saint Anselm College	1,896	0	4	0	0	1	8	0	0	7	197
Saint Bonaventure University	2,514	0	3	0	0	1	0	0	0	25	371
Saint John's University	2,036	0	1	0	0	0	8	0	1	70	438
Saint Joseph's University	8,916	0	0	0	1	1	47	0	0	60	794
Saint Mary's College of California	3,917	0	2	0	0	1	30	1	0	55	11
Saint Michael's College	2,457	0	0	0	0	1	1	0	0	104	170
Saint Peter's College	3,010	0	0	0	0	0	3	3	0	14	47
Salisbury University	8,397	0	6	0	1	4	23	0	0	4	180
Samford University	4,715	0	0	0	0	0	12	0	0	2	4
Santa Clara University	8,687	0	4	0	0	7	2	1	2	140	565
Sarah Lawrence College	1,670	0	0	0	1	0	8	0	1	28	48
Scripps College	965	0	3	0	0	1	7	1	0	6	16
Seattle University	7,817	0	0	0	0	0	1	1	0	37	173
Seton Hall University	9,836	0	4	0	0	0	12	1	0	16	241
Sewanee—The University of the South	1,536	0	2	0	0	0	13	0	1	51	119
Simmons College	4,983	0	2	0	0	0	8	0	0	7	19
Skidmore College	2,783	0	4	0	0	0	24	0	4	86	179
Smith College	3,113	0	6	0	0	0	20	1	0	0	70
Sonoma State University	8,395	0	2	0	0	3	5	0	0	18	18
Southern Methodist University	10,938	0	1	0	0	0	35	1	2	17	240
Spelman College	2,177	0	0	0	1	0	1	0	0	0	0

(continued)

| | | Criminal offenses | | | | | | | | | Violations | |
Name	Size	Murder	Negligent homicide	Forcible sex	Nonforcible sex	Robbery	Aggravated assault	Burglary	Vehicle theft	Arson	Drug	Liquor
Spring Hill College	1,601	0	0	2	0	0	0	10	3	0	20	70
St. John's College	538	0	0	0	0	1	0	0	0	0	4	26
St. John's University—New York	21,354	0	0	1	0	0	3	19	0	1	156	262
St. Lawrence University	2,423	0	0	3	0	0	0	12	4	0	130	193
St. Mary's College of Maryland	2,017	0	0	0	0	0	0	3	0	0	71	149
St. Olaf College	3,156	0	0	4	0	0	0	3	0	0	14	155
Stanford University	19,535	0	0	21	0	1	4	180	14	1	3	52
Stephens College	1,123	0	0	0	0	0	0	2	0	0	2	6
Stetson University	3,756	0	0	2	0	1	0	4	1	0	56	108
Stevens Institute of Technology	5,629	0	0	0	0	0	0	2	1	0	7	33
Stony Brook University	24,363	0	0	7	0	3	4	113	11	7	137	207
Suffolk University	9,068	0	0	2	0	1	0	8	0	0	176	325
SUNY-Albany	17,615	0	0	8	0	1	2	27	3	3	81	183
SUNY-Binghamton	14,895	0	0	5	0	0	0	17	0	3	87	75
SUNY-Geneseo	5,665	0	0	6	0	0	0	15	0	3	20	171
SUNY-Purchase College	4,167	0	0	9	0	0	0	22	0	3	111	29
SUNY College-Buffalo	12,419	0	0	2	0	0	5	40	2	2	126	46
Susquehanna University	2,305	0	0	4	0	0	3	6	0	1	56	348
Swarthmore College	1,524	0	0	1	0	0	0	16	0	0	0	12
Sweet Briar College	760	0	0	1	0	0	0	2	0	0	1	19
Syracuse University	20,407	0	0	9	0	0	2	46	0	0	82	1,084
Temple University	37,367	0	0	6	0	9	2	6	1	1	1	202
Texas A & M University—College Station	49,129	0	0	4	0	1	3	21	5	2	2	87
Texas Christian University	9,142	0	0	1	0	0	0	2	3	0	67	489

Institution											
Texas Tech University	31,637	0	5	0	1	4	22	3	1	126	272
The College of New Jersey	7,115	0	2	0	0	1	2	0	0	11	347
The College of Wooster	2,003	0	2	0	0	0	28	1	2	23	133
The Evergreen State College	4,833	0	0	0	0	1	25	0	0	286	196
The New School	10,678	0	2	0	0	0	0	0	0	50	119
The University of Alabama	30,127	0	9	0	7	3	46	4	1	142	518
The University of Montana	15,642	0	3	0	0	3	0	0	5	264	740
The University of Tennessee	30,300	0	1	0	0	0	16	4	3	74	515
The University of Texas—Austin	51,195	0	12	0	1	4	36	4	1	45	186
Transylvania University	1,110	0	0	0	0	0	2	0	0	0	79
Trinity College	2,396	0	6	0	4	0	24	10	1	184	458
Trinity University	2,498	0	2	0	1	0	12	9	0	36	250
Truman State University	6,035	0	2	0	0	2	3	0	2	0	26
Tufts University	10,480	0	10	0	0	2	20	1	0	4	91
Tulane University of Louisiana	12,144	0	5	0	0	1	14	4	0	19	286
Union College	2,197	0	1	0	1	0	23	1	1	129	586
U.S. Merchant Marine Academy	1,000	0	1	0	0	0	33	0	0	0	0
University at Buffalo	29,117	0	2	0	5	1	96	4	1	316	811
University of Arizona	39,086	0	1	0	1	3	30	25	2	55	347
University of Arkansas	21,405	0	1	0	0	0	45	11	1	60	461
University of California—Berkeley	35,833	0	6	0	14	8	63	13	13	125	610
University of California—Davis	31,392	0	14	0	1	4	71	9	2	87	202
University of California—Irvine	26,994	0	3	0	0	4	27	6	5	14	414

(continued)

Name	Size	Murder	Negligent homicide	Forcible sex	Nonforcible sex	Robbery	Aggravated assault	Burglary	Vehicle theft	Arson	Drug	Liquor
				Criminal offenses							Violations	
University of California—Los Angeles	38,157	0	0	21	1	2	2	125	14	2	122	681
University of California—Riverside	20,692	0	0	5	0	7	5	18	12	4	146	20
University of California—San Diego	29,176	1	0	3	0	0	2	40	21	2	94	1,050
University of California—Santa Barbara	22,218	0	0	6	0	0	1	51	2	1	267	772
University of California—Santa Cruz	17,187	0	0	5	0	2	3	34	4	1	894	3,566
University of Central Florida	56,106	0	0	4	0	0	6	36	24	0	74	294
University of Chicago	15,152	0	0	3	0	1	0	20	0	0	5	13
University of Cincinnati—Main Campus	32,283	0	0	0	0	0	0	0	1	0	0	0
University of Colorado—Boulder	32,697	0	0	8	0	2	2	31	5	4	1,340	1,848
University of Colorado—Denver	24,108	0	0	3	0	2	2	14	12	0	58	124
University of Connecticut	25,498	0	0	9	0	0	0	23	0	4	3	714
University of Dallas	2,843	0	0	1	0	0	0	3	0	0	4	56
University of Dayton	11,199	0	0	9	0	6	5	29	0	3	161	1,205
University of Delaware	21,177	0	0	2	0	4	3	15	1	2	114	985
University of Florida	49,827	0	0	3	0	7	6	27	12	0	20	200
University of Georgia	34,677	0	0	3	0	3	1	75	18	9	24	256
University of Hawaii—Manoa	20,337	0	0	12	0	2	11	48	39	1	238	524
University of Idaho	12,302	0	0	3	3	1	2	13	1	0	1	79

University of Illinois—Urbana-Champaign	43,862	0	7	0	9	4	63	4	0	145	833
University of Iowa	29,518	0	6	0	1	5	29	0	4	175	508
University of Kansas	28,697	0	5	0	0	2	44	2	3	165	752
University of Kentucky	27,108	0	8	0	11	8	27	6	2	55	187
University of Louisiana—Lafayette	16,763	0	1	0	2	3	11	0	0	18	34
University of Maine	11,501	0	9	0	0	3	5	0	13	208	423
University of Mary Washington	5,203	0	1	0	0	0	2	0	1	13	160
University of Maryland—Baltimore County	12,888	0	1	0	0	0	9	0	1	35	137
University of Maryland—College Park	37,641	0	9	0	8	9	75	46	6	34	1,062
University of Massachusetts—Amherst	27,569	0	12	0	1	15	59	5	0	22	1,588
University of Miami	15,657	0	1	0	3	0	33	2	0	153	427
University of Michigan—Ann Arbor	41,924	0	14	0	7	10	27	10	1	208	483
University of Minnesota—Morris	1,811	0	0	0	0	0	1	0	0	0	3
University of Minnesota—Twin Cities	51,721	0	12	0	2	1	38	6	2	116	761
University of Mississippi—Main Campus	17,085	0	3	0	1	0	47	2	0	0	53
University of Missouri—Columbia	32,341	0	5	0	1	9	4	3	0	1	848
University of Nebraska—Lincoln	24,610	0	2	0	1	1	7	2	1	62	367
University of New Hampshire—Main Campus	15,095	0	12	0	1	4	8	3	1	42	339
University of New Mexico—Main Campus	28,688	0	2	0	2	8	33	31	4	46	105

(continued)

Name	Size	Murder	Negligent homicide	Forcible sex	Nonforcible sex	Robbery	Aggravated assault	Burglary	Vehicle theft	Arson	Drug	Liquor
						Criminal offenses					Violations	
University of New Orleans	11,276	0	0	0	0	5	0	10	5	0	0	11
University of North Carolina—Asheville	3,967	0	0	3	0	0	1	13	0	1	41	64
University of North Carolina—Chapel Hill	29,390	0	0	19	0	1	4	28	0	0	3	326
University of North Carolina—Greensboro	18,771	0	0	0	0	0	0	23	1	0	14	103
University of North Dakota	14,194	0	0	5	0	0	0	6	1	1	8	696
University of Notre Dame	11,992	0	0	7	0	0	0	58	4	1	12	238
University of Oklahoma—Norman Campus	26,476	0	0	2	0	0	1	26	5	0	74	421
University of Oregon	23,342	0	0	7	0	1	2	14	2	18	101	1,030
University of Pennsylvania	25,007	0	0	9	0	3	13	12	4	1	22	117
University of Pittsburgh—Pittsburgh Campus	28,823	0	0	7	0	2	2	46	0	0	20	357
University of Puget Sound	2,823	0	0	1	0	0	0	12	5	0	52	213
University of Redlands	4,431	0	0	2	0	2	2	28	1	0	64	219
University of Rhode Island	16,294	0	0	4	0	3	0	19	3	2	98	518
University of Richmond	4,405	0	0	4	0	1	1	26	4	3	14	219
University of Rochester	10,111	0	0	17	0	3	4	27	2	0	134	328
University of San Francisco	9,557	0	0	5	0	1	1	11	1	1	73	260
University of Scranton	6,070	0	0	3	0	2	0	1	2	0	33	196
University of South Carolina—Columbia	29,599	0	0	2	0	2	7	87	26	0	201	854
University of South Dakota	10,151	0	0	2	0	0	0	3	0	0	8	246
University of South Florida—Main Campus	40,431	0	0	9	0	1	2	68	11	0	45	151

Institution											
University of Southern California	36,896	0	5	0	3	5	34	0	2	110	238
University of the Ozarks	630	0	0	0	0	2	2	0	0	1	10
University of the Pacific	6,717	0	4	1	1	1	28	8	0	20	3
University of Tulsa	4,185	0	0	0	2	0	15	0	0	18	58
University of Utah	30,819	0	4	0	0	0	37	0	0	68	179
University of Vermont	13,554	0	8	0	1	1	46	0	2	474	1,301
University of Washington—Seattle Campus	42,451	0	4	0	1	1	56	9	4	76	327
University of Wisconsin—Madison	42,180	0	9	0	3	1	57	9	3	189	1,107
University of Wyoming	12,911	0	9	0	0	0	51	0	1	17	92
Ursinus College	1,802	0	2	0	0	2	15	1	1	19	115
Valparaiso University	4,056	0	1	0	0	1	12	0	1	0	132
Vanderbilt University	12,714	0	10	0	0	7	20	0	1	52	228
Vassar College	2,446	0	6	0	0	0	10	0	1	54	118
Villanova University	10,605	0	4	0	1	1	23	0	0	104	577
Virginia Polytechnic Institute and State University	31,006	0	2	0	0	3	37	5	1	20	415
Wabash College	872	0	0	0	0	0	8	0	0	4	17
Wagner College	2,275	0	0	0	0	1	11	0	0	29	115
Wake Forest University	7,162	0	7	0	0	0	74	4	1	40	255
Warren Wilson College	992	0	8	0	0	2	11	0	0	76	104
Washington and Lee University	2,173	0	0	0	0	0	9	1	0	30	91
Washington State University	26,308	0	6	0	2	3	21	3	1	213	639
Washington University in St. Louis	13,820	0	5	0	0	1	15	2	0	44	304
Webb Institute	80	0	0	0	0	0	0	0	0	0	3
Wellesley College	2,546	0	0	0	0	0	4	1	0	7	9
Wells College	559	0	0	0	0	0	0	0	0	4	56

(continued)

		Criminal offenses									Violations	
Name	Size	Murder	Negligent homicide	Forcible sex	Nonforcible sex	Robbery	Aggravated assault	Burglary	Vehicle theft	Arson	Drug	Liquor
Wesleyan College	690	0	0	0	0	0	0	0	0	0	0	0
Wesleyan University	3,215	0	0	4	0	0	0	17	1	0	136	375
West Chester University of Pennsylvania	14,490	0	0	5	0	1	1	14	1	1	14	59
West Virginia University	29,306	0	0	7	0	5	2	20	1	3	104	1,501
Westminster College	1,585	0	0	2	0	0	0	0	0	0	4	54
Westminster College	3,163	0	0	2	0	0	0	8	1	0	17	243
Wheaton College (IL)	3,026	0	0	0	0	0	0	2	0	0	5	0
Wheaton College (MA)	1,635	0	0	8	0	0	0	7	0	1	49	86
Wheeling Jesuit University	1,363	0	0	1	0	0	0	6	0	0	5	315
Whitman College	1,555	0	0	0	0	0	0	1	1	0	17	26
Whittier College	2,288	0	0	0	0	0	0	0	0	0	0	0
Willamette University	2,851	0	0	3	0	0	3	12	2	0	49	66
William Jewell College	1,060	0	0	1	0	0	0	3	0	0	3	41
Williams College	2,101	0	0	3	0	0	0	10	1	4	1	10
Wittenberg University	1,909	0	0	2	0	0	0	7	0	2	4	74
Wofford College	1,541	0	0	0	0	2	0	9	1	0	21	112
Worcester Polytechnic Institute	5,360	0	0	0	0	1	2	5	0	0	7	67
Xavier University	7,019	0	0	2	0	0	0	3	1	0	67	703
Xavier University of Louisiana	3,391	0	0	1	0	0	0	0	1	0	6	2
Yale University	11,701	0	0	10	0	3	0	29	2	0	9	2

References

Abbey, A. (1991). Acquaintance rape and alcohol consumption on college campuses: How are they linked? *Journal of American College Health, 39,* 165–169.

Abbey, A. (2002). Alcohol-related sexual assault: a common problem among college students. *Journal of Studies on Alcohol,* 118–128.

Aldridge D. (2008). Duke lacrosse: life after the rape scandal. *Philadelphia Inquirer,* March 4.

Armstrong, E. A., Hamilton, L., & Sweeney, B. (2006). Sexual assault on campus: a multilevel, integrative approach to party rape. *Social Problems, 53*(4), 483–499.

Astin, A. W. (1993). *What matters in college? Four critical years revisited.* San Francisco: Jossey-Bass.

Babor, T. (2003). *Alcohol: no ordinary commodity: research and public policy.* New York: Oxford University Press.

Bachar, K., & Koss, M. P. (2000). From prevalence to prevention. In C. Renzetti, J. L. Edleson, & R. K. Bergen, eds., *Sourcebook of violence against women* (pp. 117–142). Thousand Oaks, CA: Sage.

Barnett, J. H. (1932). College seniors and the liquor problem. *Annals of the American Academy of Political and Social Science, 163*(September), 130–146.

Barnett, N. P., Goldstein, A. L., Murphy, J. G., Colby, S. M., & Monti, P. M. (2006). "I'll never drink like that again": characteristics of alcohol-related incidents and predictors of motivation to change in college students. *Journal of Studies on Alcohol, 67,* 754–763.

Baum, K., & Klaus, P. (2005). Violent victimization of college students, 1995–2002. NCJ Publication No. 206836. Washington, DC: US Department of Justice, Office of Justice Programs, Bureau of Justice Statistics.

Baum, S., & Ma, J. (2007). *Education pays: the benefits of higher education for individuals and society.* Washington, DC: College Board.

Baumgartner, F. R., & Jones, B. D. (1993). *Agendas and instability in American politics.* Chicago: University of Chicago Press.

Bell, R., Wechsler, H., & Johnston, L. D. (1997). Correlates of college student marijuana use: Results of a US National Survey. *Addiction, 92*(5), 571–581.

Best, J. (1995). *Images of issues: typifying contemporary social problems* (2nd ed.). New York: Aldine de Gruyter.

Bickel, R. D., & Lake, P. F. (1999). *The rights and responsibilities of the modern university. Who assumes the risks of college life?* Durham, NC: Carolina Academic Press.

Biden, J. R. (2002). *Excessive drinking on America's college campuses.* Washington, DC: U.S. Senate.

Birckmeyer, J. (1999). Minimum drinking age laws and youth suicide, 1970–1990. *American Journal of Public Health, 89,* 1365–1368.

Blane, H. T., Hewitt, L. E., & United States National Technical Information, S. (1977). *Alcohol and youth: An analysis of the literature, 1960–1975.* Rockville, MD: National Institute on Alcohol Abuse and Alcoholism.

Bliwise, R. J. (2007). One year later. *Duke Alumni Magazine,* May–June.

Bogle, K. A. (2008). *Hooking up: sex, dating, and relationships on campus.* New York: New York University Press.

Bok, D. C. (2006). *Our underachieving colleges: a candid look at how much students learn and why they should be learning more.* Princeton, NJ: Princeton University Press.

Bolman, L. G., & Deal, T. E. (1984). *Modern approaches to understanding and managing organizations.* San Francisco: Jossey-Bass.

Bonnie, R. L., & O'Connell, M. E. (2003). *Reducing underage drinking: a collective responsibility.* Washington, DC: Institute of Medicine of the National Academies.

Boston Women's Health Book Collective. (2005). *Our bodies, ourselves: A new edition for a new era.* New York: Simon & Schuster.

Boyer, E. L., & Carnegie Foundation for the Advancement of Teaching. (1987). *College: the undergraduate experience in America.* New York: Harper & Row.

Butler, K. (2006). Our inconvenient truth. *The Chronicle of Higher Education,* September 8.

Califano, J. A. (2007). Wasting the best and the brightest alcohol and drug abuse on college campuses. *America 196*(19), 16.

Carey, K. B., Scott-Sheldon, L. A. J., Carey, M. P., & DeMartini, K. S. (2007). Individual-level interventions to reduce college student drinking: a meta-analytic review. *Addictive Behaviors, 32*(11), 2469–2494.

Carter, S. D., & Bath, C. (2007). The evolution and components of the *Jeanne Clery Act*: Implications for higher education. In B. S. Fisher & J. J. Sloan, eds., *Campus Crime: Legal, Social, and Policy Perspectives* (pp. 27–44). Springfield, IL: Charles C. Thomas.

CASA. (1994). *Rethinking rites of passage: Substance abuse on America's campuses.* New York: National Center on Addiction and Substance Abuse at Columbia University.

CASA. (2007). *Wasting the best and the brightest: Substance abuse at America's colleges and universities.* New York: National Center on Addiction and Substance Abuse at Columbia University.

Chapman, R. J., ed. (2006). *When they drink: practitioner views and lessons learned on preventing high-risk collegiate drinking.* Glassboro, NJ: Rowan University.

Chapman, R. J. (2008). *Is collegiate drinking the problem we think it is?* Glassboro, NJ: Rowan University.

Chronicle of Higher Education. (2006a). 2006 Almanac. *Chronicle of Higher Education.*

Chronicle of Higher Education. (2006b). By the numbers; How higher education has changed in 40 years. *The Chronicle of Higher Education,* November 24.

Clapp, J. D., Lange, J. E., Russell, C., Shillington, A., & Voas, R. B. (2003). A failed norms social marketing campaign. *Journal of Studies on Alcohol, 64*(3), 409–414.

Clydesdale, T. T. (2007). *The first year out: understanding American teens after high school.* Chicago: University of Chicago Press.

Collins, J. J. (1989). Alcohol and interpersonal violence: Less than meets the eye. In N. A. Weiner & M. E. Wolfgang, eds., *Pathways to Criminal Violence* (pp. 49–67). Newbury Park, CA: Sage.

Conrad, P. (2004). *The sociology of health & illness: critical perspectives* (7th ed.). New York: Worth Publishers.

Cook, P. J. (2007). *Paying the tab: the economics of alcohol policy.* Princeton, NJ: Princeton University Press.

Crawford, M., Dowdall, G. W., & Wechsler, H. (1999). College women and alcohol use: Implications for learning environments. In S. N. Davis, M. Crawford, & J. Sebrechts, eds., *Coming into her own: Educational success in girls and women* (pp. 295–310). San Francisco: Jossey-Bass.

Dawson, D. A., Grant, B. F., Stinson, F. S., & Chou, P. S. (2004). Another look at heavy episodic drinking and alcohol use disorders among college and non-college youth. *Journal of Studies on Alcohol, 65*(4), 477–488.

DeJong, W. (2007). How to address alcohol problems on campus: An emerging consensus." Ivy Plus Conference on Alcohol, Brown University, June 6.

DeJong, W., Anderson, J., Colthurst, T., Davidson, L., Langford, L. M., Mackay-Smith, V. L., Ryan, & Stubbs. (2007). *Experiences in effective prevention.* Newton, MA: Higher Education Center for Alcohol and Other Drug Abuse and Violence Prevention.

DeJong, W., & Langford, L. M. (2002). A typology for campus-based alcohol prevention: moving toward environmental management strategies. *Journal of Studies on Alcohol,* 140–147.

DeJong, W., Schneider, S. K., Towvim, L. G., Murphy, M. J., Doerr, E. E., Simonsen, N. R., Mason, & Scribner. (2006). A multisite randomized trial of social norms marketing campaigns to reduce college student drinking. *Journal of Studies on Alcohol, 67*(6), 868–879.

DeJong, W., Towvim, L. G., & Schneider, S. K. (2007). Support for alcohol-control policies and enforcement strategies among US college students at 4-year institutions. *Journal of American College Health, 56*(3), 231–236.

Dimeff, L. A. (1999). *Brief alcohol screening and intervention for college students (BASICS): a harm reduction approach.* New York: Guilford Press.

Douglas, K. A., Collins, J. L., Warren, C., Kann, L., Gold, R., Clayton, S., Ross, & Kolbe. (1997). Results from the 1995 National College Health Risk Behavior Survey. *Journal of American College Health, 46*(2), 55–66.

Dowdall, G. W. (1996). *The eclipse of the state mental hospital: policy, stigma, and organization.* Albany: State University of New York Press.

Dowdall, G. (2006). How public alcohol policy shapes prevention. In R. J. Chapman, ed., *When they drink* (pp. 80–96). Glassboro, NJ: Rowan University.

Dowdall, G. W., Crawford, M., & Wechsler, H. (1998). Binge drinking among American college women: a comparison of single-sex and coeducational institutions. *Psychology of Women Quarterly, 22*(4), 705–715.

Dowdall, G. W., DeJong, W., & Austin, B. (2002). *Finding out what works and why: A guide to evaluating college prevention programs and policies.* Newton. MA: Higher Education Center for Alcohol and Other Drug Prevention.

Dowdall, G. W., & Wechsler, H. (2002). Studying college alcohol use: widening the lens, sharpening the focus. *Journal of Studies on Alcohol Supplement, 14,* 14–22.

Dufour, M. C. (1999). What is moderate drinking? Defining "drinks" and drinking levels. *Alcohol Research & Health, 23*(1), 5–14.

Ehrenburg, D. E., & Hacker, G. (1997). *Last call for high-risk bar promotions that target college students: A community action guide.* Washington, DC: Center for Science in the Public Interest.

Eigen, L. D. (1991). *Alcohol practices, policies, and potentials of American colleges and universities.* An OSAP white paper. Washington, DC: Office of Substance Abuse Prevention.

Emmons, K. M., Wechsler, H., Dowdall, G., & Abraham, M. (1998). Predictors of smoking among US college students. *American Journal of Public Health, 88*(1), 104–107.

Engs, R. C., & Hanson, D. J. (1994). Boozing and brawling on campus: A national study of violent problems associated with drinking over the past decade. *Journal of Criminal Justice, 22,* 171–180.

Faupel, C. E., Horowitz, A. M.. and Weaver, G. S. (2004). *The sociology of American drug use.* New York: McGraw-Hill.

Federal Trade Commission. (1999). *Self-regulation in the alcohol industry: A review of industry efforts to avoid promoting alcohol to underage consumers.* Washington, DC: Federal Trade Commission.

Fillmore, K. (1974). Drinking and problem drinking in early adulthood and middle age. *Quarterly Journal of Studies on Alcohol, 35,* 819–840.

Fisher, B. S., & Cullen, F. T. (1999). *The extent and nature of sexual victimization of college women: A national-level analysis.* Rockville MD: National Criminal Justice Reference Service.

References

Fisher, B. S., Cullen, F. T. and Turner, M. G. (2000). *The sexual victimization of college women*. NCJ 182369, Washington, DC: Bureau of Justice Statistics, National Institute of Justice, Department of Justice.

Fisher, B., & Sloan, J. J. (1995). *Campus crime: legal, social, and policy perspectives.* Springfield, IL: Charles C. Thomas.

Fisher, B., & Sloan, J. J. (2007). *Campus crime: legal, social, and policy perspectives* (2nd ed.). Springfield, IL: Charles C. Thomas.

Fisher, B. S., Sloan, J. J., Cullen, F. T., & Lu, C. M. (1998). Crime in the ivory tower: the level and sources of student victimization. *Criminology, 36*(3), 671–710.

Fiske, E. (2007). *Fiske guide to colleges 2008*. Naperville, IL: Sourcebooks, Inc.

Foss, R., Marchetti, L., Holladay, K., & Scholla, K. (1999). BACs of university students returning home at night. Paper presented at the 78th Annual Meeting of the Transportation Research Board, Washington, DC.

Freidson, E. (1986). *Professional Powers: A Study of the Institutionalization of Formal Knowledge*. Chicago: University of Chicago Press.

Gfroerer, J. C., Greenblatt, J. C., & Wright, D. A. (1997). Substance use in the US college-age population: differences according to educational status and living arrangement. *American Journal of Public Health, 87*(1), 62–65.

Goldman, M. S., Boyd, G. M., & Faden, V. (2002). College drinking: What it is and what to do about it: A review of the state of the science. *Journal of Studies on Alcohol Supplement.*

Government Accountability Office. (2008). Most college students are covered through employer-sponsored plans, and some colleges and states are taking steps to increase coverage. Washington, DC: U.S. Government Accountability Office.

Grazian, D. (2008). *On the make: the hustle of urban nightlife*. Chicago: University of Chicago Press.

Greenfield, L. A. (1998). *Alcohol and crime: An analysis of national data on the prevalence of alcohol involvement in crime*. Washington, DC: U.S. Department of Justice, Bureau of Justice Statistics.

Griswold, W. (2004). *Cultures and societies in a changing world*. Thousand Oaks, CA: Pine Forge Press.

Guest, S. M. (2007). The importance of enforcing alcohol rules. *The Chronicle of Higher Education*, June 1, pp. B10–B11.

Gumport, P. J. (2007). *Sociology of higher education: contributions and their contexts*. Baltimore: Johns Hopkins University Press.

Gusfield, J. R. (1981). *The culture of public problems: drinking-driving and the symbolic order*. Chicago: University of Chicago Press.

Gusfield, J. R. (1996). *Contested meanings: the construction of alcohol problems*. Madison: University of Wisconsin Press.

Haines, M. P., Barker, G., & Rice, R. M. (2006). The personal protective behaviors of college student drinkers: evidence of indigenous protective norms. *Journal of American College Health, 55*(2), 69–75.

Hallfors, D., Cho, H., Sanchez, V., Khatapoush, S., Kim, H. M., & Bauer, D. (2006). Efficacy vs. effectiveness trial results of an indicated "model" substance abuse program: implications for public health. *American Journal of Public Health, 96*(12), 2254.

Harford, T. C., Yi, H. Y., & Hilton, M. E. (2006). Alcohol abuse and dependence in college and noncollege samples: a ten-year prospective follow-up in a national survey. *Journal of Studies on Alcohol, 67*(6), 803–809.

Hart, T. C. (2003). *Violent victimization of college students.* Washington, DC: U.S. Department of Justice, Office of Justice Programs.

Herman, A. I., Philbeck, J. W., Vasilopoulos, N. L., & Depetrillo, P. B. (2003). Serotonin transporter promoter polymorphism and differences in alcohol consumption behaviour in a college student population. *Alcohol and Alcoholism, 38*(5), 446–449.

Hilgartner, S., & Bosk, C. L. (1988). The rise and fall of social problems: a public arenas model. *American Journal of Sociology, 94*(1), 53.

Hingson, R., Heeren, T., Winter, M., & Wechsler, H. (2005). Magnitude of alcohol-related mortality and morbidity among US college students ages 18–24: changes from 1998 to 2001. *Annual Review of Public Health, 26*, 259–279.

Hingson, R. W., Heeren, T., Zakocs, R. C., Kopstein, A., & Wechsler, H. (2002). Magnitude of alcohol-related mortality and morbidity among US college students ages 18–24. *Journal of Studies on Alcohol, 63*(2), 136–144.

Hingson, R. W., & Howland, J. (2002). Comprehensive community interventions to promote health: implications for college-age drinking problems. *Journal of Studies on Alcohol,* 226–240.

Hoover, E. (2005). For the 12th straight year, arrests for alcohol rise on college campuses. *The Chronicle of Higher Education,* June 24.

Horowitz, H. L. (1988). *Campus life: undergraduate cultures from the end of the eighteenth century to the present.* Chicago: University of Chicago Press.

Jennison, K. M. (2004). The short-term effects and unintended long-term consequences of binge drinking in college: a 10-year follow-up study. *American Journal of Drug and Alcohol Abuse, 30*(3), 659–684.

Johnston, L. D., O'Malley, P. M., & Bachman, J. G. (1986). *Drug use among American high school students, college students, and other young adults: National trends through 1985.* DHHS Publication No. ADM86-1450. Washington, DC: U.S. Government Printing Office.

Johnston, L. D., O'Malley, P. M., Bachman, J. G., & Schulenberg, J. (2007). *Monitoring the future: National survey results on drug use, 1975–2006. Volume II: College students and adults ages 19–45.* Bethesda, MD: National Institute on Drug Abuse.

Kanin, E. J. (1957). Male aggression in dating-courtship relations. *American Journal of Sociology, 63*(2), 197.

Knapp, C. (1996). *Drinking: a love story.* New York: Dial Press.

Koss, M. P., Gidycz, C. A., & Wisniewski, N. (1987). The scope of rape: Incidence and prevalence of sexual aggression and victimization in a national sample of higher education students. *Journal of Counseling and Clinical Psychology, 55,* 162–170.

LaBrie, J. W., Lamb, T. F., Pedersen, E. R., & Quinlan, T. (2006). A group motivational interviewing intervention reduces drinking and alcohol-related consequences in adjudicated college students. *Journal of College Student Development, 47*(3), 267–280.

LaBrie, J. W., Pedersen, E. R., Lamb, T. F., & Bove, L. (2006). Heads UP! A nested intervention with freshmen male college students and the broader campus community to promote responsible drinking. *Journal of American College Health, 54*(5), 301–304.

Langford, L. (2005). *Preventing violence and promoting safety in higher education settings: Overview of a comprehensive approach.* Newton, MA: Higher Education Center for Alcohol and Other Drug Abuse and Violence Prevention.

Larimer, M. E., & Cronce, J. M. (2007). Identification, prevention, and treatment revisited: individual-focused college drinking prevention strategies 1999–2006. *Addictive Behaviors, 32*(11), 2439–2468.

Lederman, L. C., & Stewart, L. (2005). *Changing the culture of college drinking: a socially situated health communication campaign.* Cresskill, NJ: Hampton Press.

Lees, K. (2003). Alcohol remains back-burner issue. *The Chronicle of Higher Education,* January 17.

Levine, A., Cureton, J. S., & Levine, A. (1998). *When hope and fear collide: a portrait of today's college student.* San Francisco: Jossey-Bass.

MADD (Mothers Against Drunk Driving). (2002). *Rating the states: an assessment of the nation's attention to the problem of drunk driving and underage drinking.* Irving, TX: MADD.

Maddox, G. L., & Society for the Study of Social Problems. (1970). *The domesticated drug: drinking among collegians.* New Haven, CT: College & University Press.

Mantel, B. (2006). Drinking on campus. Have efforts to reduce alcohol abuse failed? *CQ Researcher, 16*(28), 649–672.

Marlatt, G. A. (1998). *Harm reduction: pragmatic strategies for managing high-risk behaviors.* New York: Guilford Press.

Martin, S. (1992). The epidemiology of alcohol-related interpersonal violence. *Alcohol Health & Research World, 16,* 230–237.

Martin, S., ed. (1993). *Alcohol and interpersonal violence: Fostering multidisciplinary perspectives.* Rockville, MD: National Institute on Alcohol Abuse and Alcoholism.

Martin, S., ed. (1995). *The effects of the mass media on the use and abuse of alcohol.* Bethesda MD: National Institute on Alcohol Abuse and Alcoholism.

Massing, M. (1998). *The fix.* New York: Simon & Schuster.

Matthews, A. (1997). *Bright college years: inside the American campus today.* New York: Simon & Schuster.

Meilman, P. W., Cashin, J. R., McKillip, J., & Presley, C. A. (1998). Understanding the three national databases on collegiate alcohol and drug use. *Journal of American College Health, 46*(4), 159–162.

Melbin, M. (1978). Night as frontier. *American Sociological Review, 43*(1), 3–22.

Middlebrooks, C. W. (2004). History of The Network. NASPA Conference, March 28.

Mills, C. W. (1959). *The sociological imagination.* New York: Oxford University Press.

Milner, M. (2004). *Freaks, geeks, and cool kids: American teenagers, schools, and the culture of consumption.* New York: Routledge.

Moffatt, M. (1989). *Coming of age in New Jersey: college and American culture.* New Brunswick, NJ: Rutgers University Press.

Mohler-Kuo, M., Dowdall, G. W., Koss, M. P., & Wechsler, H. (2004). Correlates of rape while intoxicated in a national sample of college women. *Journal of Studies on Alcohol, 65*(1), 37–45.

Moore, M. H., & Gerstein, D. R. (1981). *Alcohol and public policy: beyond the shadow of prohibition.* Washington, DC: National Academy Press.

Moritsugu, K. P., U.S. Surgeon General. (2007). *The Surgeon General's call to action to prevent and reduce underage drinking.*

Morrison, D. A. (2004). *Marketing to the campus crowd: everything you need to know to capture the $200 billion college market.* Chicago: Dearborn Trade Publishing.

Mosher, J. F. (2002). *Partner or foe? The alcohol industry, youth alcohol problems, and alcohol policy strategies.* Policy Briefing Paper. Chicago: American Medical Association Office of Alcohol and Other Drug Abuse.

Nathan, R. (2005). *My freshman year: what a professor learned by becoming a student.* Ithaca, NY: Cornell University Press.

NIAAA (National Institute on Alcohol Abuse and Alcoholism). (1976). *The whole college catalog about drinking: a guide to alcohol abuse prevention.* Washington, DC: U.S. Government Printing Office.

NIAAA (National Institute on Alcohol Abuse and Alcoholism). (1983). *The Secretary's conference for youth on drinking and driving, Washington, DC, March 26–28, 1983.* Rockville, MD; Washington, DC, U.S. Department of Health and Human Services Public Health Service, Alcohol Drug Abuse and Mental Health Administration National Institute on Alcohol Abuse and Alcoholism.

NIAAA (National Institute on Alcohol Abuse and Alcoholism). (2000). *10th special report to the U.S. Congress on alcohol and health.* Rockville, MD: U.S. Department of Health and Human Services, Public Health Service, National Institutes of Health, National Institute on Alcohol Abuse and Alcoholism.

NIAAA (National Institute on Alcohol Abuse and Alcoholism). (2002a). *A call to action: changing the culture of drinking at U.S. colleges.* Rockville, MD: National Institute on Alcohol Abuse and Alcoholism.

NIAAA (National Institute on Alcohol Abuse and Alcoholism). (2002b). *How to reduce high-risk college drinking: Use proven strategies, fill research gaps. Final report of the Panel on Prevention and Treatment, Task Force on College Drinking.* Rockville, MD: National Institute on Alcohol Abuse and Alcoholism.

NIAAA (National Institute on Alcohol Abuse and Alcoholism). (2002c). *High-risk drinking in college: What we know and what we need to learn. Final report of the Panel on Contexts and Consequences, Task Force on College Drinking.* Rockville, MD: National Institute on Alcohol Abuse and Alcoholism.

NIAAA (National Institute on Alcohol Abuse and Alcoholism). (2003). *State Trends in Drinking Behaviors, 1984–2003.* Bethesda, MD: National Institute on Alcohol Abuse and Alcoholism.

NIAAA (National Institute on Alcohol Abuse and Alcoholism). (2006). *Alcohol use and alcohol use disorders in the United States: main findings from the 2001–2002 National Epidemiologic Survey of Alcohol and Related Conditions (NESARC):* Rockville, MD: National Institute on Alcohol Abuse and Alcoholism.

NIAAA (National Institute on Alcohol Abuse and Alcoholism). (2007a). *What colleges need to know now: an update on college drinking research.* Rockville, MD: National Institute on Alcohol Abuse and Alcoholism.

NIAAA (National Institute on Alcohol Abuse and Alcoholism). (2007b). *Five year strategic plan, FY08–13.* Bethesda, MD: National Institute on Alcohol Abuse and Alcoholism.

Neighbors, C., Larimer, M. E., Lostutter, T. W., & Woods, B. A. (2006). Harm reduction and individually focused alcohol prevention. *International Journal of Drug Policy, 17*(4), 304–309.

Nelson, T. F., Naimi, T. S., Brewer, R. D., & Wechsler, H. (2005). The state sets the rate: the relationship among state-specific college binge drinking, state binge drinking rates, and selected state alcohol control policies. *American Journal of Public Health, 95*(3), 441–446.

Nutt, D., King, L. A., Saulsbury, W., & Blakemore, C. (2007). Development of a rational scale to assess the harm of drugs of potential misuse. *The Lancet, 369*(9566), 1047–1053.

Nuwer, H. (1999). *Wrongs of passage: fraternities, sororities, hazing, and binge drinking.* Bloomington: Indiana University Press.

O'Malley, P. M., & Johnston, L. D. (2002). Epidemiology of alcohol and other drug use among American college students. *Journal of Studies on Alcohol Supplement, 14,* 23–39.

Pacific Institute for Research and Evaluation. (1999). *Costs of underage drinking.* Washington, DC: U.S. Department of Justice, Office of Justice Programs, Office of Juvenile Justice and Delinquency Prevention.

Pascarella, E. T., & Terenzini, P. T. (2005). *How college affects students: a third decade of research.* San Francisco: Jossey-Bass.

Perkins, H. W. (2002). Social norms and the prevention of alcohol misuse in collegiate contexts. *Journal of Studies on Alcohol,* 164–172.

Perkins, H. W. (2003). *The social norms approach to preventing school and college age substance abuse: a handbook for educators, counselors, and clinicians.* San Francisco: Jossey-Bass.

Presley, C. A., Leichliter, M. A., & Meilman, P. W. (1998). *Alcohol and drugs on American college campuses: A report to college presidents: Third in a series, 1995, 1996, 1997.* Carbondale, IL: Core Institute. Southern Illinois University.

Princeton Review. (2007). *The best 366 colleges, 2008 edition.* New York: Princeton Review.

Pryor, J. H., Higher Education Research Institute (Los Angeles Calif.), & Cooperative Institutional Research Program (U.S.). (2007). *The American freshman: forty year trends, 1966–2006.* Los Angeles, CA: Higher Education Research Institute, Graduate School of Education & Information Studies, University of California, Los Angeles.

Reinarman, C. (1988). The social construction of an alcohol problem: The case of Mothers Against Drunk Drivers and social control in the 1980s. *Theory and Society, 17*(1), 91–120.

Reitman, J. (2006). Sex & scandal at Duke: lacrosse players, sorority girls and the booze-fueled culture of the never-ending hookup on the nation's most embattled campus. *Rolling Stone,* June 1.

Report of the Campus Culture Initiative Steering Committee. (2007). February 15. http://news.duke.edu/reports/ccireport.pdf, accessed February 20, 2008.

Robert Wood Johnson Foundation. (2001). *Substance abuse: The nation's number one health problem.* Princeton, NJ: Robert Wood Johnson Foundation.

Ryan, B. (1997). *College alcohol risk assessment guide: environmental approaches to prevention* (2nd ed.). Newton, MA: Higher Education Center for Alcohol and Other Drug Prevention.

Saltz, R. F. (2004). Preventing alcohol-related problems on college campuses: summary of the final report of the NIAAA Task Force on College Drinking. *Alcohol Research & Health, 28*(4), 249–251.

Saltz, R., & Elandt, D. (1986). College student drinking studies, 1976–1985. *Contemporary Drug Problems, 13,* 117.

Sampson, R. (2000). *Acquaintance rape of college students.* Washington, DC: U.S. Department of Justice, Office of Community Oriented Policing Services.

Sanday, P. R. (2007). *Fraternity gang rape: sex, brotherhood, and privilege on campus* (2nd ed.). New York: New York University Press.

Schneider, J. C., & Porter-Shirley, B. (1989). *Peterson's drug and alcohol programs and policies at four-year colleges.* Princeton, NJ: Peterson's Guides.

Schwartz, M. D., & Pitts, V. L. (1995). Exploring a feminist routine activities approach to explaining sexual assault. *Justice Quarterly, 12,* 9–31.

Scribner, R., Mason, K., Theall, K., Simonsen, N., Schneider, S. K., Towvim, L. G., & DeJong, W. (2008). The contextual role of alcohol outlet density in college drinking. *Journal of Studies on Alcohol, 69*(1), 112–120.

Seaman, B. (2005). *Binge: what your college student won't tell you: campus life in an age of disconnection and excess.* Hoboken, NJ: John Wiley & Sons.

Shailagh, M., & Gruley, B. (2000). Uneasy alliance: on many campuses, big brewers play a role in new alcohol policies: Anheuser and rivals sponsor programs that encourage drinking in moderation—legacy of a death at U.Va. *Wall Street Journal*, November 2, p. A-1.

Sher, K. J., & Rutledge, P. C. (2007). Heavy drinking across the transition to college: predicting first-semester heavy drinking from precollege variables. *Addictive Behaviors, 32*(4), 819–835.

Singleton, R. (2007) Collegiate alcohol consumption and academic performance. *Journal of Studies on Alcohol and Drugs, 68,* 548–553.

Sperber, M. (2000). *Beer and circus: how big-time college sports is crippling undergraduate education.* New York: Henry Holt.

Stepp, L. S. (2007). Sex and scandal at Duke. *Rolling Stone,* June 1.

Straus, R. (1970). *Drinking in College* in the perspective of social change. In G. L. Maddox, ed., *The domesticated drug: drinking among collegians.* New Haven, CT: College & University Press.

Straus, R., & Bacon, S. D. (1953). *Drinking in college.* New Haven, CT: Yale University Press.

Stevens, M. L. (2007). *Creating a class: College admissions and the education of elites.* Cambridge, MA: Harvard University Press.

Tilly, C. (2006). *Why?* Princeton, NJ: Princeton University Press.

Timberlake, D. S., Hopfer, C. J., Rhee, S. H., Friedman, N. P., Haberstick, B. C., Lessem, J. M., et al. (2007). College attendance and its effect on drinking behaviors in a longitudinal study of adolescents. *Alcoholism: Clinical and Experimental Research, 31*(6), 1020–1030.

Toomey, T. L., Lenk, K. M., & Wagenaar, A. C. (2007). Environmental policies to reduce college drinking: an update of research findings. *Journal of Studies on Alcohol, 68*(2), 208–219.

Toomey, T. L., & Wagenaar, A. C. (2002). Environmental policies to reduce college drinking: options and research findings. *Journal of Studies on Alcohol Supplement, 14,* 193–205.

U.S. Department of Education, Office of Safe and Drug Free Schools. (2005). *The handbook for campus crime reporting.* Washington, DC: U.S. Department of Education.

U.S. Department of Education, Office of Safe and Drug Free Schools, Higher Education Center for Alcohol and Other Drug Abuse and Prevention. (2007). *Experiences in effective prevention: the U.S. Department of Education's alcohol and other drug prevention models on college campuses grants.* Washington, DC: U.S. Department of Education.

U.S. Department of Health and Human Services, Office of the Surgeon General. (2007). *The Surgeon General's call to action to prevent and reduce underage drinking.* Rockville, MD: U.S. Department of Health and Human Services, Office of the Surgeon General.

Upcraft, M. L., Gardner, J. N., & Barefoot, B. O. (2005). *Challenging and supporting the first-year student: a handbook for improving the first year of college* (1st ed.). San Francisco: Jossey-Bass.

Vaillant, G. E. (1996). A long-term follow-up of male alcohol abuse. *Archives of General Psychiatry, 53*(3), 243–249.

Wagenaar, A. C., & Toomey, T. L. (2002). Effects of minimum drinking age laws: review and analyses of the literature from 1960 to 2000. *Journal of Studies on Alcohol,* 206–225.

Wall, A. F. (2007). Evaluating a health education web site: the case of Alcohol.Edu. *NASPA Journal, 44*(4), art. 4.

Walsh, D. C. (1990). The shifting boundaries of alcohol policy. *Health Affairs, 9,* 47–62.

Walters, S. T., & Baer, J. S. (2006). *Talking with college students about alcohol: motivational strategies for reducing abuse.* New York: Guilford Press.

Warshaw, R. (1988). *I never called it rape: The Ms. report on recognizing, fighting, and surviving date and acquaintance rape.* New York: Harper & Row.

Warshaw, R., & Koss, M. P. (1988). *I never called it rape: the Ms. report on recognizing, fighting, and surviving date and acquaintance rape.* New York: Harper & Row.

Wechsler, H., & Austin, S. B. (1998). Binge drinking: the five/four measure. *Journal of Studies on Alcohol, 59*(1), 122–123.

Wechsler, H., Davenport, A., Dowdall, G., Moeykens, B., & Castillo, S. (1994). Health and behavioral consequences of binge drinking in college. a national survey of students at 140 campuses. *Journal of the American Medical Association, 272*(21), 1672–1677.

Wechsler, H., Davenport, A. E., Dowdall, G. W., Grossman, S. J., & Zanakos, S. I. (1997). Binge drinking, tobacco, and illicit drug use and involvement in college athletics. *Journal of American College Health, 45,* 195–200.

Wechsler, H., Dowdall, G. W., Davenport, A., & Castillo, S. (1995). Correlates of college student binge drinking. *American Journal of Public Health, 85,* 921–926.

Wechsler, H., Dowdall, G., Davenport, A., & Rimm, E. (1995). A gender-specific definition of binge drinking among college students. *American Journal of Public Health, 85,* 982–985.

Wechsler, H., Dowdall, G. W., Maenner, G., Gledhill-Hoyt, J., & Lee, H. (1998). Changes in binge drinking and related problems among American college students between 1993 and 1997: results of the Harvard School of Public Health College Alcohol Study. *Journal of American College Health, 47*(2), 57–68.

Wechsler, H., & Isaac, N. (1992). 'Binge' drinkers at Massachusetts colleges: prevalence, drinking style, time trends, and associated problems. *Journal of the American Medical Association, 267*(21), 2929–2931.

Wechsler, H., Kelley, K., Weitzman, E. R., San Giovanni, J. P., & Seibring, M. (2000). What colleges are doing about student binge drinking: a survey of college administrators. *Journal of American College Health, 48*(5), 219–226.

Wechsler, H., Kuo, M. C., Lee, H., & Dowdall, G. M. (2000). Environmental correlates of underage alcohol use and related problems of college students. *American Journal of Preventive Medicine, 19*(1), 24–29.

Wechsler, H., Lee, J. E., Kuo, M., Sebring, M., Nelson, T. F., & Lee, H. (2002). Trends in college binge drinking during a period of increased prevention efforts: findings from 4 Harvard School of Public Health College Alcohol Study surveys: 1993–2001. *Journal of American College Health, 50*(5), 203–217.

Wechsler, H., Lee, J. E., Kuo, M. C., & Lee, H. (2000). College binge drinking in the 1990s: a continuing problem: results of the Harvard School of Public Health 1999 College Alcohol Study. *Journal of American College Health, 48*(5), 199–210.

Wechsler, H., Lee, J. E., Kuo, M., Sebring, M., Nelson, T. F., & Lee, H. (2002). Trends in college binge drinking during a period of increased prevention efforts: Findings from 4 Harvard School of Public Health College Alcohol Study surveys: 1993–2001. *Journal of American College Health, 50*(5), 203–217.

Wechsler, H., & Sands, E. S. (1980). *Minimum-drinking-age Laws: An Evaluation*: Lexington Books.

Wechsler, H., & Wuethrich, B. (2002). *Dying to drink: confronting binge drinking on college campuses*. Emmaus, PA: Rodale.

Weitzman, E. R., Nelson, T. F., Lee, H., & Wechsler, H. (2004). Reducing drinking and related harms in college evaluation: evaluation of the "A Matter of Degree" program. *American Journal of Preventive Medicine, 27*(3), 187–196.

Wiener, C. L. (1981). *The politics of alcoholism: Building an arena around a social problem*. New Brunswick, NJ: Transaction Books.

Wiener, C. L. (1981). *The politics of alcoholism: building an arena around a social problem*. New Brunswick, NJ: Transaction Books.

Willimon, W. H., & Naylor, T. H. (1995). *The abandoned generation: rethinking higher education*. Grand Rapids, MI: W. B. Eerdmans.

Wolfe, T. (2004). *I am Charlotte Simmons*. New York: Farrar, Straus, Giroux.

Wuthnow, R. (2007). *After the baby boomers: how twenty- and thirty-somethings are shaping the future of American religion*. Princeton, NJ: Princeton University Press.

Yaeger, D., Good, R. S., & Pressler, M. (2007). *It's not about the truth: the untold story of the Duke lacrosse case and the lives it shattered*. New York: Threshold Editions.

Young, A. M., Morales, M., McCabe, S. E., Boyd, C. J., & D'Arcy, H. (2005). Drinking like a guy: frequent binge drinking among undergraduate women. *Substance Use & Misuse, 40*(2), 241–267.

Zailckas, K. (2005). *Smashed: story of a drunken girlhood*. New York: Viking.

Zegart, A. B. (2007). *Spying blind: the CIA, the FBI, and the origins of 9/11*. Princeton, NJ: Princeton University Press.

Zemsky, R. (2007). The rise and fall of the Spellings Commission. *The Chronicle of Higher Education*, January 26.

Zhao, E. (2007). Drug use misperceived on campus. *The Chronicle of Higher Education*, September 21.

About the Author

George W. Dowdall is professor of sociology at Saint Joseph's University. He has also been a faculty member at Indiana University and Buffalo State and has held visiting appointments at UCLA, the University of Pennsylvania, Harvard, and Brown. His publications include *The Eclipse of the State Mental Hospital*, *Adventures in Criminal Justice Research*, and journal articles on college drinking, including one commissioned by the National Institute of Alcohol Abuse and Alcoholism's Task Force on College Drinking. He serves on the Pennsylvania Advisory Council on Drug and Alcohol Abuse and on the Board of Directors of the Clery Center for Security on Campus, Inc.

Index

The letter *f* following a page number denotes a figure. The letter *t* following a page number denotes a table.

Also available from Stylus

Contested Issues in Student Affairs
Diverse Perspectives and Respectful Dialogue
Edited by Peter M. Magolda and Marcia B. Baxter Magolda

What is your level of understanding of the many moral, ideological, and political issues that student affairs educators regularly encounter? What is your personal responsibility to addressing these issues? What are the rationales behind your decisions? What are the theoretical perspectives you might choose and why? How do your responses compare with those of colleagues?

Contested Issues in Student Affairs augments traditional introductory handbooks that focus on functional areas (e.g., residence life, career services) and organizational issues. It fills a void by addressing the social, educational and moral concepts and concerns of student affairs work that transcend content areas and administrative units, such as the tensions between theory and practice, academic affairs and student affairs, risk taking, and failure; and such as issues of race, ethnicity, sexual orientation, and spirituality. It places learning and social justice at the epicenter of student affairs practice.

The book addresses these issues by asking 24 critical and contentious questions that go to the heart of contemporary educational practice. Each chapter is followed by a response that offers additional perspectives and complications, reminding readers of the ambiguity and complexity of many situations.

Authoring Your Life
Developing an Internal Voice to Navigate Life's Challenges
Marcia B. Baxter Magolda
Illustrated by Matthew Henry Hall
Foreword by Sharon Daloz Parks

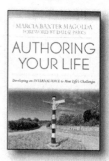

"Geared for a popular rather than an academic audience, this book is designed to assist young adults in moving from dependence on external authorities to taking charge of their own life decisions. Secondly, the book serves as a guide to significant others who wish to help these individuals more effectively address the challenges that life brings. As in her earlier work, Baxter Magolda relies extensively on quoted material from her participants' interviews as the foundation for *Authoring Your Life*. As a result, Baxter Magolda's discussion is richly textured and her theoretical concepts and applications are well-supported.

Authoring Your Life adds to the growing body of literature on self-authorship. Written in comprehensible language that student staff as well as professionals unfamiliar with the concept of self-authorship can understand, it contains fascinating in-depth narratives that demonstrate the evolution of life during the young adult years."—*Journal of College Student Development*

"This book should be considered an essential addition to the library for the young professional just entering a career in academic advising. The emphasis placed on developing the skills to become a more independent thinker is essential to understanding the needs of college and university students who are in the early stages of understanding the complexities of becoming successful contributors to society as a whole."—*NACADA Journal* (National Academic Advising Association)

22883 Quicksilver Drive
Sterling, VA 20166-2102

Subscribe to our e-mail alerts: www.Styluspub.com